THE MAN I KNEW

THE MAN I KNEW

Herbert Barness in the Press

1957-1998

Edited by Lynda Barness

I have made every effort to credit the original publications and authors; however, some of the clippings saved were missing the name of the publication, the author, or the date. In some cases, I have included only an excerpt of the original article, the part that pertains to the life and work of Herbert Barness. Some articles have also been abridged for length.

Copyright

© 2018 by Lynda Barness

All Rights Reserved. No part of this publication may be used or reproduced in any form or by any means, graphic, electronic, or mechanical, including scanning, photocopying, recording, taping, or by any information storage retrieval system or otherwise, without prior written permission of the copyright holder except in the case of brief quotations as part of critical articles or reviews.

ISBN-10: 1-942489-49-8

ISBN-13: 978-1-942489-49-8

Published by SkillBites Publishing

First Printing, 2018

Printed in the United States of America

This book is dedicated to

Henny-Penny-Jenny and M.J.-Lissa

To Jen and Melissa, who were privileged to know their Popee and to be showered by his love: "You can't spoil them with love," their grandfather (my father) used to say. He loved his daughters and granddaughters beyond measure, and we all knew and felt it. We were so lucky!

Sollydolly, Allie-B, and Izzy-B

To Solomon, Alexandra, and Isabella: I only wish that he had lived long enough to know you. You would have been the center of his universe. He too, would have loved you "all the much in the whole wide universe." And more. I created this book because I wanted you to know about your great-grandfather. You are his legacy. And he is a part of all of us.

Dan and Charlie

And finally, to my sons-in-law, Daniel and Charles: My father would have loved you and found real joy in talking to you about politics, food, sports, and countless other things... but most of all he would have loved you because you love two major lights-of-his-life, his granddaughters—and because you are the wonderful fathers of the great-grandchildren he never knew.

Contents

Preface 1

Introduction 7

The Early Years: Before 1960 11

The 1960s 43

The 1970s 193

The 1980s 235

The 1990s 279

Epilogue 395

Afterword 399

Acknowledgments 413

Appendix A: List of Articles by Year and Title 415

Appendix B: Resume of Herbert Barness 425

Appendix C: Barness Brochures 429

Appendix D: Barness Offices 449

Preface

Looking back, I'm not sure how it happened. But it seems like I first became the family historian when I was only a child.

Some 40 years ago, my grandmother gave me a collection of letters that she had saved from the time when her two sons were away at college and then away—very far away from their country life in Bucks County, Pennsylvania—during World War II. Several years ago, I finally tackled the project of reading these letters and organizing them into a book. *The Man I Knew Was Once A Boy: The Letters of Herbert Barness 1938-1948* was a compilation of letters written by my dad from the time he was 14 until he was 24, from childhood, to college, through his military service in World War II, to his completion of college and his marriage to my mother.

Shortly thereafter, when I moved from the suburbs to the city, I turned my attention to the cartons filled with newspaper articles about my father. I knew that if I left the articles in the cartons they would eventually get tossed, so I put them in clear sheet protectors and sorted them into binders by decade, and they moved with me.

Recently, I was inspired to tackle these clippings. Almost every one has a source and date on the back, written in my childish handwriting. I am now 68, and what amazes me the most is that the first clippings are from 1958, when I was just 9 years old. I certainly wasn't reading the newspapers daily as a child, so I am positive that it was my father who handed me the clippings and told me to date them, wanting to share this endeavor with me. Later, much later, when I worked for and with him in the real estate business, from 1985-1998, I was well poised to collect information. I am still amazed, though, at what was collected over the decades.

Ever since that time, I have saved family information and memorabilia. Much of what I have collected is NOT included here—such as the items from political conventions, events that my dad hosted, family vacations, and other personal memories—but, suffice it to say, I have been the repository of much of our family history.

The Man I Knew Was Once a Boy provided me with a bird's-eye view of the very private thoughts and dreams of a young man. This book presents a very public view of his life, consisting solely of what others thought and wrote about him. Through these articles, I learned more about my father as he flourished and grew, from the time he returned to the U.S. from military service, finished college, married my mother, and started his life back in what he always called "beautiful Bucks County." The traits that I saw in the first book—devotion to family and community, his entrepreneurial spirit, his love of sports—are in full view here. Nevertheless, what follows is not a comprehensive story of my dad's life, but a glimpse from the articles that were accumulated and saved.

There may be articles that are missing, but I made a conscious decision not to go back to the newspapers of the time to find them. This book contains only the articles that he personally saved and my reminiscences. In some cases, I have included only an excerpt of the original article, and some articles have also been edited for length. I also put brackets in just a few places, with notes from me, where I couldn't resist adding or correcting something! There are some discrepancies with dates of certain events, but I left most of them as the article noted, since I am not sure of the exact timeline.

Part of me was hesitant to include certain articles in this book because readers have the hindsight of decades with which to measure people and events. My father was always socially liberal (he was pro-choice, a member of the NAACP, and more), but he lived during a time when you could be socially liberal and fiscally conservative and still be a Republican. The Republican Party of 2017, as I write this, bears little resemblance to the Party of 1998 when my dad died. I hope that readers will consider the context and times in which he lived.

I have so many wonderful memories of my father beyond what is in the pages here. For example, I could write a whole book about our family vacations! We traveled annually during my high school winter breaks to the Virgin Islands when my dad was building homes there ... and then there were other family trips, most memorably the summer when my dad took off from work for a month and my parents, sister, and I flew to Denver, Colorado, and went west from there. I actually have my mother's travelogue from that trip that included Colorado, Wyoming, Yellowstone National Park, the Snake River Raft ride, Salt Lake City, Zion National Park, Bryce Canyon, the Grand Canyon, Las Vegas, Los Angeles and Disneyland, San Simeon, Hearst Castle, Yosemite, San Francisco, and more! Other amazing and memorable family trips were with three generations: my parents, their children, and their grandchildren ... to Hawaii, England, Switzerland, Disneyland, Key West, and our last trip, shortly before my father's passing, to Ireland. I have more memories ... about family holidays, when we all sat around the table at my Barness grandparents' home in Warrington, and when we helped ourselves to the contents of the candy drawer in the side table there; when we went to New York City each year to celebrate Thanksgiving with my mother's family; exposure to all sorts of people (some very famous, most just kind and interesting), places, and things including sports, politics, and business—and fun. And family always coming first. Always.

As I read through the articles, there were a few that really touched me. In general, they were not about a particular accomplishment of my father, but rather about the man I knew or something about his family background that I didn't. Here are a few of my favorites:

- From an article by W. Lester Trauch, *The Daily Intelligencer*, May 24, 1965, about my grandfather, Joseph Barness:

"Joe Barness's father died when he was 12 years old and living in Russia. He left school at 14 and was 16 years old when he arrived in the United States. He never saw his mother again after he left Russia and many of his relatives became scattered and lost because of the pogroms ... He couldn't speak any English when he got to New York but he got work in the clothing industry. From 1918-24 he was in Philadelphia and worked at Snellenberg's. In 1920 he married Mrs. Barness. Her name is Mary and she too came from Russia very young ... In 1924 Mr. and Mrs. Barness came to Warrington Township to live on a farm on Bristol Road. There was no electricity in rural Warrington."

- From an editorial/obituary of Joseph Barness, my grandfather, in *The Daily Intelligencer*, Sept. 18, 1973: "He passed on his ambition, cooperation, integrity and success to his two sons, one carrying on his dynasty, and the other a physician." Yes, he certainly did!

- From an article by Jeffrey Fleishman, "Herb Barness—A Quiet Force," *The Intelligencer/Record*, June 1990: "'I don't get impassioned. I get dedicated,' he [Herbert Barness] said."

- From an article by Margaret Quann, *The Intelligencer/Record*, February 24, 1995:

"When Herbert Barness was a child in the 1920s, the region was bucolic. Rolling farmland. Cows grazing in open fields. One-room schoolhouses such as Castle Valley in Doylestown Township, the school he attended ... Electricity, that newfangled invention that lit the cities and small towns, still hadn't gone country. Kerosene lamps provided the lighting in farmhouses. And baths? Well, they were taken in a washtub of water that had been warmed on the wood-burning kitchen stove ... It was to this very rural area that his parents came in 1922 after arriving in Philadelphia from their native Poland and Russia. Joseph and Mary Barness were from farming families, and they wanted to farm ... At 71, Barness is still going strong. Still a shrewd businessman. Still active in politics. Still looking to the future. Still building on the past."

- From *The Bucks County Courier Times*, June 9, 1996, about Herbert Barness: "Over the past 47 years, Mr. Barness has made people, community, promise and commitment the cornerstone of his career."

And, I might add, those were the cornerstones of his life as well.

Introduction

In 1989, my father Herb Barness wrote a letter to his grandchildren, describing his early life. I found it and I used it as the introduction to *The Man I Knew Was Once A Boy* as well, but I am sharing it again here because it offers a unique glimpse into those early years, in his own words.

Dear [Grandchild by name]:

I was born in Philadelphia, Pennsylvania, on December 1, 1923.

My parents were immigrants who were married on October 24, 1920. My father came to this country at the age of 14, by himself. More difficult to believe is the fact that my mother came to this country at the age of 10—by herself—to join her father who had come to the United States two years before. She arrived in the United States in 1903. They met in 1919, were married in 1920, and had a son, Lewis, in July of 1921.

In April of 1924, shortly after I was born, my parents moved to Warrington, Bucks County, Pennsylvania, from Philadelphia. They bought a farm of 98 acres on Bristol Road for $5,000. That was a lot of money in 1924, so they had a mortgage on the farm because they did not have $5,000. They worked on the farm, and my father was really a farmer. At that time, Bristol Road was just a mud road and there was no electricity or any improvements on the farm. Because of this, my mother had to boil water or heat water on a big old stove that burned wood or coal and then would pour the hot water, together with some cooler water, in the tub so that we could bathe or get washed. There was a well and a hand pump outside that we would use to pump water into buckets and carry the buckets of water into the house. In the wintertime it was very, very cold, but the water in the well did not freeze because it was much below the surface of the ground. They were certainly very difficult times for our parents, but they made sure we really never knew of many of the difficulties.

There were a few children within a mile or two with whom we could play, but for the first 8 or 9 years of my life, we really did not see many other children other than relatives who would come to visit us (or we could go to visit them).

The school we attended for the first 8 grades was about two miles from our home, and of course we walked to and from school every day. There was no such thing as school buses, and very few people had automobiles. School had one big room in it with a potbelly stove in the middle of the room. There were two outhouses, one for the girls and one for the boys if we had to use bathroom facilities. I can remember in the wintertime, the schoolroom was very cold, and we always wore sweaters and jackets during the school day. In the one room there were 8 grades, with only one teacher for all 8 grades. As a result, if we were interested, we could listen to her teaching all the subjects in every grade. As you know, my brother (your Great Uncle Lewis) went from 1st grade to 3rd grade to 5th grade, because when he got into 2nd grade or 4th grade he already knew all the questions and all the answers.

When I was 8 years old, my parents sold their farm and we moved to Easton Road, which is also known as Route 611. We moved there because by that time my father was trying to make a living selling real estate rather than farming, and there was more automobile traffic on Route 611, which was a paved road, than there was on Bristol Road. Being an immigrant, my father spoke Russian and Polish very fluently. He was selling farms then to other immigrants who came from Russia and Poland because he could speak to them very well. When we moved to the house on Easton Highway we had electricity and all the other conveniences that we take for granted today. Of course, we did not have television, but we did have radios; we did not have refrigerators, but we had iceboxes. The ice man would come several times a week and bring big blocks of ice which would be put into the top of the ice box so that the cold from the ice would go through the box and keep everything relatively cold. Of course in the summertime he had to come more often than the wintertime, and in the wintertime frequently we would just go outside and get some ice and bring it and put it into the box.

I started high school in 1936 in Doylestown, Pennsylvania. The high school was 4 miles from our home, so we either had to take a bus or get a ride to and from school by hitch-hiking or sometimes with a friend or our father. There still was no such thing as a school bus, but rather we went on the Philadelphia Rapid Transit Bus, which is now SEPTA. It cost 10 cents to go to Doylestown and 10 cents to return. Almost all kinds of candy was only 1 cent; ice cream cones, as well as Coca-Cola and other types of junk food, were 5 cents. In Doylestown, there was a Woolworth "5 and 10 cent store" and other stores, which we really were not accustomed to, having lived in Warrington. There was even a movie house in Doylestown, so once a week my parents would take us to the movies. For my mother, father, brother, and myself to go to the movies cost a total of $1.

In the summertime we always worked in the garden to raise vegetables for the summer and try to keep them also for the winter. Very occasionally we would go swimming in a pond that was also used for the cows and other animals. We had no swimming pools in our area, but there was a swimming pool in Doylestown that we used after we started high school. For us a long trip would be to go into Philadelphia with our parents, and once every few years we might even go to New York to visit some other relatives. Money was very scarce in those days, but we ate well and we were always properly clothed. I suppose we ate well because we lived on a farm and grew almost all of our own vegetables and fruits. We even raised our own chickens and cows, so we had plenty of eggs and plenty of milk.

In 1940, I graduated from high school, and for the first time in my life, I left home without my parents or brother. I entered college at Bucknell University, which created an entirely new atmosphere. I was studying engineering, and although I was not a particularly great student, I was doing fairly well. On December 7, 1941, World War II started, and at that time I was too young to go into the Armed Forces. However, on December 7, 1942, I enlisted in the Army Air Forces and was called to active duty two weeks later. I came home for the Christmas holidays, and then my parents took me to Harrisburg to get on a train, where we left for Florida, and my military career started.

I was placed into a school to study meteorology and graduated as a meteorologist from the University of Illinois in 1943. While in the Army, we were required to go to school from 8 a.m. to 9 p.m. because an emergency existed. That is why they took my 2-½ years that I attended Bucknell University and, with the accelerated program in the Army, they gave me a degree. I then worked as a meteorologist for approximately six months, and since I had some previous engineering education, I had applied for some schooling in electronics and communications. After six weeks of this accelerated course, I was shipped to the Pacific, where I spent almost three years as an officer in the Army Air Force. My last position in the Air Force was as a Squadron Commander, headquartered on the island of Guam. I then returned home in 1946 and re-enrolled in Bucknell University, where I had started to get my degree in 1940.

I met your Grandmother, Irma Shorin, shortly after I returned to Bucknell, where she was also a student. I graduated in February of 1948, and we were married after she graduated, in June of 1948.

Love,
Popee

THE EARLY YEARS
Before 1960

I know bits and pieces about the early days of my grandparents.

Joseph Barness and Mary Silverstein Barness, both immigrants, were married on October 24, 1920. He had been a contract manufacturer of children's clothing in Philadelphia, and she was employed as a seamstress. Their son Lewis was born in 1921, and Herbert was born in 1923. They lived in Philadelphia until maybe 1924, when they purchased a farm in Warrington, Pa. And that was the start of a new life in the country for the Barness family.

The family lore says that the house had no water, heat, or electricity. In the summer of 1924, with assistance from hired labor, running water and a heating system were installed. They purchased a few cows and a few horses. The fields were planted with the usual—corn, wheat, hay, and oats. Hired laborers worked the fields, while Joseph Barness continued to commute to Philadelphia.

Around 1925, they purchased 2,000 chickens, which were Mary's responsibility. For several years, Mary operated an informal restaurant at home to earn extra money, primarily on Sundays. As the story goes, chicken farming didn't really work out as expected, so they built a second house they hoped to sell on part of the land they had acquired when they first came to Bucks County. It was hard to make a living as a chicken farmer, and my grandfather looked for another way to provide for his family.

My grandparents spoke several languages, including Yiddish, English (with an accent), and, I think, others. (Although I am not exactly sure where they were born, I believe it was a place where borders changed, perhaps Russia/Poland). So it happened that the immigrants who traveled to the "country"—that is, rural Bucks County—met this country farmer who invariably spoke their language. A bond of trust was formed because of this, and so was a subsequent business.

Joseph and Mary Barness worked together, he with the construction, and she with the bookkeeping, purchasing, and other office work. They were inseparable, and I can still picture them walking together, holding hands. It was said that my grandfather never purchased a piece of ground without showing it to my grandmother first and asking for her input. They built one house for sale. And then they built another. One by one, these homes were built. A belief and a vision made it all possible. The goal was the American Dream: home ownership. Better housing and better roads came to the country, and a larger parcel of land was bought. Success was measured not in dollars, but by neighbors emerging in a farming landscape. Then electricity was brought to the country, and a community grew.

Joe and Mary Barness were my grandparents. I knew them well and long—he lived to be 80 and she to 94. They were simple people, really, in the best sense of the word. They cared about their family, their neighbors, and their country. They were pioneers, and they helped to change their world. And it is their spirit, their belief, and their integrity that set the stage for the lives and successes of their children, grandchildren, great-grandchildren, and great-great-grandchildren—and for the generations to follow.

Business then was conducted by a handshake. One's word was a promise. That was real, and that was how it was. Pop-pop was not only the home builder; he was the friend, the lender, the translator, the advisor. He and my grandmother were involved. They cared. Each house mattered, because the people who were going to live there mattered. Community mattered. Reputation mattered. So did promises, commitment, and follow-through.

And memories. They built not only homes, but also traditions and histories. They helped other pioneering families develop roots, foundations, and meaning in their new surroundings. And those who worked on Barness homes became a part of this, too. The homes were built with pride by each person who touched a tool, designed a plan, and finished a house. Loyalty, pride, craftsmanship, responsibility, respect—these are the characteristics, on a very human level, that have defined the home-building business for our family.

Over the years, everything changed and nothing changed. My dad, Herb Barness, returned from active duty after World War II and went back to Bucknell University to finish his education. He met my mother there, and they were married in June of 1948 and moved to Warrington. My mother had grown up in Brooklyn, New York, so she was entering a very different world! My parents bought a piece of ground on Stuckert Road in Warrington, and my father and grandfather built a house there; for the first six months of their marriage, while their house was being constructed, my parents lived with my father's parents in their home on Easton Road (Route 611) in Warrington.

Our home on Stuckert Road was the large parcel in the foreground, surrounded by a tree line and crops.

My father was eager to begin working in the real estate business with his father, and he was on the job sites at the beginning. The post-war boom played a large part in the development of Bucks County because it was such a desirable place to live, and some major businesses, such as U.S. Steel, had moved in, and their employees needed homes. My father took the lead in the business when, as the story goes, the cost of land became $100 per acre. My grandfather felt that time had passed him by, and he couldn't imagine spending that kind of money. He stepped aside—although he still came to the office daily—so that his son's entrepreneurial spirit and vision could embrace the future. My father expanded the business in a manner that his parents could not have dreamed possible, even as they lived to witness much of it.

My sister and I both grew up in Warrington, and we went to what was then Warrington Elementary School on Barness Road (my grandfather built houses on that road early on). I actually missed going to a one-room schoolhouse like my dad and uncle did by only a few years! We moved to Abington Township when I was going into seventh grade. But Bucks County has always been H-O-M-E. My parents moved back when I was in college, and the "country" still touches my heart when I drive through or stop to visit. I have wonderful memories of my own childhood there, and even more tender recollections of visiting my parents on their farm with my own young children. My dad had a chicken coop, and some of my favorite memories have to do with my young daughters "picking eggs."

My dad always spoke fondly of the early years of his involvement in the business, when he was on the site of each home under construction in his work boots and work clothes. Although his wardrobe changed over the years, his love of the business never did. He was always the first one in the office in the morning. The first Barness office was an add-on to my grandparents' home on Route 611 in Warrington. The next was across the driveway, in a small strip shopping center that my family built. The third office was behind the second, in another shopping center that my family had built, above the hardware store. The final home of The Barness Organization was a large stone building that my father built when I was working with him, less than a mile from his parents' home and the original office. A roll-top desk graced my dad's office, just like the one his father used. This was a gift from my sister and me for his birthday one year, and it's the only gift I ever remember him requesting. For every other gift, he always said that all he wanted was "love and affection."

Hanging over my father's desk was a huge black and white photograph of a farmer in overalls, his wife, and two young sons—the Barness family of the 1920s. He'd come a long way, but he never forgot the cherished beginnings of our family story.

1920s: The First Barness House

GEORGE KLEIN BOUGHT FIRST BARNESS HOUSE IN 1920s
The Warrington Township Report
Published by the Board of Supervisors
Summer 2005

This article, which discusses the very early days of the Barness real estate business, was written and provided by the Warrington Township Historic Commission. See their website for the entire article.

In the early 1920s, Joseph Barness and his wife Mary, at one time chicken farmers, purchased 80 acres of land in Bucks County. George and Ethel Klein were the first to buy a Barness home in the late 1920s, which still stands, pretty much in its original condition, at 3064 Bristol Road. Mary Barness baked and delivered a welcome cake to the Kleins and invited them to dinner.

The Beardsleys became the second Barness buyers, and Mary Barness repeated the cake-and-dinner process. The same happened with the third family to purchase, the Hancocks.

In 1935, Joseph Barness bought an additional 100 acres, which included the corner of Easton and Lower Barness roads, where his residence and office would reside for many years. [*It was actually near the corner of Bristol Road.*] This structure still stands at 1334 Easton Road and is now the home of several businesses.

The Barnesses were one of the first to envision a "total" community and homes where electricity was an included feature. In the 1930s you could purchase a Cape Cod house on one acre of land for $4,990. Remember, this was a time where the economic conditions of the Great Depression were still fresh in the minds of all Americans.

The houses built on Upper and Lower Barness roads were built by Barness during World War II. Since there were wartime restrictions on building homes, Mr. Barness obtained permission to build 30 to 32 homes on the old Dobbins Farm off of Easton Road, with the stipulation that they be rental properties for defense workers. Most of the original occupants worked for Brewster Aircraft, which later became NADC in Warminster. Each house was situated on one acre of land; all were constructed of brick and had slate roofs. However, no two houses were exactly alike due to the materials that were available for use at that time. To this day the houses on this street still retain much of their original charm, even though many have been added on to, and some properties have been subdivided, with newer-styled houses built on them.

The Barnesses are the namesake to many recreational areas in the township including the Mary Barness Tennis and Swim Club located at 2501 Freedoms Way and Barness Park located at 2750 Bristol Road. [*These facilities are still in existence and used extensively by children and families of the community!*]

1932-36: What Is Home Without a Garden?

I received a letter dated September 2, 1998, just a few days before my dad passed away. Ben Kristol and his wife were early residents of Warrington, and he enclosed the only copy (and this was an original!) of a Joseph Barness brochure that I had never seen.

He wrote: "Joseph and Mary Barness and the 1924-1936 imprints came to memory ... Beyond the burning down of our and your [grandparents'] *barn the same afternoon as it was the turning event that edged Barness into new aspirations, October 1927.* [This had never been mentioned to me, and I checked with my Uncle Lew, who also had no recollection of it.] ... Since we have been diminishing most of our papers and albums and collections for some time, you may keep the original **What Is Home Without A Garden?** We worked and dreamed with your family on that 1932-1936."

The brochure is printed on paper similar to construction paper. The paper is folded, and each page of the brochure is about 5½ x 7½ -inches.

Inside the cover:
YOU WILL FIND FREEDOM … ON A MINIATURE GARDEN FARM

We wish to be frank. The purpose of describing and showing one of our homes is: To first attempt to show you why you should own your own home and, next, if possible, to sell you that home. If we succeed in both purposes we shall be very happy, but if we are successful in the first purpose only, this description will have served its course. We sincerely mean every word printed in this edition, and to those who seek a *country home*, we wish that you consult us. We take our profession seriously, and attempt to build and sell properties that can give you the most for your money. So, then, keeping this in mind continually, we ask you to read our copy carefully, and remember that we are ready to serve you.

Rent receipts multiply in number but not in value. Why not invest that rent money in a home instead of spending it for something less substantial and less permanent? A home of your own is now in the reach of every man and every pocketbook. It is simple. A small down payment, and the balance monthly, the same amount as your rent is today. Your choice may be had from the different designs and prices that we shall describe.

"Health and Happiness," these real things in life may be found on a little garden farm, which is located in Warrington, Bucks Co., 8 miles north of Willow Grove or 14 miles north of Philadelphia's City Line, and only 78 miles from New York.

Page two:
Here are 10 advantages in owning A GARDEN HOME IN WARRINGTON

1. PRIDE. Pride of possession inspires you to work around home and garden, giving you healthful exercise in the open air and sunshine.

2. INDIVIDUAL EXPRESSION. You will take pleasure in making the exterior and interior of your home express your individuality. The home is yours!

3. INDEPENDENCE. Owning your home, you can live as you please with no interference from anyone.

4. TAXES. The taxes are at least 50 per cent lower than those in the city. Thus the monthly payment on the 20-year plan is no higher than the monthly payment on the city's 25-year plan.

5. PETS. The home owner can have as many pets as he wants, both indoors and outdoors, but there are adequate restrictions to ensure you that your home will not decrease in value.

Page three (continuation from Page Two):

6. POSSIBLE INCOME. You could, for instance, make your property produce an income by building a poultry house and raising poultry or gardening.

7. PEACE OF MIND. You know that you have provided a home for your family. When you finish paying for it, you will have small expense in maintaining it.

8. A CASH EQUITY. Owning a home is like having a savings account. In an emergency, money can always be borrowed with the home as security.
9. EASY PAYMENTS. You pay for the home you desire on monthly payments suited to your income. At no time will you have to renew the mortgage.
10. WEALTH. A man's greatest asset is planning a home of his own for the happiness of his wife and children.

———

If you contemplate home-ownership, come to our office at once. You will not be high pressured, as such tactics are not our policy, but you will learn how to proceed to own your home with the least expense and worry.

Page four:
It is more than an investment to own your own home. It is a tradition! A tradition made of the satisfaction men and women have always had in the joys of a gracious garden, the privacy to live as they pleased, the advantages they could offer their children, the unmistakable glow of being "Lord of the Manor."

To Warrington the roads are good; the stores, churches, and buses are accommodating, the surroundings are very pleasant; the community is ideal, the neighbors are your dear friends.

You may buy a five-room and bath Cape Cod bungalow which is built of masonry and beautifully designed. This home contains a large living room with a real log-burning fireplace; dining room; beautiful kitchen with a double drain-board sink and a built-in all-wall cabinet, linoleum floor covering, and electric range;

two bedrooms with three closets; tile bathroom with a built-in tub and shower, Venetian Mirror Wall Hanging Cabinet over the wash-stand, and linen closet; unfinished attic which can be converted into two large additional bedrooms; large basement with concrete floor and plastered walls, laundry trays, artesian well with automatic electric pump; hot and cold running water, hot water heat; hardwood floors; nice graded lawn; garage; on one acre tract of land. Price, $4,990. More ground available if desired. This home can be financed through the Federal Housing Insured Mortgage, or any other way you would desire. Never before were these easy terms available to those who love *country life.*

Our homes can be bought for 10 percent cash, the balance in small monthly payments (like rent) that cover everything: the principle payment, the interest, the taxes ...

Page five: (continued)

... and the insurance. "No Extras." No second mortgage. No lump-sum payments now or later!

Sidestep the "waste" of five years of renting... decide now you will turn those "rental checks" into "home-payment" checks. That is one way to escape the bother and uncertainty of month-to-month leases, the one sure way to escape increasing higher rents and the one sure way to saving, security, and independence!

If you are in business or working "full time," you'll find plenty of time to keep some chickens and raise a garden for pleasure. If you work "part-time," you'll find that your garden and chickens will be a great help to you and your family. By spending $3.00 for seeds and by doing a little work, which is really more pleasure than labor, you may supply your family with vegetables for the whole year. In time of recession, think of how much help this would be to you.

We have other beautiful modern homes with 2, 3, or 4 bedrooms, some have 2 baths, on tracts of 1 to 10 acres. Prices range from $3,990.00

We are also specializing in building homes to order. We find that among the outstanding ambitions of people, one is to build their own home, to see it grow before his or her eyes, and to have it consist of whatever he or she desires.

The investor who puts $1,000 down into a $6,000 home should see its worth of $8,000 within the next five years. NO OTHER INVESTMENT CAN EQUAL THIS!

If a home is bought on a 20-year plan, monthly payments are less than would go for rent, and the buyer has his home, which is better than any other investment of fluctuating value.

Page six:
CAPE COD BUNGALOW, 5 rooms and bath, shower, heat, electric, laundry trays, hot and cold water, open fireplace, Artesian well, garage, one acre of land.

Price $3,990.00

ENGLISH BRICK BUNGALOW, 7 rooms and two baths (one tile), shower, hot water heat, hardwood floors, electric range, linoleum in kitchen, open fireplace, hot and cold running water, laundry trays, Artesian well, garage, one acre of land.

Price $5,575.00

CAPE COD SEMI-BUNGALOW, 6 rooms and bath, shower, heat, electric, laundry trays, hot and cold water, Artesian well, garage, three acres of land.

Price $4,490.00

TWO-STORY COLONIAL SIX-ROOM HOUSE, tile bath, shower, hot water heat, open fireplace, hardwood floors, electric range, linoleum, hot and cold running water, laundry trays, Artesian well, two-car garage, one acre of land.

Price $5,990

ENGLISH COLONIAL, stone, seven rooms and two tile baths, shower, electric range, oil burner, hot water heat, Artesian well, hot and cold running water, open fireplace, hardwood floors, linoleum in kitchen, two-car garage, one acre of land, surrounded with beautiful woodland.

Price $7,750.00

DUTCH COLONIAL, built of brick and clapboard, 6 rooms, 6 large closets, and a storage room, tile bath, hardwood floors, hot water heat, Artesian well, electric pump, separate laundry, garage, cemented and plastered cellar, hot and cold running water, electric range, linoleum, double drain-board sink and full wall cabinets in kitchen. One acre of land.

Price $5,290.00

And many, many others

Back page (a short budget worksheet):
Warrington Miniature Garden Farms

Price $____

Cash $ ____

Interest and Principal $

FHA Premium

Taxes (approx.)

Fire Insurance Premium

Total monthly charge

Average monthly saving

New monthly expenses

After paying this amount for twenty years, the home remains yours free and clear.

We have other plans where your monthly payments are less and your mortgage extended for a longer period.

1940: Welcoming People to Warrington

My grandparents made new friends with every house they built. They lived a rural, country life. Even when I was growing up in Warrington in the 1950s not far from my grandparents' home, there was a general store on the corner of Route 611 and Bristol Road that housed the post office, the butcher, and the local grocer. A ride to Doylestown was considered going "into town." As in many farming communities, it seemed that everyone knew everyone. I remember Althea Bloom, who remained friendly with my grandmother throughout her life.

Letter from Herbert Barness on Joseph Barness & Son, Inc. stationery
975 Easton Road
July 15, 1997

TO: Mrs. Althea Bloom
1309 School Lane
Warrington, PA 18976

Dear Althea:

Thank you so much for the wonderful letter we received. It is just about 57 years ago that my father built your home and you moved to Warrington. It was so different in that era that it would be impossible for anyone in today's world to be able to realize what it was like to move to Warrington in 1940 or in that time. Not only did you move into a small community, but it was almost like becoming part of a large family. I know that my parents felt that you were not a customer or a client but rather you were almost like their children and they had to look after you.

Best,
Herb

[*I also have the original receipt from the deposit on the Bloom home, dated Oct. 5, 1940:* "Received of William R. Bloom, Two Hundred Dollars, Deposit on Bungalow #52 School Lane. Price to be Fifty Nine Hundred Ninety Dollars. Agreement to be prepared by Oct. 10, 1940. Signed, Joseph Barness."]

1941: The Warrington Lions Club Is Established

The establishment of a Lions Club in Warrington was a big deal in its day, and it quickly became a major social organization. In a farming community, the homes were fairly spread out, so various groups were formed to give the community a social life. My grandparents were always part of the fabric of their community, so it is not surprising to me that my grandfather was involved in the Lions Club early on. The club started the Warrington Horse Show in 1958, and I have fond memories of my grandmother baking cakes for the bake sale every year. The Show was an annual event until 1988. In 2004, I was invited to become an Affiliate Member of the Lions Club, and I did so for two years, to continue the Barness tradition.

Lions Club 50th Anniversary Program
December 7, 1991
Fountainhead
New Hope, PA

In October of 1941, with war raging in Europe, Warrington with a population of about 1,200 people, was only a small rural community.

The idea of a social or community service club was initiated by a small group of men: Elvy Crouthamel, Al Clarence, Joe Barness and C. Edwin Mayer ... Informal dinner meetings were held at Vincent's Warrington Inn, and the men eventually visited the Perkasie Lions Club ... Erwin Mayer's

Post Office and General Store [*which I remember!*] was a natural focal point to organize 69 local men, anxious to form a "Lions" Club.

Charter Night was held at Casa Conti in Glenside on Monday Evening, Dec. 8th, 1941, with Perkasie as the sponsoring club. The cost of the Gala was $2 per plate. District Governor Earle S. Tomlinson presented the International Charter to Dr. John Prickett, our club's first president ... Under the clouds of war, and the tragedy of Pearl Harbor on the previous day, the Warrington Lions began their first 50 years of service.

There were plenty of club projects during the World War II years, for a young patriotic organization. The early Lions held scrap drives, blood donations, food & gift collections for service men, and even had "War Bond" drives ... It soon became evident that local community groups needed a meeting place. The Lions met the challenge.

Joe Barness, a leader in this project, donated a lot on 611. The Community Building formed a corporation in 1945, broke ground in Sept. 1950, dedicated the building in May 1952, and burned the mortgage in April 1960. What a job! Older members remember Al Clarence being a tough construction foreman. [*I think this is where I went to preschool!*]

The community had their building, but the Lions had operating and maintenance expenses. Another challenge; we needed a good fundraiser.

Arnold Blythe & L. Erwin Mayer came up with the idea of a Horse Show in 1944. The decision to go ahead was made in 1957, and we held our first "one day" show in August 1958 on the Norris Farm in Edison. It was some job building the ring and necessary jumps.

The horse show was a big success, and we eventually had to relocate to a larger "Rothrocks Farm" on Pickertown Road ... The show grew to two days in 1965. And then in 1978 we took on the "Class A" three-day show. A tent was rented to stable horses overnight, and everyone prayed for a clear weekend. We learned that the end of July is a very rainy period.

After 30 years, we ended the horse show project in July 1988, when our facilities needed updating and the property was sold for development.

1955: Dawson Manor

I don't remember this particular community as I was only 5 years old when it was built, but I found a flyer in my files about it. The homes started at $12,490, and the features included:

- Three Full Bed Rooms—each will accommodate twin beds
- Full Basement
- Baseboard Hot Water Heat
- Natural Wood Kitchen Cabinets
- Ceramic Colored Tile Bath (your choice)
- Built-in Bath Vanity with Sliding Door Medicine Cabinet
- Improvements of Sewer, Sidewalk, Curb, Water, Paved Streets
- Minimum Lot Size 60' x 150' [slightly less than ¼ acre]

There was also a Barness Playground in Dawson Manor that was donated to the township in 1959.

RECEIVE PRIZES FOR NAMING DEVELOPMENT
Hatboro Newspaper
April 1955

A new real estate development in Hatboro was named this week by students from the Hatboro-Horsham High School.

The development will be called Dawson Manor, and the name was submitted by Pat Tinney and James Sell. Both were awarded $25 prizes.

Dawson Manor will be developed by Joseph Barness & Son, of Warrington, who made the awards to the students following a school-wide contest.

The name Dawson is derived from John Dawson, who, in 1705, became the first settler of Hatboro. Dawson, a hatter by trade, later built the Crooked Billet Inn, which still stands.

Six awards were made to students for selecting street names in the new settlement. They are: Boileau, Sarah Haigler; Jarrett, Paul Coe; Keith, Edward Lavish and Nicholas Lucera; Lukens, Gerald Jackson and Nancy Pool; Cornell, Jean Morse; Moore, anonymously.

The name Boileau is derived from Nathaniel Boileau, who lived next to Loller School early in the 19th century and was very active in Pennsylvania politics, serving as Secretary of State for nine years. He was one of Hatboro's prominent citizens during its early development.

Jarrett stems from John Jarrett, born in 1702 and a life-long resident of Horsham. Jarrett was one of the original officers of the Hatboro Library Association in 1775.

The name Cornell comes from the well-known family, which came to this area in the early 1900s. The name was given in honor of Warren Cornell, Sr.

Lukens is derived from an old family in the area, Jon Lukens being the original settler. He came to Horsham in 1734.

John Keith was one of the early notables of Montgomery County. In 1717 he was appointed Lieutenant Governor of Pennsylvania. His estate in Horsham still stands and is occupied by the Strawbridge family.

Moore stems from Dr. Nicholas Moore, who came here from London in 1682. He was the first Chief Justice of Pennsylvania. He was granted the Manor of Moreland by William Penn.

1957: Profile of Joe Barness

WARRINGTON—A CROSS ROADS FROM THE EARLY 1700s TO THE LATE 1930s, TODAY A SUBURBAN COMMMUNITY: *JOSEPH BARNESS: WARRINGTON'S 20TH CENTURY PIONEER*
The Bucks County Realtor Magazine
1957

In 1924 Joseph Barness, familiarly known to our members as Joe, came to Warrington, where he purchased 80 acres of ground facing Bristol Road. It was not until 1928, four years later, that he built and sold his first house, thus becoming a pioneer in furthering the expansion of the area from a mere crossroad to the fast-growing community you see today.

In 1935 he bought an additional 100 acres, which included the corner site on which his office and residence now stands. Prior to Joe's arrival in Warrington, he resided in Philadelphia. His first house sold for $3,900. Recently he built one, which sold for $32,500.

Many of our Directors and board members spent much time at his home in Warrington during the year he served as President of our Board [*in 1954*], graciously entertained afterwards by his wife May [*my grandmother was often called May*]. They have two sons. Herbert Barness, member of our Board, was also the first President of the Home Builders Association, which he helped organize. He has been associated with his father for the last 10 years. He served in the armed forces and graduated from Bucknell University with a degree in Mechanical Engineering, and now lives in Warrington.

1958: *Fortune* Magazine Ad Featuring Herb Barness

Fortune Magazine
August 1958

My father built Warrington Country Club on Almshouse Road, and it opened on Memorial Day Weekend, 1958. I remember it well. Both of my parents learned to play golf, and my sister and I were given every opportunity to learn to play (including having the golf pro give us lessons in our basement!). My parents loved golf and played as long as they were able—and often played together—but my sister and I never took to it.

This ad was part of a campaign by the Bucks County Industrial Development Corporation to bring companies and new businesses to Bucks County. My dad, who served as President of the corporation from 1958-1962, is the golfer in the forefront of the photo, hitting out of the stream! On the back of this piece, there was a Post-It note from my dad to me that said, "LB—For posterity. Warr. CC 1958." Clearly, I was destined to be the family historian!

Deciding on a New Location

Man in the foreground is about to move to a new location in Bucks County. Knows where he's going, too. He should.
He owns the golf course.
He's Herb Barness who recently built the Warrington Country Club and already over 300 golfing executives and their families are members. Warrington, by the way, is right in the heart of Bucks County.

Executives who work in Bucks —
and there are a lot of them —
are only a chip shot away from their favorite outdoor sports.
Even more sedentary types find Bucks uncommonly salubrious.
Book shops report a brisk business.

The reason that most of these executives live in Bucks County is because they enjoy working there.
Leading companies have found that point by point the advantages of doing business in Bucks are unmatched. Worth investigating, too, is Pennsylvania's tax setup and a 100% financing plan which Bucks can make available.

Relocation, we know from experience, is an important and involved decision. We will cooperate with your representatives **in complete confidence**.
Better yet,
come see Bucks for yourself.
And bring your clubs.

write:

Gordon R. Exley, 2d
Bucks County Industrial
Development Corporation
Doylestown, Pennsylvania

It's pleasant to do business in

BUCKS COUNTY,
Pennsylvania

Typical hex sign that appears on buildings in this colorful Pennsylvania Dutch country. Thought to bring good fortune to the building.

1959: County Distinguished Service Award

The Board of Commissioners

of

Bucks County, Pennsylvania

is pleased to award this

Distinguished

Public Service Award

to

HERBERT BARNESS

In recognition of Distinguished Service in the interests of

Bucks County

Board of Commissioners

Dated DECEMBER 31, 1959

1959: Brochure from the National Agricultural College

The idea for a farm school in Bucks County came from Dr. Joseph Krasukopf, whose goal and vision was to establish a school to train young Jewish men in the art of farming. He founded the school in 1896, and it was renamed The National Farm School and Junior College in 1946 and then the National Agricultural College in 1948. The name was changed again to Delaware Valley College of Science and Agriculture in 1960, so this brochure pre-dates that era. It seems natural to me that my dad cared about Jewish boys learning to farm in Bucks County, since he himself was one of them. He served on the Board of Trustees of Delaware Valley College for years, and in 1983 he stepped aside and I was given a seat on the Board to continue the Barness tradition. I served as a Trustee for five years.

The brochure outlines the college's five-year progress program of expansion and physical development, and it notes that two dormitories housing a total of 130 students and two faculty families were currently under construction. The articles from 1960 that follow (see pages 49-51) describe the dedication ceremony for the dorms, one of which was named for my grandparents, and note that Herbert Barness and Leon L. Berkowitz were Associate Chairmen of the fundraising effort. Herbert Barness's photo and comments on the importance of this project were included in the brochure. In his own words:

"An educational institution which occupies the largest campus of any private college in the United States, and is the only college in Bucks County, while at the same time, possessing the advantage of proximity to the cultural center of Philadelphia, is unquestionably, a college of tremendous potential.

"National Agricultural College's importance should be weighed in terms of the educational opportunities it offers as an asset of the fast-growing Delaware Valley. What we do now to increase our College's ability to keep pace with future student enrollment needs will reflect credit and add prestige to Delaware Valley's cultural reputation.

"Everyone concerned with the future of higher education in our country, and in particular with the educational needs of our own Delaware Valley community, should share in shaping the future of National Agricultural College as though it were considered a most important industry."

The 1960s

I TURNED 11 YEARS OLD IN 1960, and my father turned 38. In 1961, we moved from Warrington and what was still a rural life (my best friend's family had a farm and we used to play in the cow barn), to Rydal, Pennsylvania, in Abington Township, a more classically suburban setting. I remember how excited I was to live on a street with a sidewalk! My parents designed and built our house, a split-level home with a large great room and an area for my mother's art studio. It had a formal dining room, which we used, and a formal living room, which we did not! There was even a putting green, with real putting green grass, outside. That fall, I started 7th grade at Huntingdon Junior High School.

The summer of 1965 was especially memorable for our family, because my father took a month off from work, and we traveled from Denver westward as a family. To this day, it is remarkable to me that in an age with no cell phones or fax machines, he left his business for an entire month! But it was well worth it, as we talked about that trip for our entire lives. In other summers, my sister and I both attended overnight camp in the Poconos. We also started traveling to the Virgin Islands during the winter school vacations. In 1967, I was graduated from Abington High School and entered Tufts University as a freshman.

My dad was very busy during this time too; the business flourished, and I have many clippings from this decade. Post-World War II construction continued to boom in Bucks County, and many new communities were built. It was also a time of great change and cultural turbulence in our country, with the Civil Rights Movement and the Vietnam War as the backdrop to our lives. My father's interest in his community continued, with leadership in the local Boy Scouts organization, work on behalf of the Bucks County Industrial Development Corporation—a long-range drive to promote the area to new businesses and bring industry to Bucks County—and a donation to Delaware Valley College with his brother Lewis in honor of their parents.

My father also loved sports, and it was during this time that his enthusiasm turned into a business interest, first in harness racing (where the driver sits in a two-wheeled sulky) and then flat racing (where the rider sits on the horse). He also bid for a National Basketball Association franchise team and the Philadelphia Eagles football team, and became the sponsor and President of the Philadelphia Golf Classic. I think his involvement in all of these sports was an extension of his genuine interest in them, and since the only one he could actually play was golf, he found other ways to be involved. I'm sure that the business part of owning a pro-sports team or launching harness racing in Philadelphia appealed to him, but he was also very interested in the "fun" part too. When he finally became a part owner of the Eagles in 1969, we had a great time going to games and even the Super Bowl.

My dad had always been interested in politics—he said it stemmed from the time of FDR's third term—and it was during this decade that he began to take on a more active role behind the scenes.

1960

The first major set of clippings I have came from The Evening Bulletin, The Philadelphia Inquirer, Levittown Times, The Daily Free Press *(Quakertown),* The Yardley News, The Trenton Evening Times, The Public Spirit *(Hatboro),* The Daily Intelligencer, The Fairless Hills News, Bristol Daily Courier, The Newtown Enterprise, Delaware Valley News, The Star *(Southampton),* The Morning Call *(Allentown),* The News Herald *(Perkasie) and* Delaware Valley Advance *(Langhorne). They are all from February 1960, and each of them covered the same information about the campaign for a new and expanded camp for the Boy Scouts, with my father named the General Chairman of that campaign. I don't know if my dad had someone collect and label these articles or whether they were assembled and sent to him, but they were all together, mounted on the same colored paper, and had the source and date typed in small labels. This Boy Scout campaign was obviously big news in Bucks County!!*

SCOUTS LAUNCH TO EXPAND CAMP, $360,000 DRIVE TO BUY POCONO SITE: Warrington Man Named As Chairman
The Levittown Times
February 4, 1960

The Bucks County Council Boy Scouts of America, whose Scout membership has tripled in the past decade, today launched a campaign for $360,000 that will expand and improve its present camp and acquire a new site in the Pocono Mountains.

At the same time, Council President W. Atlee Burpee III announced that Herbert Barness, Warrington land developer and builder, would serve as general chairman of the campaign.

Announcement of the campaign comes just four days before the observance of the 50th anniversary of the founding of Scouting in America.

Barness, a partner in Joseph Barness and Son and president of the Warrington Country Club, said he had accepted the general chairmanship of the Boy Scout Development Fund because this jump in population and Scout membership "creates a very great need for the boys of Bucks County and a challenge to all adult leaders."

Barness, a native of Bucks County, former Scout and father of two daughters, said that because Scouting and its camp operation are non-profit, the council must turn to all residents of the area to make this needed expansion.

Mr. Barness, a graduate of Doylestown High School and Bucknell University, was a major in the Air Force [*No, he was a Captain and Commander of the U.S. Army Air Force's Communication Squadron in Guam*], with four years' service during World War II. He is a director of Welcome House, president of the Bucks County Industrial Development Corporation and Park Foundation, and a trustee of National Agricultural College.

The Advance Gifts campaign was set off at an enthusiastic kickoff dinner at the Warrington Golf and Country Club, attended by 100 volunteer workers and their wives. Campaign General Chairman Herbert Barness was toastmaster at the kickoff dinner and noted that this is the first time in its history that Bucks County Council has conducted a county-wide fund drive.

"We have already had success in recruiting a top-notch team for this historic campaign," Barness said.

INDUSTRIAL UNIT PICKS BARNESS
The Daily Intelligencer
February 5, 1960

Herbert Barness of Joseph Barness & Son, Warrington, was reelected president of the Bucks County Industrial Development Corporation Wednesday evening, at the annual meeting of the membership held at the Warrington Golf and Country Club.

In his annual report to the membership, President Barness stated that in the 22-month period, 21 firms, capable of employing 3,204 persons, have been convinced to locate their plants in Bucks County. In this same period, four local firms, employing 2,979 persons, have been assisted in strike mediation and plant expansion problems by our Corporation.

The annual income produced by the firms relocated or otherwise assisted is estimated equal to the support of 41,000 people, and increase in volume of trade to $61,500,000 and a tax value to the municipalities affected that would provide for the amortization and maintenance of 3,250 school rooms.

GIFTS FOR GENERATIONS
The Daily Intelligencer
November 5, 1960
Editorial

Dedication of two new dormitories at Delaware Valley College lends renewed emphasis on the growing importance of this institution in our regional educational scheme.

The buildings represent part of an extensive expansion program at the school where more than 400 students are enrolled and whose dramatic growth since it was founded in 1896 is one of the more thrilling sagas of America's smaller colleges and universities.

That these two modern, nicely equipped dormitories—each housing 60 students—representing a total cost of $400,000, were made possible through the generosity of members of the college board and people who are much a part of Bucks County is warm commentary indeed on public spirited interest of men devoted to lasting and enduring values for generations to come.

Significance of the work of the college, of the unheralded thoughtfulness of the donors was not lost on the some 200 business, industrial, professional, and governmental leaders who attended the dedicatory service.

It was more than a dedicatory. It was a quiet, appreciative, and understanding salute as well to Herbert Barness, his brother, Dr. Lewis Barness and Samuel Cooke, who made the attractive dormitories possible.

VALLEY COLLEGE DEDICATES DORMS: To House 130; Honor to Parents
The Daily Intelligencer
November 1960

Two new dormitories to house 130 students were dedicated Saturday by Delaware Valley College, Doylestown, as part of Homecoming Day.

Constructed at cost of $400,000 through the Housing and Home Finance Agency of the Federal Housing Authority, the two buildings are named Ethel Cooke Hall and Joseph [*and Mary*] Barness Hall and represent completion of the first stage of the current five-year development program.

The dormitories are named in honor of the parents of two benefactors of the college—Samuel Cooke, president of the Penn Fruit Company, and Herbert Barness, Bucks County realtor and developer—both members of the Board of Trustees. Dr. Louis [*Lewis*] Barness, brother of Herbert Barness, of Pennsylvania University [*University of Pennsylvania*] also took part in the ceremony.

SONS HONOR PARENTS. Two sons, Herbert and Dr. Lewis Barness, honored their parents, Joseph and Mary Barness, Warrington, on Saturday when a dormitory at Delaware Valley College of Science and Agriculture was dedicated to them. Shown, left to right, are James Work, college president; Herbert Barness, opening the door to Barness Hall; Samuel Cooke, Morris H. Goldman, chairman of the board of trustees. Staff photo by Charles Norton.

BARNESS NAMES 7 TO TASK FORCE
The Philadelphia Inquirer
August 19, 1960

Herbert Barness, President of the Bucks County Industrial Development Corporation, Wed. night appointed a seven-man "task force" Committee to study the feasibility of an urban renewal program for Bucks County.

The appointments were made at a special meeting of the Corporation's Board of Directors at the Warrington Golf & Country Club.

The task force will make a preliminary physical study of these areas, draft a preliminary report to the full Board of Directors, and after a discussion and evaluation of the report, the entire Board will make a final physical observation tour before drafting a recommendation to the County Commissioners.

PLEASE, KRIS, TAKE CARE OF OUR FRIENDS
The Daily Intelligencer
December 24, 1960
Editorial Comment

Here we are again, Christmas. Maybe the world is spinning faster; or perhaps the years are coming to pass more rapidly; quite possible we're growing younger. Whatever the reason, the Yule season seems to be here more frequently.

You will understand, we are sure, that this is not the standard Yuletide essay. We've dispatched our editorial piece elsewhere on this page and today, on this very eve of that significant time when most people (young people, that is) stack up the loot and convince themselves it is more blessed to receive, we wander off on another beat.

If this isn't giving, it is at least generous thinking about many of our very fond and personal friends whose stockings, we pray, will be bulging with old Kris' response to our pleas.

So, our entreaty to St. Nick is for others and not for ourselves. We're sure he'll agree they've earned the right to a very special cup of joy, such as, for example:

HERB BARNESS: Four fine new industries for his Industrial Development Corporation, which would mean at least four more afternoon-evening golf matches and receptions at his country club.

1961

INDUSTRIAL PARK PLANS BARED FOR WARRINGTON: 9 Plants To Build On Site
The Daily Intelligencer
October 12, 1961

Nine manufacturing firms, which will initially employ 600 persons, have arranged to build plants in the Warrington Industrial Park.

The announcement was made this morning by Gordon R. Exley II, executive director of the Bucks County Industrial Development Corp., and Warrington builder and developer Joseph Barness, president of J. Barness and Son.

Barness owns the 87-acre tract in Warrington Township on which the plants will be built and, along with Industrial Development Corp, is negotiating with other firms.

Representatives of the firms will meet at the Warrington Golf and Country Club this afternoon to be greeted by county and state officials.

BUCKS RACING ASSN. AWARDED LICENSE
The Daily Intelligencer
Undated

The State Harness Racing Commission ended a series of legal and political battles yesterday by awarding a harness racing license to the Bucks County Racing Assn.

The action was taken in Harrisburg with Democratic Commissioners Martin Cusick and Edward Kane voting for the award to the Bucks group and Chairman Lawrence B. Sheppard abstaining. The commission also awarded a license to the Washington Trotting Association, Washington County.

The Bucks group will lease the $12 million Liberty Bell Race Track now under construction at Knight Rd. and Woodhaven Blvd., Philadelphia. A portion of the track grounds will extend into Bensalem Township, Bucks County.

Both the Bucks unit and the Liberty Bell Racing Assn., headed by Philadelphia trucking magnate James P. Clark, will each sponsor 5-day racing seasons. It is reported that in return for use of the one-mile oval and the 35,000-seat grandstand, the Bucks Racing Assn. will pay an annual $150,000 rental and turn over half its profits.

Liberty Bell was awarded its license April 5. At that time Lawrence voted against the award and heatedly charged that Clark was setting up a "racing monopoly."

On July 19, the State Supreme Court upheld Liberty Bell's license, which had been contested by the Keystone Racing Assn., an organization which had hoped to operate in Bensalem Township. The commission is empowered to issue one more license.

The Bucks County Racing Association is headed by its president, Daniel Parish of Pittsburgh, a close friend of Gov. Lawrence. John T. Welsh, Doylestown realtor and Bucks Democratic leader, is secretary. Art Rooney of Pittsburgh, owner of the National Football League's Pittsburgh Steelers, is vice-president and treasurer. Herbert Barness, Warrington builder and developer, is, along with Welsh and the others, a director and incorporator.

Welsh said today that he was happy with the commission's decision and added that present plans call for the track to begin operations in Aug. 1962.

1962

'GREAT DAYS' ARE UNDERWAY AT LIBERTY BELL PARK
The Daily Intelligencer
June 2, 1962
Sports Beat by Bill Brown

START OF SOMETHING BIG. Susan Robinson, Miss Pennsylvania, cuts the ribbon officially opening Liberty Bell Park and the first thoroughbred racing in the history of the state. Looking on at Saturday afternoon's ribbon cutting are Herbert Barness, President of Continental Racing Association and Warrington realtor (left), and Roy Wilkinson, Jr., Chairman of the Pennsylvania State Horse Racing Commission.

ACCEPTS PORTRAIT
The Daily Intelligencer and Realty Record
Undated

Herbert Barness, of Joseph Barness and Son, prominent developer and retiring President of the Bucks County Industrial Development Corp., and his wife, Irma, admire a portrait presented at the Corporation's recent annual meeting in recognition of his years of community service on the Planning Commission, Sewer and Water Commission, Park Board, Boy Scout Fund Raising Drive, Delaware Valley College Board of Trustees and as Corporation President for two years. The presentation was made by retiring Corporation Vice President George Burnham, IV, Asst. Vice President of U.S. Steel Corp. The portrait was painted by James Schuker of Quakertown, a well-known artist who had never seen Mr. Barness. He painted the portrait from recent photos.

1963

$12 MILLION COMMUNITY FOR BUCKS TRACT
Philadelphia Daily News, December 21, 1962
The Jewish Exponent, December 29, 1962
Real Property News, January 2, 1963
The Evening Bulletin, January 6, 1963
Building and Realty Record, January 7, 1963

A $12 million home development, replete with its own swim club for residents and its own sewage plant, is being planned in Warrington, Bucks County.

The development, which will begin with 233 acres and homes starting at $17,990, is located on Route 611, three-quarters of a mile north of Street Road. The area at one time was famous for the breeding of world-famous Palomino horses. Hence, the development will be known as Palomino Farms.

The development firm is headed by Herbert Barness, president of Joseph Barness & Son, Warrington realtor and builder.

Barness said three, possibly four, builders will participate in the home development. The first models are now under construction, with official opening planned for February.

The Palomino Farms area will include a school site, sites for religious buildings, wide winding streets for extra safety, and bridle trails bordering historic Neshaminy Creek. The latter runs through the 233-acre site.

"The officers of Palomino Farms will maintain a strict supervision of the new Bucks County development to make certain that only the finest-quality products are used, and that dignity in design and promotion follows a plan to be established," stated Barness.

The land area is marked by a tall water tower, which will provide water to the 440 homes initially to be built.

BUCKS CO. BOARD NAMES A.M. MOYER
The Bulletin
January 12, 1963

Chairman of the Bucks County Planning Commission for this year is A. Marlyn Moyer Jr., president of the Trevose Savings and Loan Association and of the Lower Bucks County Chamber of Commerce.

Herbert Barness of Warrington was elected vice chairman, and Mrs. Elinor R. Ridge of Lower Makefield was reelected secretary.

Brochure from Welcome House

Looking back, I realize what a dynamic place Bucks County was in the 1960s. It had attracted some major cultural and literary stars, and with that, some important and good works.

Pearl S. Buck, noted novelist and winner of the Pulitzer Prize for The Good Earth, *was the first American woman to win the Nobel Prize in literature. She established Welcome House, which was an interracial adoption agency, the first of its kind, which helped place children who were fathered by American soldiers in Asia during World War II. On a personal note, a forever memory: I was assigned by my English teacher in junior high school to do an interview with someone, and my dad arranged for me to go to Pearl Buck's house and interview her. I can still picture her coming down a winding staircase in a velvet dress to meet me. And somewhere I still have that interview.*

Another renowned Bucks County resident was Oscar Hammerstein II, the famous lyricist and collaborator who wrote the classic musicals of my youth: Show Boat, Oklahoma!, Carousel, South Pacific, The King and I, *and* The Sound of Music. *He lived at the Highland Farm in Doylestown from 1940 until his death 20 years later.*

James A. Michener, author of so many novels, including Tales of the South Pacific *(which won a Pulitzer Prize for fiction in 1948 and which Oscar Hammerstein and Richard Rodgers adapted as a musical),* Hawaii,

Centennial, Chesapeake, Alaska, *and more, grew up in Doylestown, Bucks County, and graduated from Doylestown High School in 1925 (which was my father's alma mater, although they were there about two decades apart).*

Bucks County was still a small community in those days, and these illustrious and talented artists contributed their time and money to numerous worthy causes. My dad knew them, and he worked alongside Pearl Buck and Oscar Hammerstein for Welcome House, even serving as the President.

I am not sure of the year of this piece, but I know it had to be after 1960, which is when Oscar Hammerstein died, and before 1964, when the Pearl S. Buck Foundation was established and my dad was no longer involved. Note the interesting Board of Directors!

Welcome House was established over a decade ago by Pearl S. Buck to provide permanent "family homes" or foster homes for American-born children of Asian or part-Asian ancestry. These children had been considered "unadoptable" because of their unusual background.

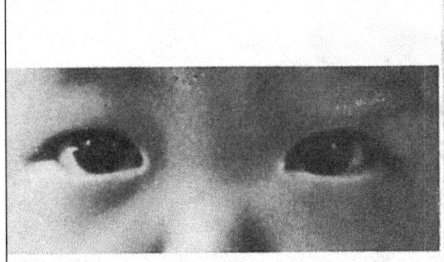

WELCOME HOUSE was established over a decade ago by Pearl S. Buck to provide permanent "family homes" or foster homes for American-born children of Asian or part-Asian ancestry. These children had been considered as "unadoptable" because of their unusual background.

As information about WELCOME HOUSE and its work was given to the public, adoptive parents of Asian and non-Asian background came to WELCOME HOUSE to apply to adopt such children. The program of the agency then changed focus and children began to be placed for adoption rather than for permanent foster care. WELCOME HOUSE pioneered in the placement of the part-Asian child, and its happy experience in this field has made a notable contribution to American adoption policy. While "matching" of a child is considered important, the Board of Directors

CHAIRMAN OF THE BOARD OF DIRECTORS
PEARL S. BUCK

BOARD OF DIRECTORS
MR. AND MRS. HERBERT BARNESS
MRS. EDWARD BIESTER
MR. AND MRS. NATHANIEL BREWER
MR. AND MRS. DAVID BURPEE
DR. AND MRS. RICHARD DARNELL
MR. AND MRS. ROBERT DODDRIDGE
MR. AND MRS. MICHAEL ELLIS
MR. AND MRS. KERMIT FISCHER
MRS. MARGARET ROESS FISCHER
MRS. OSCAR HAMMERSTEIN, II
MR. AND MRS. WILLIAM HAMMERSTEIN
MR. AND MRS. JOSEPH M. McDANIEL
MRS. CLARE NELSON
MR. AND MRS. EDWARD RITTENBERG
MR. AND MRS. WILLIAM A. SMITH
MR. AND MRS. W. BUZBY TAYLOR
MR. AND MRS. ST. JOHN TERRELL
MRS. RICHARD J. WALSH
MR. AND MRS. CHARLES A. WELLS

HONORARY BOARD MEMBERS
DR. RALPH J. BUNCHE
MR. EUGENE BURDICK
DR. MARTIN LUTHER KING, JR.
MR. WILLIAM J. LEDERER
MR. AND MRS. JAMES A. MICHENER
DR. GENEVIEVE BOWEN SHAW

2 PHILA. GROUPS IN N.B.A. BIDS

The Bulletin and *The Philadelphia Inquirer*
January 16, 1963
By Bill Conlin

It's interesting to me that I have very few memories of my dad's involvement in basketball. Then again, I was 14 years old when all this was happening and had recently moved to a new home and school in Rydal, so I guess I had other things on my mind!

A syndicate of Philadelphia district businessmen, headed by Herbert Barness, Warrington builder and real estate developer, wants to put this city back in the National Basketball Association next season.

The group has contacted the office of Maurice Podoloff, NBA President, and asked for a meeting regarding acquiring a franchise as soon as Podoloff returns from Wednesday night's NBA All-Star game in Los Angeles.

Allen Sommer, spokesman for the group, said it was understood that the Detroit club might be available for purchase.

Two groups of businessmen today reported they are ready, willing and hoping to bring a National Basketball Association franchise back to Philadelphia …

The second group is headed by Herbert Barness, a Bucks County realtor… Barness is reportedly in the venture with two other area businessmen.

"We made our minds up to pursue a franchise several weeks ago," said Barness by telephone from his office in Warrington.

"We have been in contact with Mr. Podoloff [*president of the National Basketball Association from 1949-1963*], and he plans to sit down with us after his return from the meeting in Los Angeles. Money is the least of our worries. We hope we can bring a team back to Philadelphia and make it work. The Warriors haven't done well in San Francisco, and we think Philadelphia should be an NBA town."

Barness said it is his understanding that the Detroit franchise is for sale, but that his group would also be willing to back a new franchise ... Barness is the vice president of the Bucks County Racing Association, which will lease the new Liberty Bell track for its 50-day meeting.

Other cities with representatives at the NBA meeting reportedly interested in an NBA franchise are Cleveland, Kansas, and Baltimore.

BUCK'S BARNESS
The Trenton Times
Editorial by Jimmie McDowell, Executive Sports Editor
Undated

Herb Barness, sports-minded Bucks County builder and developer from Warrington, is keenly interested in the possibility of owning a professional basketball team in Philadelphia. However, he isn't in a great hurry to push the issue in the middle of the current season, figuring that the time to talk and act is at season's end.

When the Warriors left Philly, Herb, an ardent fan, began thinking about buying an existing franchise or being a part of an expansion program in the National Basketball Association. "I figure that Philadelphia was and still is a good pro basketball city," he said yesterday.

He wished to deny the published report that he planned to buy the Detroit Pistons and move this team to Philadelphia. He would be interested in any available franchise, true, but he has done nothing towards acquiring the Pistons, he told the *Trenton Times*.

Herb has been a part of several sports undertakings, including two country clubs featuring 18-hole golf courses, and quite a few swimming clubs in recent years. He was impressed with the excellent turnout of the Philadelphia-New York football exhibition game at Princeton's Palmer

Stadium and believes that such a crowd could very well indicate that this area could support a professional football team. However, he is not involved with any of the people mentioned as prospective buyers of Harry Wismer's New York Titans.

Barness was not a part of the group that appeared on the West Coast in quest of a NBA franchise. The action there does not discourage him. Herb believes that at the end of the season the NBA will review the entire pro basketball picture, particularly in view of the fact that the rival hoop, the ABL, folded. He thinks there is sufficient talent available to stock additional franchises in the NBA. He'll be in there pitching for Philadelphia.

HOMES BY 3 BUILDERS OPEN AT PALOMINO FARMS
The Bulletin
February 9, 1963

Three builders working at Palomino Farms will each show a sample of their craftsmanship tomorrow in the new community on Route 611, three-quarters of a mile north of Street Road, Warrington, Bucks County.

Diversity of design is assured in the development by reason of the fact that three builders, each having their own styles, are building there ... Palomino Farms will have a swimming club for residents, its own sewage and water systems, and an area set aside for an elementary school and bridle paths. [*This really heralded modern real estate development!*]

Joseph Barness & Son of Warrington and Stanton E. Lipschutz of the Philadelphia firm of Becker, Lipschutz and Prussan are the developers. Bankers Bond & Mortgage Co. offered the financing.

The Philadelphia Inquirer
March 2, 1963

The announcement of my dad's election to be a director of the Philadelphia Lyric Opera Company was covered by multiple publications, including The Jewish Times. *I have no idea how he became involved, as he was definitely not an opera buff. I am assuming that someone he knew asked him ... and that's probably why he became a part of this organization. It seems to me that he frequently said YES when asked!*

Herbert Barness of Warrington, vice president of the Bucks County Planning Commission, has been named to the board of directors of the Philadelphia Lyric Opera Co.

BARNESS SAYS GROUP STILL SEEKS NBA PACT FOR CITY
The Daily Intelligencer
March 4, 1963

Following is a statement by Herbert Barness, Warrington land developer and realtor, regarding his position on obtaining a National Basketball Association franchise for Philadelphia, which has been issued because of numerous inquiries by the press.

"The group of businessmen which I represent is still interested in obtaining an NBA franchise for Philadelphia, and we are still negotiating towards this end. Numerous conversations have been held with representatives of the league. Conversations will continue after the termination of the current season. There are many details to be covered, which must wait until time is available with all the parties involved during which they can be discussed and ironed out."

The Jewish Exponent
April 1, 1963

Once again, I'm not sure how my father became involved with this particular organization, which provides football programs for youth. I do remember some of his friends from this organization, however, so I assume that someone he liked asked and he became active.

Herbert Barness, Bucks County developer and engineer, has been named to the national board of the Pop Warner Little Scholars.

Likely from *The Daily Intelligencer*
April 3, 1963

This is the first mention of my father wanting to build outside of the Bucks County/Philadelphia area. His entrepreneurial spirit definitely led him to new challenges and possibilities, and I think he saw a new and unique opportunity in the Caribbean. According to the 1964 Philadelphia Magazine profile on page 95, he began learning Spanish in anticipation of doing business in Puerto Rico and had acquired land there by 1963. We visited Puerto Rico on a family vacation, so I can only assume that this had something to do with it, but as far as I know, my dad never actually built a hotel there.

Herbert Barness, the Bucks County developer, has a bid from a national hotel chain to put up an ocean-front hotel in Puerto Rico.

HERBERT BARNESS BIDS FOR BIRDS AT 4.5 MILLION; FACES FIGHT FROM PAUL BROWN 7 ASSOCIATES
The Daily Intelligencer
August 20, 1963
By Russ Green

The Philadelphia Eagles football team was for sale during the 1960s, and my father was a bidder. There was a huge amount of press about this, but I have included only some of the many articles in my possession.

Paul Brown, fired Cleveland Browns coach and general manager, and Herbert Barness, a real estate tycoon, ran neck and neck today in what appeared to be a two-man race to buy the Philadelphia Eagles.

Barness reportedly made a bid of $4,550,000 at an Eagles stockholders' meeting yesterday.

Barness, a vice president and director of the William Penn Harness Racing Association, is ready to make a "cash deposit of any amount within 24 hours," according to his attorney, Paul Schwartz.

Owners of the Eagles put the club up for sale yesterday, with the price tag in excess of $4.55 million and a proviso the team be kept in Philadelphia.

Schwartz was quoted as telling the stockholders Barness wanted to "keep the ownership in Philadelphia," instead of "turning it over to outsiders." Barness was declared ready to buy 51 percent of the stock and retain as many of the original stockholders who wished to stay.

EAGLES' STOCKHOLDERS DECIDE TO SELL TEAM, LOCAL BID PRESENTED: BROWN STILL BEST BET TO TAKE OVER
The Philadelphia Inquirer
April 20, 1963
By Herb Good

As a side note, this piece includes the first mention of Engineering & Planning Associates, an offshoot of Joseph Barness & Sons that Herb started in the 1950s. This associate company did the engineering and planning that was necessary prior to development—securing zoning changes, putting in water and sewer lines, and so on. Joseph Barness & Son did the actual real estate development and home building—purchasing ground, financing development, building homes, marketing, and more. The two companies worked together, but Engineering and Planning Associates worked for others as well. The 1964 Philadelphia Magazine profile of my father on page 95 provides further insight into the work of this second company.

Stockholders of the Eagles agreed Friday by a "substantial majority" to sell their assets in the professional football club. They immediately received a bid for $4,550,000 from a local group headed by Herbert Barness, a resident of Warrington in Bucks County.

This bid was made, *The Inquirer* learned, in the hope of keeping the Eagles in the hands of Philadelphia-area civic leaders and sportsmen rather than having the franchise taken over by a syndicate headed by Paul Brown, former coach and general manager of the Cleveland Browns.

The stockholders gave authority to Frank McNamee, Eagles' president, and Michael J. O'Neill, representing the estate of the late James P. Clark, to negotiate the sale with prospective purchasers. This was done after they voted to sell at a meeting that lasted approximately one hour and 20 minutes in the boardroom of the Fidelity-Philadelphia Trust Co.

McNamee said that no bids were presented or discussed at the meeting. But Friday night he admitted receiving a written offer from Barness' group prior to the meeting but said he didn't read it until after the meeting. He said it would be considered along with other anticipated offers.

O'Neill said at least four other individuals or groups have evidenced interest in the club, and he expects to hear from several of them now that the stockholders have made their decision.

The offer on behalf of Barness and his group was made by lawyer John Swartz, who reportedly assured Eagles officials that his client was ready to begin immediate negotiations.

Barness, who heads one of the country's largest independent engineering and planning companies, is the founder and builder of the Warrington Golf and Country Club; vice president of the William Penn Racing Association, in which he's an associate of Art Rooney, Pittsburgh Steelers owner; and a national director of Pop Warner's Little Scholars.

Barness' letter explained that his group comprised residents of the Philadelphia metropolitan area who have supported the club over the years. It said that because of the affection that the fans hold for the Eagles the club should not be entrusted to anyone other than those who have supported it.

Barness and his associates are willing to acquire all of the outstanding stock, but would be willing to permit as many of the present stockholders to remain in the company as might desire to do so just as long as Barness takes over at least 51 percent of the stock.

O'Neill said that in his opinion they couldn't consider the Barness offer as a formal bid until he and McNamee knew the identity of Barness' associates and other factors involved.

Brown has had several conversations with McNamee about the sale, and it is believed that McNamee is strongly in favor of working out a deal with one of the most successful coaches in the game.

It is also known that O'Neill is against absentee ownership in any form, and therefore is expected to favor selling to Barness's group.

PROFILE: ENJOYS GOLF, RACING [*a box within this article*]
Herbert Barness, who heads a group that Friday declared itself ready to buy the Eagles for $4,500,000, is a husky six-footer whose interest in football was intensified, if anything, when he broke a leg playing the game as a schoolboy.

Native of Bucks County and long-time resident of Warrington, he is a graduate of Bucknell University (mechanical engineering) whose company, Engineering and Planning Associates, Inc., is one of the country's largest independent land developers. He has a wide range of other interests, including sports, the arts and philanthropies. He is the founder and builder of the Warrington Golf and Country Club—he shoots in the 80s—vice president and a director of the William Penn Racing (harness) Association, and a national director of the Pop Warner Little Scholars.

Barness served as president of Bucks County Industrial Development Corp., Bucks Park Foundations, and the Bucks County Home Builders

Association. He is now vice chairman of the Bucks County Planning Commission and president of the Pearl Buck Welcome House.

REALTOR BARNESS OFFERS $4.5 MILLION FOR EAGLES
The Philadelphia Inquirer
April 20, 1963
By Hugh Brown

... Asked about Barness' offer and its alleged delivery, McNamee had this to say:

"Yes, it was delivered to the Eagles office. But I ignored it deliberately. I put Barness' letter in the drawer of my desk and when I returned to the Eagles' office after the meeting, I opened it and read it in the presence of Mike O'Neill (Eagles voting trustee with McNamee), Jim Gallagher (Eagles personnel director) and Eddie Hogan (team publicist).

"The reason I delayed opening the letter was to avoid any haggling at the meeting. I had made clear several days earlier that the only issue before the stockholders would be to sell or not to sell."

Besides his real estate activities, Barness is vice president and director of the William Penn Racing Association which will lease the new Liberty Bell harness track for a Fall meeting, founder of the Warrington Country Club, a national director of the Pop Warner (football) Little Scholars, a member of the Bucks County Industrial Development Corp., and a director of the Philadelphia Lyric Opera Co. His father, Joseph, is director of a Doylestown bank and a partner with his son in the land development concern of Joseph Barness & Son.

In January, Barness announced his intention of pursuing a National Basketball Association franchise for this city, but apparently, that was shelved when Philadelphia was ruled out as an NBA site for 1963-1964.

McNamee, who is interested in the Liberty Bell track, was asked if (1) he knew Barness, and (2) whether he and O'Neill could consider his $4,500,000 or put it before the stockholders.

"I've met him," McNamee replied. "I understand he's got some stock in the track. As for his offer, it's below the minimum. The minimum—with 91 shares priced at $50,000—is $4,550,000."

Barness admitted "making a bona fide offer through my attorney ... and I am ready to make a cash deposit in 24 hours. There are others involved, but I don't want to divulge their names. I'm not trying to buy this team through newspapers."

BARNESS IN RUNNING TO BUY EAGLES
The Levittown Times.
April 20, 1963

Herbert Barness, a Warrington realtor, was running neck and neck today with Paul Brown, fired Cleveland Browns coach, in what appeared to be a two-man race to buy the Philadelphia Eagles ...

Barness, who said this morning that he had heard nothing new on the negotiations since his offer yesterday afternoon, lives at 1334 Easton Road, Warrington. [*That's actually the home of his parents!*]

Barness is a husky, six-foot Bucks County native. A longtime resident of Bucks, he is an engineering graduate of Bucknell University whose company, Engineering and Planning Associates, Inc., is one of the country's largest independent land developers. He has served as president of the Bucks County Industrial Development Corp, Bucks Park Foundation, and the Bucks County Home Builders Association.

Herb Barness new owner of the Eagles?

Maybe not at the moment, but the popular Bucks Countian has offered $4,500,000 cash for the former NFL champions, and it could be that the stockholders, eager to sell, will very seriously consider the offer in preference to some nebulous dickering from a Midwestern syndicate headed by Paul Brown.

BARNESS BID SHRUGGED OFF, BROWN SEEN AS EAGLES' BUYER
The Philadelphia Inquirer
Undated
By Herb Good

Although Paul Brown has yet to come forward with a formal offer, there is more reason than ever to believe that his syndicate will wind up with the Eagles.

The manner in which Frank McNamee, Eagles' president, and Michael J. O'Neill have shrugged off an offer from a group headed by Herbert Barness, Warrington land developer, serves to strengthen claims of insiders that the sale to Brown is all but an accomplished fact.

McNamee and O'Neill were authorized to negotiate the sale of the Eagles by the pro football club's stockholders on Friday.

McNamee pointed out that the written offer received from Barness Friday was for a mere $4.5 million, which is $50,000 under the Eagles' asking price.

"For that reason we don't have any authority to consider it," said McNamee.

O'Neill said the Barness offer couldn't be considered a formal one, since the identity of Barness' associates was not known.

Barness, who operates the largest independent engineering and planning firm in the country, said Saturday he was sure his associates would be willing to increase the bid by the required $50,000.

However, he said he isn't prepared to reveal publicly the names of the people with him at this time, since he doesn't want it to appear that he is trying to purchase the team through the newspapers.

TELLIN' ALL ABOUT SPORTS
The Daily Intelligencer
April 22, 1963
By Jim Hackett

There are several ways to meet a person and assess his personality and credentials when he's aspiring to a high position.

Herb Barness of Warrington has made a bona fide bid to purchase controlling interest in the Philadelphia Eagles.

As I read of Herb Barness' accomplishments, service and philanthropies, they impress me. But they take a backseat to an opinion I formed 15 years ago when I had never seen Herb Barness, didn't know him—and only heard about him through a mutual friend.

Sell-Perk hired a football coach fresh off the campus of Bucknell University. He brought with him a charming, beautiful, piano-playing and concert-contralto wife. This man was Chet Dawson, his wife was Judy. Dawson was the rugged son of a New York factory worker. Judy was the daughter of a Western Pennsylvania auto dealer.

Dawson was hired after a committee went to see Bucknell play football. The Bisons received a battering—but Dawson stood as a tiger in defeat. The minister who headed the committee was the most enthusiastic for his selection.

Herb Barness was a classmate of this pair.

Chet and Judy settled down to what promised to be a lifetime of happiness for two people deeply in love. The love burns deeply still—but it has been fueled by heartbreak and tragedy.

Dawson's first child was a son born with a digestive ailment. The oldest age ever attained by a child with this pancreatic affliction is 14. Their second child, a daughter, was born with the same deficiency. The son has since died. Today Dawson teaches school in Orange, New Jersey.

But it's back to those trying years when the couple lived in Perkasie. They did not have time to establish deep roots and a wide group of friends. Those who knew them intimately assisted in the best way they could and prayed for a medical discovery that was not forthcoming.

During all of these trying days, the Dawsons spoke very warmly of their college friend Herb Barness. His interest, his assistance, his fast friendship in their heartbreak was a treasure to them.

Herb Barness is more than a success—he's a person. The Eagles can use that commodity.

PLANNING MUST BE IMPLEMENTED
The Daily Intelligencer
1963
By W. Lester Trauch

Two Bucks County Planning Commission members, Charles R. Witmer, Sellersville, and Herbert Barness, Warrington, after hearing about $3 million dollars being spent on a Penn-Jersey transportation study to which the Bucks County Commissioners contributed $6,000, took their hair down about studies.

But it was Herbert Barness, young, dynamic Warrington realtor, builder, and developer, who with his father, Joseph, have done more to make Warrington Township the fine, modern, progressive municipality it is than practically anyone else, tore into the uselessness of making plans and then not carrying them out.

"It seems," said Barness, "that for years, at least 15 years or more, that we have been hearing about highway plans and rerouting Routes 202 and 611 in and around Doylestown, but nothing ever happens.

"The money," he emphasized, "is spent to make the plans and surveys, but they are never carried out. So what is the use of making studies if they never get used?"

Barness said Route 611 is in deplorable shape, and that it is ridiculous to build a four-lane highway up to Doylestown and then have no place for four lanes of vehicular traffic to get through the congested County Seat streets.

Barness said, "Plans and studies are fine, but getting them off paper and into the working stages is what counts in the end, which the State Highway department hasn't been doing in this community."

TELLIN' ALL ABOUT SPORTS
The Daily Intelligencer
April 25, 1963
By Jim Hackett

A LITTLE BIT ABOUT A LOT OF THINGS: Herb Barness, Warrington realtor who made a $4.5 million bid for the Philadelphia Eagles, told the *Intelligencer* he has not heard from the Eagles since he made his bid ... There is a strong feeling in these parts, and I share it, if the Eagles management was so intent on keeping the franchise with a local flavor, why doesn't Herb Barness get first call over Paul Brown? Barness is as local as Franklin Field, or Chuck Bednarik.

MUM'S WORD ON EAGLE SALE: Brown Missing Again
The Philadelphia Inquirer
April 25, 1963
By Fred Byrod

On the Eagles front, it was wordless Wednesday: one prospective buyer wasn't talking again, and another who was ready to talk had no one to listen.

Paul Brown, former head coach and manager of the Cleveland Browns, was missing again—or at least had not answered his phone for two days—after making his first appearance at home in more than two weeks Sunday night.

Herbert Barness, Warrington, Pa., land developer who heads a syndicate which submitted a written bid to buy the team last Friday at the time the stockholders voted to sell, said he had heard nothing from Eagles' president Frank. L. McNamee.

"I'm going to contact McNamee again," Barness said, "just to make sure he understands that while the price we offered was $4,500,000, we are ready to pay the minimum set, $4,550,000 (91 shares at $50,000 apiece)."

Barness said that five of the present stockholders have asked to be included in his group, and that six other stockholders telephoned him to say they hope he is successful in his attempt to buy the National Football League franchise.

TELLIN' ALL ABOUT SPORTS
The Daily Intelligencer
April 26, 1963
By Jim Hackett

There is a very strong feeling of hope in these parts that Herb Barness of Warrington should get first call to buy the Philadelphia Eagles after he made a bid when the stockholders voted to sell on Friday.

I don't know much about $4.5 million, but I did write an incident that reflects the human side of Herb Barness and his family. From the comments, many people agree. Here is a sample:

> Dear Jim:
>
> Had to tell you how deeply we enjoyed your recent column on the Herb Barnesses. All the other news articles, which I clipped from the Intell and the Philadelphia papers to ship to our children in college, were full of business and club details. None showed their very human appeal. We were very happy to read it.
>
> We moved here to Warrington in 1941. We moved into one of Joe's new homes on School Lane, newly married and starting a family. The Barnesses could not have been kinder. They acted very much like parents in many cases.
>
> When Bill, my husband, got interested in the Bux-Mont baseball league, the local team needed moral support or money. Joe was always

overwilling to provide—baseball field, trucks for moving equipment, lawn mower (a 4-foot cutter that was Herb's, I believe), advice or money. This human side is so often missed. So glad you caught it.

Althea Bloom, 1309 School Lane, Warrington

FIRE BLOWS WHISTLE ON 'COOL' EAGLE TALK
The Bulletin
By Hugh Brown
April 30, 1963

The meeting of minds yesterday between the Fourth Estate and the Messrs. O'Neill and McNamee produced nothing much other than considerable yak from the journalists' prosecuting attorney and the impression that the nation's piggy banks are safe from a mass stampede.

... Apparently, the only entrant in the Eagles sweepstakes who has really taken the bit in his teeth or if you prefer, a hook in his mouth—is Herbert Barness, the Warrington realty developer who is rich enough to afford a sporting proposition. O'Neill and McNamee confirmed that they had sat down with Barness, that he had upped his offer $50,000 to the negotiable minimum, and he'd be considered.

TELLIN' ALL ABOUT SPORTS
The Daily Intelligencer
April 30, 1963
By Jim Hackett

It is good to hear that Frank L. McNamee and Michael O'Neill, who have been designated by the stockholders to sell the Philadelphia Eagles, have talked to Herb Barness of Warrington. The pair announced their contact at a press conference yesterday.

They revealed that Paul Brown does not have a solo track to the purchase; that Barness verbally agreed to add $50,000 to his initial bid of $4.5 million to meet stockholders' requirements; that there are at least six parties interested in purchasing the club; they have no intention of developing an auction.

BARNESS WITHDRAWS BID FOR EAGLES AFTER FAILING TO GET CLEVELAND MONEY

The Bulletin
May 16, 1963
By John Brogan

A group of local businessmen, headed by Herbert Barness, Warrington Pa., realtor, has withdrawn its $4,550,000 offer to purchase the Eagles.

The offer was withdrawn in a letter sent more than a week ago to club president Frank L. McNamee, after Barness had failed in an attempt to interest a Cleveland faction in joining his group to purchase Philadelphia's National Football League franchise.

McNamee said this morning that Barness' letter of withdrawal, submitted by his attorney, John Swartz, was in "good taste." But the Eagles president expressed that the Barness group was reported "tired of waiting."

McNamee said it was made clear in a meeting with Barness that the Eagles were "in no hurry to sell and would take a long, thorough look at prospective buyers to get the best management possible for the team."

Barness' attempt to get Cleveland backing wasn't connected with Paul Brown. Barness indicated that his Philadelphia group—incidentally the only known bidders for the Eagles franchise—was fading away.

Barness contacted a Cleveland broker who had been interested in the Eagles. He had the broker fly here and asked him if he could get Cleveland backing to join his local group.

At his home this morning, Barness refused to confirm or deny that his group had withdrawn.

"I have no comments," Barness said, "until I find out what's going on."

"I don't want to make a fiasco of this thing," he continued. "I don't know whether I'm in the picture or not, so I don't want to say anything until I find out."

Asked if this meant that he had not submitted a letter of withdrawal, Barness said: "No comment."

Only yesterday, Barness said: "I'm not out of the picture. I haven't heard from the Eagles. I'm still waiting to hear from them. I have not forwarded a check because I haven't heard whether or not they are interested."

TIRED OF DELAY, BARNESS ENDS BID FOR EAGLES
The Philadelphia Inquirer
May 16, 1963
By Fred Byrod

The only known bidders for the Philadelphia Eagles franchise have withdrawn their $4,550,000 offer to buy the pro football team, *The Inquirer* learned Wednesday.

A group of Philadelphia district businessmen headed by Herbert Barness, Warrington, Pa., land developer, took this action, an informed source reported, because they had heard nothing from the Eagles' management following an interview April 28 with Frank L. McNamee and Michael O'Neill, who were designated by the stockholders to handle negotiations for the sale of the club.

"When the Barness group heard nothing more," the source said, "they concluded there was no interest in their offer and they decided not to let it stand indefinitely."

Asked to verify the report, Barness said: "I have no comment."

McNamee, the club president, declined to discuss the matter, saying that he thought "anything to be said should come from Barness."

The Barness syndicate made its offer in a letter submitted April 19, the day the stockholders voted to sell at a minimum price of $4,550,000 or $50,000 per share for the 91 shares of stock outstanding.

At a press conference April 29, McNamee and O'Neill said that there were "about a half dozen other firm bids" but the Barness group was the only one that had been interviewed at length up to that time. They said that nothing had developed in their meeting with Barness that would preclude selling to his group.

EAGLES' SALE SEEMS UNLIKELY NOW
The Bulletin
May 23, 1963

... Concerning the interest of Herbert Barness, which also appears as dead as last autumn's falling leaves, McNamee revealed that members of the suburban real estate developer's group included Bob Hall, former Philadelphia attorney and ex-director of Yale athletics, and "a Norristown trucking firm owner named Tose."

"I received formal notice of Barness' withdrawal as an Eagle bidder," McNamee said. "I understand he was unable to secure the backing of a couple of people in Cleveland."

HALL IS INTERESTED IN EAGLES
The Philadelphia Inquirer
June 27, 1963
By Fred Byrod

... O'Neill admitted that the only "bona fide" offer received since the club was officially offered for sale last March was from a syndicate headed by Herbert Barness, Warrington, Pa., land developer. The Barness group withdrew its offer when, it said, the Eagles failed to answer.

'COME BLOW YOUR HORN' PREMIERE AT COUNTY

The Daily Intelligencer
July 19, 1963

"Come Blow Your Horn," the film version of the Broadway comedy originally produced at the Bucks County Playhouse in 1960 and in New York in 1961, will have its premiere performance at the County Theater in Doylestown at 7 and 9 p.m. on Wednesday, August 7. The proceeds for both performances that evening are for the benefit of Welcome House, an adoption center for children of mixed American Parents. Welcome House was originally founded by novelist Pearl S. Buck and Oscar Hammerstein II, and Herbert Barness is current president.

Michael Ellis and William Hammerstein are on the Board of Directors, and these two men were the original producers of "Come Blow Your Horn" in New York. This will be the only fundraising event of the summer for Welcome House. Tickets for these two performances are now on sale at the County Theater in Doylestown and at the Bucks County Playhouse in New Hope.

"Come Blow Your Horn" stars Frank Sinatra, Lee J. Cobb, Molly Picon, Barbara Rush, and Jill St. John.

BARNESS PUSHING NOVEL ZONING PLAN

The Philadelphia Inquirer
August 4, 1963
By Oscar B. Teller, Real Estate Editor

A new approach to the problem of suburban zoning that would leave more ground available for recreation and garden areas is being urged by Herbert Barness, prominent Bucks county planner and land developer.

"Instead of zoning one area for apartments, another for semi-detached homes, a third for single homes and a fourth for the professional offices needed in every suburb, why not put them all in one attractive community?" asks Barness.

He calls the concept "coordinated zoning." A key point would be to leave enough playground space, green-belts and parking area to serve all the housing units instead of trying to provide such facilities hit-or-miss.

"One spacious land area could provide the type of leisure living demanded by Americans and yet leave large areas for both beauty and recreation, which planning commissions throughout the country are stipulating," he added.

And while he didn't say so, it would seem that public transportation could be provided at relatively low cost, since a single bus stop would serve the whole community.

Although the coordinated zoning concept has never been tried in this country, there are plenty of examples of it in the postwar suburbs of Europe and the Far East, Barness pointed out.

BARNESS NAMED
The Bulletin
August 17, 1963

This appointment was also covered in The Daily Intelligencer *and* The Jewish Times. *Once again, my dad was involved in this organization, but I don't know what fueled his connection to it ... except that he was clearly civic minded and liked to help out.*

Herbert Barness, president of Welcome House, Inc., and vice president of the Bucks County Planning Commission, has been named chairman of fund-raising for the Big Brothers of Bucks County.

The campaign for $100,000 will begin about Oct 1. The organization helps boys without fathers to find a "guidance father."

BARNESS WANTS ZONING PLANS TO ELIMINATE SLUMS
Real Property News
August 15, 1963

The coordinated communities that my father was describing were something new at the time. When my grandfather started building houses, he built one at a time. As time went on, and after the demand for housing grew, larger parcels were purchased for development, and planning took on a different look.

With choice available land for residential and apartment construction along the East Coast becoming scarce, a new approach to planning has been strongly recommended to integrate most zoning classifications into one plan and help eliminate future slums, stated a prominent Warrington builder.

Herbert Barness said the plan includes a coordinated community on one segment of land to include apartment structures, individual homes, recreation areas for children and adults, landscaped garden areas, parking and professional offices. Barness is president of Engineering & Planning Associates and vice president of Joseph Barness & Son.

"Eventually," he predicted, "apartments can be incorporated into such an integration of zoning classifications." He said that this type of coordinated planning can increase the efficient use of raw ground.

The builder added, "One spacious land area can provide the type of leisure living demanded by Americans and yet leave large areas for both beauty and recreation, which planning commissions throughout the nation are stipulating. More important—this type of planning can eventually eliminate the slums of tomorrow."

Barness pointed out that if builders take the time and trouble to incorporate such overall plans in future construction programs, they can contribute greatly to the communities in which they have business.

BUCKS DEVELOPER AIMS AT CARIBBEAN: ST. THOMAS PLANS
The Daily Intelligencer
August 22, 1963

I don't know the exact history or reason that my father started looking at the Caribbean, except that it was an opportunity for growth. And I am sure it must have been exciting! According to the Philadelphia Magazine *profile on page 95, he made his first investments there in 1961. We took a number of family trips to the US Virgin Islands, and my father ended up building an apartment building on St. Thomas, overlooking Charlotte Amalie, called Plantation Manor Apartments. I recall that they were rentals then, but I think they are condos now (or maybe I just don't remember accurately!) He also built the Golden Roc garden apartments in St. Croix in 1964.*

A major development of land for residential and apartment building in the Caribbean area was disclosed by Herbert Barness, president of Joseph Barness and Son of Warrington. He said he is prepared to invest a "considerable amount of money" in that area in the next five to eight years.

Barness, who also heads Engineering and Planning Associates of Warrington, one of the country's largest independent land planning firms, said Joseph Barness and Son has acquired "several sizeable tracts of land" in the United States Virgin Islands, Puerto Rico, and is currently negotiating for land in the British Virgin Islands, Aruba, Antigua, Tortola and other islands in that general sector of the world.

The first step in actual building, he disclosed, will be the construction of 81 custom single-family dwellings and 200 apartments on St. Thomas, Virgin Islands, overlooking the picturesque harbor of Charlotte Amalie, capital of the Islands. Ground will be broken by October 1.

"This will be the initial phase of a larger home and apartment development on St. Thomas," Barness said. Total cost of this phase, which will include a swimming pool for residents, will be approximately $8,000,000.

"Engineering and Planning Associates has already completed the development engineering," Barness said.

The single dwellings will range from $18,000 cottages to elaborate Danish-style homes costing up to $70,000. The garden-type tropical high-rise apartments will be priced for rental to the average-income American family, Barness added.

"They will be moderately priced," he said.

The St. Thomas development by Barness will utilize public water and sewer and other utilities. He said Joseph Barness and Son has established an office for the U.S. Virgin Islands operation on St. Thomas at 19 Norre Gade, from which all developing and building operations will be directed.

Another office has also been established in San Juan, Puerto Rico, for the entire Caribbean area, Barness stated.

"We have been studying the entire Caribbean area for over two years," he declared, "and we find an acute need for homes and apartments both for residents and for North and South Americans who want an ideal vacation spot part of the year and can rent their properties for income for about 8 months."

Barness, who with his father, Joseph, has been responsible for the major development of Bucks County, said he and a group of associates and financial institutions plan to invest in the Caribbean during the next five to eight years.

The Jewish Exponent
August 23, 1963

Herbert Barness is readying a surprise building announcement concerning two major projects in the Virgin Islands.

BARNESS TO START CARIBBEAN PROJECT
The Philadelphia Inquirer
August 25, 1963
By Oscar B. Teller, Real Estate Editor

It looks like a lot of housing news in the next couple of years will be coming from the sunny Caribbean.

Levitt & Sons, Inc., the biggest home building firm of them all, is already hard at work on a development in San Juan, Puerto Rico, where sample houses are to be ready within the next couple of weeks. And last week came the announcement that Herbert Barness, millionaire Bucks county builder and land developer, is about to start an $8 million program on St. Thomas in the Virgin Islands.

The Barness project will involve 82 single-family custom dwellings and about 200 apartments overlooking the picturesque harbor of Charlotte Amalie, capital of the islands.

Some of the houses will cost as much as $70,000, Barness said, but the garden-type, high-rise apartments "will be priced for rental to the average-income American family." He plans to break ground for the project by October 1.

The Charlotte Amalie tract is one of several owned by Barness's firm, Joseph Barness & Son, in the Virgin Islands and Puerto Rico. In addition, he said he is negotiating for land in the British Virgin Islands, Aruba, Antigua, Tortola, and other islands.

"We have been studying the entire Caribbean area for over two years," said Barness, "and find an acute need for homes and apartments both for permanent residents and for North and South Americans who want a vacation home for part of the year and rental income for the rest."

'BROTHERS' TO SEEK MEMBERSHIP IN UF
The Daily Intelligencer
September 1, 1963

The Big Brothers as a new social organization is conducting an independent campaign for contributions to help get its programs underway in the county.

After demonstrating its purpose through the funds obtained from the present campaign, Big Brothers plan to request membership in the Bucks County United Fund. Meantime, until 1965, the fundraising efforts will be carried on through the cooperative and volunteer efforts of local residents and interested citizens.

Warrington realtor and developer Herbert Barness has volunteered his time to be Chairman of the Ways and Means Committee for the Big Brothers of Bucks County. In this capacity, he has a "citizen's message" for the people of Bucks County.

Said Barness: "Through the cooperation of the Bucks County press, a number of splendid men have volunteered to befriend fatherless boys through the Big Brothers Plan. This program permits volunteers to work with fatherless boys on an individual and personal basis, to invest time and themselves for the benefit of an unhappy or a confused boy."

BARNESS PLANS 116 APARTMENTS
Philadelphia Daily News
September 13, 1963

Joseph Barness & Son, Warrington, will construct 116 apartment units in Bethlehem at Catasqua Rd. near Route 22.

Herbert Barness, president, said the company has acquired an 11-acre tract of land next to the Howard Johnson Motel on Catasqua Rd. for the garden-type apartment development.

All engineering improvements and plans have already been made by Engineering and Planning Associates of Warrington, one of the East's largest independent land planning firms.

Barness also announced construction—and permanent financing of $940,000 has been arranged through Bankers Bond and Mortgage Co. of Philadelphia.

The new 116-apartment unit development in Bethlehem will include off-street parking, recreational facilities for residents and spacious landscaped areas.

The apartment building will be made of red brick and will be of Colonial design, Barness said. One-, two- and three-bedroom apartments, all moderately priced, will be offered in the new apartment development.

'FOUR FIELDS' SITE SOLD TO BARNESS
The Daily Intelligencer
Undated [*The article says that Barness is a member of the Bucks County Planning Commission, and he became a member of that organization in 1963.*]

Sale of the van Steenwyk tract in Horsham Township to Joseph Barness and Son, Warrington developer, was announced Tuesday.

Barness will apply to the Horsham Supervisors to develop the property under the planning residential (cluster) zoning classification. The 183-acre tract, called "Four Fields," adjoins Oak Terrace Country Club in the Tennis Ave.-McKean Rd. Area.

Charles Dager, owner of Dager Realtor, Jenkintown, negotiated the sale. No purchase price was announced. The offering price was listed last July as $330,000.

Dager said Herbert Barness of the Barness firm is a member of the Bucks County Planning Commission and that he will work closely with the Horsham and Montgomery County Planning Commissions "in attempting to create a unique residential community maintaining the existing beautiful natural aspects of this tract."

"We are extremely pleased to bring Barness to Horsham Township," Dager added, "because he is the developer in the Philadelphia area that can best accomplish the objectives of the planned residential zoning ordinances."

1964

BARNESS HEADS RACE GROUP: Swaps Jobs with Parish
The Philadelphia Inquirer
January 24, 1964

Herbert Barness, Warrington land developer, was elected president of the William Penn Racing Association at the harness racing group's annual meeting Thursday at the Warwick Hotel. Barness succeeded Daniel C. Parish, Pittsburgh builder.

Parish, in turn, succeeded Barness as a vice president of the association, which plans two meetings at Liberty Bell Park. The first will run 24 days, from June 8 to July 4. The second will go 26 days, from Sept. 18 through Oct. 17.

Barness, who was an unsuccessful bidder for the Eagles, switched positions with Parish because the distance of Parish's residence and business offices made it inconvenient for him to attend racing events regularly, according to an association spokesman. Barness, 40, is president of Joseph Barness and Son and of Planning and Engineering Associates, Inc. He is a director of the Philadelphia Lyric Opera Co. and was founder and first president of Warrington Golf and Country Club. A Bucknell graduate, he is a trustee of Delaware Valley College.

HERB BARNESS NAMED PENN RACING CHIEF
The Daily Intelligencer
Friday, January 24, 1964

I loved seeing the name of the newspaper written in my grandmother's handwriting on this article.

Herbert Barness of Warrington was named president of the William Penn Racing Association at a meeting of the organization yesterday at the Warwick Hotel in Philadelphia.

Barness, a well-known builder and civic leader, was advanced to the top position from the vice-presidency. He succeeds Dan Parish of Pittsburgh, last year's president.

The William Penn Racing Association will enter its second season of harness racing this fall at Liberty Bell Park in Northeast Philadelphia.

Last year the organization handled the September running and enjoyed fine success under the leadership of Parish. The association was founded slightly over a year ago.

Barness is well-known throughout the *Intelligencer* area as well as throughout the Delaware Valley. In addition to his construction business in Warrington Township, he has made notable civic contributions to the area.

This year Barness holds an official position with the Big Brothers Association in Bucks County in addition to being chairman of its ways and means committee

Barness made several major contributions to the local sports scene. One of these was the founding and building of Warrington Country Club.

He was prominent on national sports pages late last season when it was reported that he was heading a syndicate trying to purchase the Philadelphia Eagles. His group's bid was withdrawn, leading the way to the acceptance of the current owner Jerry Wolman.

BARNESS ELECTED WM. PENN RACING ASSN. PRESIDENT
Levittown Times
January 24, 1964

Herbert Barness, of Warrington, was elected president of the William Penn Racing Association at the annual meeting yesterday at the Warwick Hotel.

The nationally prominent Bucks County land developer, who had filled the office of vice-president, succeeds Daniel C. Parish, of Pittsburgh, as head of the harness racing body, which will conduct a split meeting at Liberty Bell Park from June 8 through July 4 and Sept. 18 through Oct. 17.

The 40-year-old Barness has a rich background in civic, sports and business affairs. He is the founder and first president of the Warrington Golf and Country Club, president of the Pearl Buck Welcome House, chairman of the Big Brothers Association of Bucks County, and a director of the Philadelphia Lyric Opera Company.

One of the largest land developers in the United States, Barness, who also is interested in land development in St. Thomas and St. Croix in the Virgin Islands, is president of Bucks County Industrial Development Company, Bucks County Park Foundation and Joseph Barness & Son.

Barness is a graduate of Bucknell University. He is married. The Barnesses have two daughters, Lynda, 13, and Nancy, 11.

Herbert Barness, (right), of Warrington, newly elected president of the William Penn Racing Association, chats with the Rooney twins, Pat and John (standing); their brother, Tim, (seated from left), Daniel C. Parish, outgoing president, and Arthur J. Rooney, secretary-treasurer, following harness racing association's annual meeting recently at the Warwick Hotel, Philadelphia.

The Bulletin
January 24, 1964

Daniel C. Parish, outgoing president of William Penn Racing Association, which holds its harness meetings at Liberty Bell Park, turns over portfolios to newly elected prexy Herbert Barness, Bucks County land developer and civic leader at group's annual meeting yesterday at Warwick Hotel.

WORK STARTED AT JUSTA FARM
The Philadelphia Inquirer
January 26, 1964

Four builders have started construction of model homes at Justa Farm in Huntingdon Valley, Lower Moreland Township.

Planned for the tract where members of the Elkins family once raised famous horses are 350 homes representing a construction value of some $12 million.

Located on Huntingdon Pike above Bethayres, Justa Farm is being developed by Joseph Barness & Son, of Warrington. An associated firm, Engineering and Planning Associates, is doing the engineering work, including the installation of a sewer plant. Herbert Barness said Justa Farm will be the first large community in that area with both public water and sewer.

The four builders, Eitner Homes, Emil Stahl & Son, Leonard Kaplan and Jaemar Construction, are building homes that will sell for $32,000 and up.

The Jewish Exponent
April 19, 1964

Herbert Barness, land developer and president of the William Penn Harness Racing Association, explains racing cap to Jack Steck, president of Poor Richard Club. Barness was honored by the club along with the Liberty Bell Race Track officials.

TWIN DOUBLE TRIO STRIKES IT RICH OVER COLLAR ITCH
The Bulletin
July 1964

The term "twin double ticket" should probably be "daily double ticket," which is a bet that picks winners of two (usually consecutive) races.

BIG CLEANUP. William Penn Racing Association president Herbert Barness presents a $72,837.40 check to co-holders of lone twin double ticket last night at Liberty Bell Park. The lucky trio: Harry Laughlin, William Penton, and Frank Deuter started parlay with numbers from laundry mark. Steve Brody, a laundry man, talked winners into playing second half numbers.

CONSTRUCTION BEGUN BY BARNESS IN LANCASTER
Real Property News
July 1964

Joseph Barness & Son will construct a 150-unit garden court apartment development and 117 homes on a tract on Millersville Road in Manor Township, Lancaster County. Herbert Barness, president of the firm, said that the cost of the apartment units and homes will be approximately $3,250,000.

Financing and mortgage has been obtained through Bankers Bond & Mortgage Co. Ground will be broken for the project this month.

This will be the first of a series of building projects Joseph Barness & Son will undertake in the Lancaster area. The garden court apartments will include a swimming pool, a large recreation area, and off-street parking. Herbert Barness, developer, builder and engineer, is president of the William Penn Racing Association.

BUCKS CO. BUILDER BUILDS IN ISLANDS
The Bulletin
October 10, 1964

The first of many planned developments in the Caribbean has been completed in St. Croix, Virgin Islands, by Joseph Barness & Son, Warrington, Bucks County, land developers.

It is the 37-unit Golden Roc garden apartment development adjacent to Christiansted. A second section of the development has been started.

HOW 'WHIZ KIDS' RANG THE BELL

Philadelphia Daily News
October 21, 1964
By Jack Kiser

A news flash out of Garden State informs us that Gene Mori is installing the twin double tomorrow in an effort to pump some new blood into his tired turnstiles and mutuel machines.

You can't blame Mr. Mori for such a move. When attendance and handle continues to fade faster than the Phillies, something has to be done. The downward trend started at Atlantic City Race Course and it hasn't stopped since. Maybe the twin double gimmick will halt the slide, maybe it won't.

And maybe Mr. Mori could do worse than investigate what took place up at Liberty Bell Park during the past four weeks. This harness track entered it final 26 nights of action with more strikes against it than Westinghouse Electric's Lester plant. Yet it wound up the meet in deep blue ink and set several betting records in the process.

This miracle was no fluke. It was the product of hard work and fresh thinking by a group of racing neophytes. So new at the game, in fact, that they didn't know they were licked.

The hard core of this compact group was composed of Herb Barness, Pat Rooney, John Rooney, Jerry Lawrence and Mort Berry. At first, old heads called them the "Whiz Kids" with just a trace of facetiousness in their voices. Today the nickname carries well-deserved respect when it is spoken.

So fantastic was their success that the State Harness Commission has asked them to submit a detailed report on how it was accomplished. It should be an invaluable guide to other tracks.

So what did the "Whiz Kids" do? They went out and raised attendance and handle more than 30 percent over the 1963 pace.

It's almost impossible to say who deserves the bigger credit. Barness, a highly successful Bucks County land developer and a sports buff, served as general director from his position as president of the William Penn Association. The Rooney twins, members of the board of directors and sons of Steelers owner Art Rooney—a man's man if there ever was one—came up with promotion ideas galore and carried them through themselves. So did young Lawrence, the advertising director and son of former governor David Lawrence, and Berry, one of the best public relations men around.

BUCKS' BOUNCY BUILDER
Philadelphia Magazine
Undated [*But the article states that Herb Barness is 41, so the year is 1964.*]

Bucks County is drenched in contrasts. It is the location of artsy-craftsy New Hope with its artists and antique shops and Levittown, the archetype of cookie-cutter building in suburbia. It is the home of U.S. Steel's brawny Fairless Works and of barns daubed with the traditional hex signs.

Since World War II, change has swept over Bucks, building up what was essentially a rural county at just about the fastest clip in the U.S. Doing much of the building and developing has been 41-year-old Herbert Barness, president of Warrington-based (between Doylestown and the Montgomery County line) Joseph Barness & Son and Engineering & Planning Associates.

The Barness firm has had its fingers in enough suburban pies to stock a good-sized bakery. A profusion of homes, apartments, industrial parks, shopping centers, and country clubs built by Barness have played a major part in Bucks County's wholesale map changing.

Like the county he is so closely associated with, Herb Barness is a study in contrasts. With his studious cast of face, horn-rimmed glasses and high forehead, Barness might be taken for an associate finance professor at the Wharton School. He's hardly the type that might be found hanging around a race track. Nevertheless, Barness fills both bills—he has been deeply bitten by both the education bug and the sports bug.

School days

"I started at Bucknell before the war," says the builder. "Then, when I entered the Air Force, the first thing they did was send me to the meteorology school. After the war I went back to Bucknell and got my degree in mechanical engineering, but I guess you could say I've never stopped going to school since then."

His major project was getting a master's degree in political science as a part-time student at Penn's Fels Institute. [*He didn't get a degree but attended classes.*] The ins and outs of local government are indeed well worth knowing for the engineer-builder of today. Harder to apply to his daily activity was a course Barness took at the Barnes Institute a few years ago. Barness's wife Irma paints and sculpts and was getting the full treatment at Barnes. Barness took time out from his busy schedule to attend one afternoon class a week at Barnes, getting the lowdown on modern art from the crusty Dr. Barnes' heir at the school, Violette deMazia. "She was very intense and a good teacher," says Barness. Barness isn't taking any formal classes anywhere at the present, but he'll zoom off for a seminar at the drop of a hat.

The sports bug sunk its fangs just as deeply into Barness. "To tell the truth, though," he ruefully admits, "I was never exactly a star performer. I broke my arm playing football in high school and had my head bashed in when I went out for boxing in college." Barness has long been hot after acquiring a major sports franchise. After the Warriors departed for San Francisco, he and some friends formed a syndicate to try to bring a new pro basketball team into Philadelphia. It looked like a deal was set to bring the Detroit team here when Barness and his pals decided to go after bigger game. This was back in 1963 when the Eagles were on the block. Barness made an offer, but the Eagles never took it seriously and it was withdrawn. By this time a deal had been worked out to transfer the Syracuse basketball team to Philadelphia, and the Barness group was left out in the cold.

Horse play

Barness's association with harness racing has been more successful. He was one of the principal founders of the William Penn Racing Association, one of the four licensed groups in the state. A legitimate resident of Bucks County and a Republican, Barness made a good counter-weight to the other William Penn leaders—Dan Parish and Art Rooney, two longtime Pittsburgh buddies of Democratic governor David Lawrence. Barness was elected president of the group in January 1964. Harness racing hasn't exactly caught fire in the Philadelphia area, but Barness says he hasn't been disappointed. "We didn't expect the track to be crammed from the beginning," he says. "This is a long-term proposition. Harness racing will gradually build up a loyal following, just the way an athletic team does. It takes time."

Barness tackles his vocation with the same zesty elan that he devotes to his avocations. He now builds and develops land in other urban areas and as far away as the Caribbean, but his first love is still Bucks County. His father, Joseph Barness, moved his family there in the '20s when Barness was a few months old. In the manufacturing business at first, Joseph Barness backed into real estate in a modest way, and was soon devoting his whole time to it. He is still active as chairman of the building firm and shows up at the Warrington office every day.

"The county was far different when my father moved out here," recalls Herb Barness. "I went to a one-room school house in Warrington that had a pot-bellied stove and an outhouse. I walked two-and-a-half miles to school each way and most of the buildings I passed were single farm residences."

On the line

Young Barness made an early debut in his father's construction business. "I worked on construction jobs in the summers and on weekends as far back as I can remember," he says. "I started operating a bulldozer when I was 13 or 14."

The Barness firm had developed a number of small residential communities before World War II, but it was in the post-war years that building in Bucks really boomed. Herb Barness joined the firm after finishing off his war-interrupted college work in 1948. The residential building splurge was in full swing, but there was more to Bucks than homes. The Barness firm was soon building commercial buildings, including shopping centers and industrial buildings.

As Herb Barness began taking over the reins of the building business in the 1950s he made land development a specialty through his associate company, Engineering & Planning Associates. As a standard pattern, Barness will acquire promising farmland near an urban center, perform the engineering and planning services, such as securing zoning changes and putting in sewers, water mains and other improvements, and then sell the land to a builder or group of builders, if the tract is too large for one to handle. "We handle problems that the average builder can't cope with," he explains. "The zoning laws are different all over, but some of the problems we tackle are the same every place. The advantages of acquiring already developed land are obvious—it cuts down the length of time between the construction start of a project and the time when the builder starts getting a return on his investment."

Southward ho

Barness's most challenging recent work has been in the Caribbean. Problems encountered there make suburban zoning squabbles look like Sunday school picnics. "I first started investing the Caribbean area in 1961," Barness recalls. Typically, he began studying Spanish. By 1963 Barness had acquired sizeable tracts of land in the U.S. Virgin Islands and Puerto Rico and had his eye on other land in the British Virgin Islands, Aruba, Antigua, and Tortola. The first projects were started in the Virgin Islands on St. Thomas and St. Croix. "There were a number of problems in the Caribbean that we had to overcome," says Barness. "There is an extreme water shortage. The workers aren't exactly the world's most reliable, and some building materials are scarce there. On some of the islands the land is steep and rocky and requires a lot of preparation before it can be built on."

The first Barness & Son Caribbean project was finished last fall: A 37-unit garden apartment development, called Golden Roc Apartments, near Christiansted on St. Croix. Construction was started on a second section of the development right away. The first part of a project on nearby St. Thomas, overlooking the harbor of Charlotte Amalie, was finished shortly after this. Barness's goal for the Caribbean area calls for approximately $200 million in building over a five- to eight-year period.

Barness's interest in land development in other parts of the U.S. and in building in the Caribbean have supplemented rather than replaced the firm's activities in suburban Philadelphia. Garden apartments and swank housing developments have been seeded in the nearby ground in multi-million dollar chunks.

In some of these, Barness handles the whole process. In others, Engineering & Planning Associates acts only as the land developer and planner. Perhaps the plushest local project now in the works is Justa Farms in Huntingdon Valley near Bryn Athyn. On the 200-acre former Elkins estate, once a breeding farm for race horses, 350 houses tagged from $30,000 up are being built. Another former stud farm, now know as Palomino Farms in Warrington, was divided into 400 lots and turned into houses selling for $18,000 and up.

Wide scope
All in all, Barness estimates that his father and he have done hundreds of millions in building in Bucks County. This activity plus a sense of noblesse oblige have made the Barness name associated with a number of civic activities in Bucks County. There are two streets named after Joseph Barness is Warrington and there is a Joseph & Mary Barness dormitory at Delaware Valley College in neighboring Doylestown. (The younger Barness is a college trustee.)

Herb Barness is one of these people who can't say no when he is asked to serve on a committee or civic agency. He is the longtime president of Welcome House (the chairman is Pearl Buck), an adoption agency for children for American-Asian parentage. He is a past president of the Bucks County Industrial Development Commission and is now president of the Bucks County Planning Commission—two agencies that have been instrumental in guiding the burgeoning county. But there are also the Boy Scouts, the Big Brothers, the Park Foundation, *ad infinitum*.

With building and land development projects by the bushel and an endless round of civic and community meetings to attend, Barness spends a long and arduous day, usually reaching his Warrington office at 7 in the morning. "One advantage of having the office close to my home is that at least I can have dinner with my family," he sighs. It is only fitting that Barness is president of the William Penn Racing Association. He is nearly always in harness and manages to proceed at a fast pace, sort of a human Dan Patch from Bucks County.

1965

Trenton-Evening Times
January 12, 1965

GET YOUR HORSES READY, LES. Liberty Bell president Ed Dougherty and William Penn President Herb Barness show harness racing dates to Les Pullen, Trenton area driver who is expected to appear quite often in winner's circle at Liberty Bell Park.

GROWTH OF WARRINGTON SHOP CENTER CONTINUES
The Daily Intelligencer
January 29, 1965

The Warrington Shopping Center recently completed its second section. It now has 12 stores, a major food market, a post office, luncheonette, and a State Liquor store.

According to Joseph Barness, founder and chairman of Joseph Barness & Son and head of the Warrington Shopping Center with his son, Herbert, growth of this center is far from completed.

While details have not been completed, additional plans are being made to meet the demands of the shopping public.

The first section of the Warrington Shopping Center was completed three years ago when the elder Barness snipped a ribbon to open up the sizeable parking lot to the first shoppers. Since then it has been almost filled or completely filled every shopping day.

For residents of Warrington and the surrounding Bucks County area, it has become the hub of their commercial life.

LAND IMPROVEMENT PROGRAM UPTURN SEEN BY BARNESS
The Daily Intelligencer
January 29, 2965
By Herbert Barness
President, Joseph Barness & Son, Warrington

The tremendous growth and expansion of Bucks County in the past decade has been studied—and is now being studied—by industrial and urban experts throughout the nation.

In the Delaware Valley area, the growth of Bucks County has been the most rapid and the most progressive of any of the nine counties.

Home building and apartment construction tripled in the past 15 years, and while it has slowed down in the past two years, this segment of our economic growth has far from ceased.

Engineering and Planning Associates of Warrington, one of the East's largest independent land development firms, reports that demand for land planning and improvement is now on the upturn again after striking a plateau in the Bucks-Montgomery-Philadelphia area.

Many of the newer industrial plants in the county are expanding for the fourth and fifth time since they located in our midst, and new plants are seeking sites because of ample labor, fine transportation arteries, and plentiful land.

From the time my father, Joseph, moved to Warrington in 1926 and began building until the present, is a paradox. My father's original building plans have mushroomed into industrial parks, home developments, country clubs (Warrington CC). We are proud that the Barness name is synonymous with the growth of Bucks County. We are even prouder that our development efforts have not ceased and will not halt.

Industrially, supported by the Bucks County Industrial Development Corp. and the County Planning Commission and Real Estate Board, the entire area should be in an extended period of growth and expansion.

(Herbert Barness today is one of Buck County's leading citizens. A graduate engineer, his interests extend from the past presidency of the Industrial Development Corp. and the presidency of Warrington County Club—which he founded and built—to the presidency of the William Penn Racing Association. He is also president of Recreational Pools, Inc., Warrington Industrial Park, Palomino Farms and other building corporations here and in the Caribbean.)

CHALFONT POST OFFICE GEARED FOR GROWTH
The Daily Intelligencer
Early 1965
By W. Lester Trauch, *Intelligencer* Staff Writer

Joseph Barness and son, Herbert, Warrington contractors, developers and realtors, built the new post office building, which is made of two-tone tan bricks. It is 92 feet long with the loading platform and about 43 feet wide.

A modern touch, and one of the first of its kind since the ZIP code was inaugurated, is the ZIP Code number 18914 on the wall beneath the name in big, bold metal numerals.

NEW POST OFFICE. Joseph Barness, Warrington contractor who built the new $60,000 post office for Chalfont Borough, which will open Monday, and Postmaster William I. Wolfinger, a veteran of 44 years postal service, check to see that everything is ready for the move, which will take place over the weekend. Staff photo by Rudy Millarg.

RACING IN HARNESS ENLIVENS BARNESS
American Jewish Life
April 16-20, 1965

As an energetic boy of 14, Herb Barness operated a bulldozer. It was his start in the business of construction, heeding the advice of his father, Joseph, to learn it "from the ground up."

Today, the younger Barness—he's 41—is President of Joseph Barness & Son and Engineering and Planning Associates, a prime mover in the spectacular real estate development of Bucks County out of his Warrington (Pa.)-based offices; president of the William Penn Harness Racing Association now operating at Liberty Bell Park and one of the most sports-minded men in the country.

Responsible for the erection of homes, apartments, industrial parks, shopping centers, etc., since World War II, in his home area, the tireless Barness has branched out to the Caribbean, encountering and surmounting untold problems in the Virgin Islands on St. Thomas and St. Croix. His jewel in the islands is a 37-unit apartment development on St. Croix, finished only last fall.

As a student in his war-interrupted career at Bucknell University, Herb also tried his hand (or it is his foot?) in football and boxing, but as he says, "I wasn't a great athlete at either." Yet, the competition in both sports is an example of his fiery zeal that has been a part of him all his life.

So it is not surprising that he starts his day at an early hour at his Warrington office. Neither is it surprising that he is one of the last to leave the racetrack at night. And with all this, he's a fine family man and manages to have dinner at home most nights with his lovely wife Irma and his two teenage daughters, Lynda, 16, and Nancy, 13, at his modest home, 1334 Easton Road, Warrington. [*That was the home of his parents. He had actually moved us to Rydal and commuted daily to Warrington, about a 25-minute drive away.*]

Gimbels Department Store Ad No. 510—Orig. Setting 4-16-65
The Bulletin
April 1965
Photographed by Fabian Bachrach

WELCOME HOUSE is an authorized adoption agency specializing in the placement of children of mixed Asian-American parentage, of children with physical handicaps, and children of varying racial mixtures and beyond the age of infancy. Located at Fordhook Farms, Doylestown Penna., Welcome House is supported by public contributions, which can be sent directly to the agency founded 15 years ago by Nobel Prize-winning novelist Pearl S. Buck. While the staff of Welcome House strives to find homes for these unfortunate children, funds are urgently needed in this important work to help keep these children in comfort while homes are found.

RACING GROUP HERE MOVES TO SELL STOCK: William Penn Assn. Sets Ceiling Price at $7.50 a Share
The Sunday Bulletin
April 18, 1965

The William Penn Racing Association, which runs harness racing at Liberty Bell Park, has applied to the Securities & Exchange Commission for registration to sell 230,000 shares of nonvoting stock.

The proposal calls for the stock to be sold at a maximum of $7.50 a share. The plan also has to be approved by the State Harness Racing Commission. It would be the first public offering of the stock of the racing corporation.

Herbert Barness, Bucks County real estate man and president of the racing association, said the stock would be sold to pay off bank loans, including one obtained to buy the stock last November from Daniel C. Parish, Pittsburgh asphalt contractor. He said the loans were made with Provident Tradesmens Bank.

Gimbel Ad No. 510—Orig. Setting 4-16-65—

WELCOME HOUSE is an authorized adoption agency specializing in the placement of children of mixed Asian-American parentage, of children with physical handicaps, and children of varying racial mixtures and beyond the age of infancy. Located at Ferdbook Farms, Doylestown, Penna. Welcome House is supported by public contributions which can be sent directly to the agency founded 15 years ago by Nobel Prize winning novelist Pearl S. Buck. While the staff of Welcome House strives to find homes for these unfortunate children, funds are urgently needed in this important work to help keep these children in comfort while homes are found.

Herbert Barness
President
Welcome House

Photographed by Fabian Bachrach

MR. HERBERT BARNESS
President—Joseph Barness & Sons
President—William Penn Racing Association

The man in the Society Brand suit

Nothing holds a candle to Mohair for light weight luxury and incredible resistance to the inevitable "mussing" to which clothing is subjected in warm weather. Society Brand uses a blend of 55% Mohair and 45% rare imported wool, styles it with its well known understated look, tailored with the meticulous detail and patient hours-long underpressing for built in character; the mark of Society Brand. For the man who values the poised year round look through many of our hot humid summers, we prescribe the suit sketched in a cool black Mohair blend at $115.

❋ Gimbels

PHILADELPHIA CHELTENHAM UPPER DARBY GREAT NORTHEAST MOORESTOWN

Parish sold 26,000 shares of voting stock and 234,000 shares of nonvoting stock at $5 a share. He had purchased them at $1 a share. Most of the nonvoting stock was sold at $2 a share.

The 26,000 shares of voting stock were bought by Parish's associate, Arthur Rooney, owner of the Pittsburgh Steelers. William Penn bought the 234,000 nonvoting shares. Rooney now owns 52 percent of the voting stock of the association.

Barness said the same group of about 60 to 100 persons presently own all of the 669,100 shares of nonvoting and 100,000 shares of voting stock outstanding.

Source Unknown
April 23, 1965

The four builders and the developer at Justa Farm, Huntingdon Pike above Byberry Rd., Huntingdon Valley, Lower Moreland Township, will shut down the prestigious community to the public for four weeks, beginning April 30, for private preview showings of the new models.

Developer is Herbert Barness of Jos. Barness & Son, with financing by Bankers Bond & Mortgage Co., Philadelphia. Engineering and Planning Associates, Warrington, which did the land developing and planning, is constructing a full-scale public sewer for Justa Farm. An important feature of the community is that all utilities are underground.

LIBERTY BELL MUTUEL HANDLE TOPS INDIVIDUAL U.S. NORM
The Philadelphia Inquirer
April 24, 1965
By John Dell

Money not only makes the mare go but also makes a race track a going business. That's why smiles are so wide in Liberty Bell Park's counting room nowadays. The place is in a real go situation. Business is better than ever. Attendance at the 25-night session that ends Saturday night has averaged more than 13,000. Last year the average was slightly more than 9,000 per night.

More people have brought much more money to the mutuel windows. People passed an average of about $550,000 a night to the clerk in last year's first 25 nights. This year they've put an average of about $782,000 into play.

"Our per capita figure is $63.74," Herb Barness, president of William Penn Racing association, announced after checking the figures for the first 22 nights. "The national average of per capita betting for harness racing is $50 to $55, and that includes the New York tracks, where betting is much greater than anywhere else."

Why have people here been wagering so much more than the national average? Is it because Liberty Bell had the only wheel in town, with no competition from Garden State until the final day?

Barness thinks that's only part of the answer. Howard Miller, president of Brandywine Raceway, which opens next Saturday, agrees.

"I think harness racing is really coming into its own," Miller says. "The sport's been growing every year I've been in it—since 1955. And I don't notice any diminution of interest."

"I look for continued growth," Barness says. "I don't think there's going to be any limit. I think we've just scratched the surface. Last year we were up 20 percent, and this year we're up another 40 percent. I think the growth will continue through the year."

WM. PENN PREPARES RACING WITH OUTING
The Daily Intelligencer
April 1965

Newspaper editors, columnists and sports writers will join radio-TV news commentators, personalities, and sportscasters in a friendly, divot-digging battle Friday, June 5 on the greens and fairways of Philmont Country Club.

The occasion is the first annual William Penn Racing Association Invitational Tournament, sponsored by the group which opens its night harness meet at Liberty Bell Park on Monday, June 8.

Vying for prizes with the gentlemen of the Fourth Estate will be sports figures such as Alvin Dark, field general of the Giants, and Eagles owner Jerry Wolman, coach Joe Kuharich, linebacker Ben Scott, and all-time great Chuck Bednarik.

William Penn President Herbert Barness conceived the idea of a golf outing in lieu of the usual press party signaling the start of his organization's 24-night Spring Meet at the Northeast Philadelphia harness racing plant. William Penn's Fall meeting, opening in mid-September, will wind up the second and increasingly successful season of Standardbred racing in the Delaware Valley area.

Some 200 invited golfers are expected to tee off on Philmont's South Course starting at 9 a.m., winding up their rounds with a swim and a buffet.

HOSTS AND MOSTEST. Herb Barness and Jack Kelly, Jr. host area writers and celebrities tomorrow to tell the story of the opening of the William Penn Racing Association. Sanders Russell, one of America's great harness drivers who took the Hambletonian in 1962, will be present to discuss the sport.

LIBERTY BELL SURVEYS HAMBLETONIAN NEEDS, MAY BRING CLASSIC TO TRACK
Source Unknown
1965

HORSE TALK. Herbert Barness, William Penn Racing Association president, and his assistant, Patrick Rooney, chat with Lawrence B. Sheppard, the world's foremost breeder of harness horses, at a horse sale in Harrisburg. Sheppard is the former chairman of the Pennsylvania Harness Racing Commission. The Hambletonian, which is the Kentucky Derby of harness racing, may be presented in all its pageantry at Liberty Bell Park in the foreseeable future.

BARNESS SAYS REAL ESTATE VALUES FIRM

The Daily Intelligencer
May 21, 1965
By Herbert Barness
President, Joseph Barness & Son

The real estate market in the Bucks County area has shown no signs of weakening. If anything, values are holding firm and will probably strengthen.

This is due to the fact that the entire Bucks and Montgomery County areas are still growth areas and are desirable areas for new families or new industries to locate.

While other development areas are reporting poor sales of homes, builders in our own sector report many new sales, even of homes in the $30,000s and above.

New home developments are being announced weekly, while many new industries have announced plans to build in this part of Pennsylvania. These are the best barometers of the trend of real estate values in any area.

Normally, in a declining market builders are reluctant to establish new projects and industry thinks three times before deciding to construct a new plant.

Another trend evidenced in this area is the trading-up of new residential values. Homes selling for $30,000, $40,000 and over are being purchased almost in the volume lower-priced homes are being sold. This is an important indication of the type of new families moving into the Bucks-Montgomery County area. The average home sale is around $20,000 at present, much higher than the national average.

The indication now is that, if anything, the real estate market will continue to show signs of strength during 1965.

EVENING AT RACES
Source Unknown
Undated

ORT, which stands for Organization for Rehabilitation and Training, is a Jewish vocational and educational organization. A cousin of my dad's was very involved in the local branch, so I suspect that this is how the connection was made.

Herbert Barness, president of the William Penn Racing Association, helps members of the Philadelphia Region Women's American ORT make plans for an evening at Liberty Bell Park, which the region will sponsor June 1. A race will be named in honor of ORT.

JOSEPH BARNESS FETED BY 290 IN WARRINGTON: Pioneer Business Leader

The Daily Intelligencer
By W. Lester Trauch
Undated [*1965, I think.*]

Joseph Barness, Warrington Township pioneer and crusading business leader who had topped success after success in many fields, last night was "topped" in a community celebration with honors, respect and affection.

Barness, a charter member and one of the founders of the Warrington Township Lions Club, was feted at a testimonial dinner and ladies' night in the Warrington Golf and Country Club, which is one of the many Barness landmarks.

"This community has been my life," said Barness, a realtor, contractor, developer and banker, and 290 men and women gave him a standing ovation and thundering applause, climaxing an evening of outpouring generosity and admiration.

His wife, Mary, shared in the honors bestowed on them as accolades were showered over them by friends, neighbors, two sons, and a host of successful men and women.

Their two sons, Dr. Lewis Barness, professor and chief of pediatrics at the University of Pennsylvania Medical School, and Herbert, who is associated with his father in business, and wives shared the triumphant family memories.

Arthur M. Eastburn, Jr., Doylestown attorney, served as the master of ceremonies. He gave a stirring, moving and colorful biographical sketch of Barness, who came to the United States 35 years ago from Russia. Mr. and Mrs. Barness settled in Warrington in 1924.

Taking part in honoring the 71-year-old guest of honor were the following:

- Warrington Township Justice of the Peace Irvin L. MacNair recalled that Barness and several others founded the Lions Club 24-and-one-half years ago.

- George E. Beggs Jr., who has been in Warrington since 1941, lauded Barness for his belief in people.

- Sanford Oxman, a sportsman, credited Barness with helping the Little League, which now owns 27 acres and has 500 boys playing baseball.

- Miss M. Alice Hennessy, law office secretary, in a glowingly written tribute, described the friendship that existed between the late William H. Satterthwaite Jr. and Barness, fraught with undertones of ambition, understanding and achievements.

- J. Carroll Molloy Jr., Doylestown realtor, whose father and Barness were founders of the Bucks County Realtors' Board, brought greetings from 155 realtors in Bucks County. "I have worked on the smallest real estate deals, $500, and the largest, $200,000, with Joe Barness. He is one of our foremost realtors."

- Charles E. Radcliff, president of Doylestown Federal Savings and Loan Assn., of which Barness is a director; and Howard M. Barnes, Doylestown National Bank and Trust Co., executive head and vice president, of which Barness is a member of the board, lauded his financial transactions.

- Bucks County President Judge Edward G. Biester declared that "Joseph Barness has lived through the change patterns in Warrington and has created a living part of the community."

THE BARNESS HOUR. Mr. and Mrs. Joseph Barness are presented a plaque honoring Mr. Barness at a gala testimonial attended by 290 persons at the Warrington Golf and Country Club last night for their achievements in community life and Bucks County. Staff Photo by Phil Poneck.

TRIBUTE TO A MAN WITH HEART
The Daily Intelligencer
May 24, 1965
By W. Lester Trauch

The source and date for this were written in my grandmother's handwriting.

Joseph Barness, Warrington Township realtor, contractor, banker and business leader, was recently honored by the Warrington Lions for his contributions to the community, civic mindedness and concern for his fellow-man.

Arthur M. Eastburn Jr., Doylestown attorney, emceeing the 290-person testimonial, dropped this observation about Joseph Barness.

"Joe Barness was speaking to William H. Satterthwaite, Jr., one of his best friends, when he said, 'Maybe we have lived too long and are apt to base our opinions on 30 years ago,'" said Eastburn.

The most dramatic, exciting and sensitive touch in the Barness testimonial came, just as it does in the theater, where one scene glows and rises above everything else in the play.

Miss M. Alice Hennessy, who was Mr. Satterthwaite's secretary from her graduation from Doylestown High School in 1925 until his death several years ago, was presented as "the highly intelligent right hand of Mr. Satterthwaite."

Miss Hennessy, reading a tribute to Mr. Barness, written by Attorney Eastburn, revealed such friendship, understanding, sensitivity and richness in business undertakings that it also became a moving, glowing and definitive tribute to both men.

I was sorry that Judge and Mrs. Edwin H. Satterthwaite, who were unable to attend, weren't present to share in this one-act, one-scene, one-woman performance that became a brilliant memorial to the jurist's father. Just as in the theater, this moment will never again be captured but can only be relived in the memories of everyone who heard Eastburn's character and personality analysis of two giants.

I'm always fascinated by the eyes of men and women who leave one world to see another; whose eyes have looked, loved and suffered in more than one world.

Mr. and Mrs. Barness's kindly eyes have the look of having seen, felt, enjoyed a great deal and also experienced anguish and suffering.

Joe Barness's father died when he was 12 years old and living in Russia. He left school at 14 and was 16 years old when he arrived in the United States. He never saw his mother again after he left Russia, and many of his relatives became scattered and lost because of the pogroms.

He couldn't speak any English when he got to New York, but he got work in the clothing industry. From 1918-24 he was in Philadelphia and worked at Snellenberg's. In 1920 he married Mrs. Barness. Her name is Mary, and she too came from Russia very young.

In 1924, Mr. and Mrs. Barness came to Warrington Township to live on a farm on Bristol Road. There was no electricity in rural Warrington.

In 1927 he became a real estate salesman and built his first house. Barness has the reputation of never having built a house for anyone who didn't like it after it was built.

In his banking circles, he holds the distinction of never having recommended anyone for a mortgage or loan who didn't pay it back. "He's an excellent judge of people," said one admirer, "just as he is an excellent neighbor, helper and generous."

"Barness is the story of Warrington," said Eastburn. "He is our part of America and a community."

Sanford Oxman, sportsman, delighted the assemblage when he related how he went to see Barness about an athletic field. "We have no money," he told Barness. To which Barness replied, "I will lease you a field for 11 years at $1 a year. Can you pay that?" Then Barness turned around, signed the lease and paid the bill for the 11 years himself. [*I was there at the dedication of Barness Field.*]

BARNESS NEW SPONSOR OF TEST: Philadelphia Golf Classic
The Philadelphia Inquirer
Undated
By Fred Byrod

I recall from The Man I Knew Was Once a Boy *that my dad dabbled in the game of golf as a young man. By the time he took over the Philadelphia Golf Classic, he and my mom were both avid and experienced golfers.*

The Philadelphia Golf Classic, $125,000 tournament to be played at Whitemarsh Valley County Club Aug. 5-8, had a new sponsor Tuesday— its third in as many years—when Herbert Barness became president.

Barness, a millionaire Warrington, Pa., land developer and president of William Penn Racing Association, which conducts harness racing at Liberty Bell Track, succeeded John P. Crisconi.

"We want to make sure this fine tournament continues as a fixture on the schedule of the Professional Golfers' Association," Barness said. "It's good for golf and it's good for Philadelphia in general."

PHILA. GOLF CLASSIC GETTING FINE DIRECTION WHICH IS EXPECTED TO ADD UP TO SUCCESS

Sunday News
July 25, 1965

At the press-radio-TV meeting held by the officials of the Philadelphia Golf Classic at Whitemarsh the other day, an air of hope, expectancy and firm assurance was felt that had been missing in the two previous events, which took baths of considerable proportions, we were told.

One of the reasons for this hope is Paul Warren, who moved into the management of the tournament about a month ago and began giving the event some professional directions.

Another reason for this new display of confidence is the fact that Joseph Barness [*it was actually Herbert Barness*], a Philadelphia business tycoon and sportsman, who is associated with Art Rooney, Pittsburgh Steelers' owner, in the William Penn Racing operation, and his right arm, Joseph Cascardo, have taken over the Classic, lock, stock, and barrel, and have put their own staff, headed by Mike Rooney, Art's son, in the department of ticket distributions. They are pros in this end of the promotion.

INTRODUCING ... NEW MEMBERS OF THE GOLDEN SLIPPER SQUARE CLUB
Golden Slipper Club Publication
1965

The Golden Slipper Club is a charitable organization in the Philadelphia area. It runs a summer camp and a senior center, along with other initiatives and programs.

Shown with Admissions Committee Chairman the Honorable Edward A. Kallick are the gentlemen who are now members of Slipper by virtue of their induction at this meeting. [*Herbert Barness is on the right in the back row.*]

BARNESS IS QUIETLY EFFICIENT; APPLIES BUSINESS TECHNIQUE TO GOLF
Source unknown
Undated
By Joe Schwendeman

Probably the most overlooked golfer in next Wednesday's pro-amateur tournament at Whitemarsh Valley CC will be a six-footer with thinning dark hair, black-rimmed glasses and a quiet manner that is almost courtly.

Overlooked until someone says, "That's Herb Barness."

Herbert Barness owns the pro-am. He also owns the four-day, 72-hole medal play tournament known as the $125,0000 Philadelphia Golf Classic, which will begin next Thursday on the same Whitemarsh course.

The last guy to show any expression at this lineup of airway proprietorship is Barness himself. Several things influence his attitude.

Barness is not a brash promoter of the old school, nor is he blasé. He is an assured businessman. Although he bought the franchise for Philadelphia's only national pro tournament a month ago, his confidence has been bolstered by the certainty that this year's tournament will be a financial success.

Now he's thinking of next year.

"We're going to have a tournament again next year," said the Warrington, Pa., realtor-sportsman. "We've got a commitment with the PGA and for a television show too, like this year. Our '66 plans are underway."

How does a tournament compare with operating a normal business?

"There's a parallel," Barness said. "In both you need promotion and hustle. In golf you also need a broad base of people to work with. I'd like to get as many country club people interested as we can, and this is a difficult job. We have to approach people on many different levels. For instance, we're going to have a race at Liberty Bell named for the Classic."

Barness is president of the William Penn Racing Association at the northeast track. It was his first major venture into sports after what he calls "several abortive attempts." Barness was a figure in syndicates which tried to buy an NBA club, the Eagles, and more recently, an AFL club.

Now he's into golf, and this came about almost unexpectedly. John Crisconi, auto dealer who was the '64 tourney angel, offered the franchise to Barness. Crisconi and Barness did not know each other.

Barness balked at Crisconi's first offer, but eventually the pair got together.

"John wanted to give up the tournament because of poor health and other problems," Barness said. "He convinced me a major tournament is a good thing for Philadelphia, and that we should have one here. I bought the entire stock of Philadelphia Golf Enterprises, Inc.

"John not only made me a believer, but now I hear myself telling people that the Classic is good for Philadelphia … it fits in with our concept of a major league sports city."

6 PRO-AM TEAMS SHUT OUT; BARNESS TROTS TO SIDELINES
The Philadelphia Inquirer
August 4, 1965
By John Dell of the *Inquirer* Staff

What's the use of being a big man? Herbert Barness is president of all sorts of thing, including the William Penn Racing Association and the Greater Philadelphia Golf Enterprise, Inc. The first organization sponsors harness racing and the second runs the $125,000 Philadelphia Golf Classic, which will occupy Whitemarsh Valley CC through Sunday.

Barness wanted to play in the Wednesday pro-am tournament that will precede the main event. There will be 56 teams, including virtually all of the big names except Ben Hogan. Six more teams wanted to enter, but there wasn't room. Barness was on one of the shutout teams.

BARNESS PUTS GOLF CLASSIC IN 'BLACK'; FIRST TIME EVER
The Bulletin
August 11, 1965

Herbert Barness, Warrington realtor and developer, had almost as much cause for rejoicing today as young Jack Nicklaus who walked off with the top prize of $24,500 yesterday in the Philadelphia Classic Golf Tournament at Whitemarsh Valley Country Club.

Barness, serving his first year as president of the Philadelphia Golf Classic, which ended its seven-day run yesterday, said, "Both our attendance and our receipts have exceeded last year's tournament."

NEW PRESIDENT OF CLASSIC IS A MAN OF ACTION
Philadelphia Golf Classic Program
August 2-8, 1965
by Fred Byrod [*who was also a writer for* The Philadelphia Inquirer]

Herbert Barness, new president of the Philadelphia Golf Classic, is a man who gets things done.

For more than a decade, he has been quietly putting over big ventures as a land developer in his native Bucks County and in the Caribbean. In the past year, he has been a driving force in the promotion of harness racing in Philadelphia as president of the William Penn Racing Association, one of the two groups operating at Liberty Bell track. Along with Art Rooney, owner of the Pittsburgh Steelers of the National Football League, he is a major stockholder in William Penn.

Barness brought the same spirit and zeal to his new role as a sponsor of professional golf.

"When John Crisconi (president of the group which sponsored last year's tournament at Whitemarsh) decided he no longer had the time to continue, it became apparent that someone else would have to take it over if it were to survive," Herb says.

"I'm sure others could have done it, but John asked me. I got interested—and here we are.

"It's no one-shot proposition with me. I went into it with the hope and belief that this tournament could be developed into one of the best in the country, bringing big-time golf to Philadelphia every year, and at the same time benefitting various charities and other worthwhile civic prospects."

Barness, 41, is a graduate of Doylestown High School and Bucknell University (mechanical engineering) with a wide range of interests.

He is president of Joseph Barness and Son and Planning and Engineering Associates, Inc., one of the biggest enterprises of its kind in the country. Both have their headquarters at Warrington, in Bucks County.

In the past, he served as president of the Bucks County Industrial Development Co. and is now chairman of the Bucks County Planning Commission.

Barness built and still owns Warrington Country Club.

"Back in 1957, Dave Gordon and I decided another golf course was needed in this part of the country," Herb says. (Dave Gordon, a high school classmate of Barness, is a partner with his father Bill in one of the country's leading golf architectural firms.)

"I had the land. The Gordons designed the course. One of my companies, Earth Movers, Inc., built it."

Dave Gordon recalls that most of the summer of 1957, Herb himself was on the course almost every morning at 6 a.m. After first operating it as a semi-public course, Barness leased the property to a group of club members who formed a private club four years ago.

Since then, Barness and a partner built Malvern Golf Club on the Main Line. Herb has since disposed of his interest in it.

On a family vacation trip to the West immediately after taking over the Philadelphia Golf Classic, Barness visited California's famed Pebble Beach course and was enchanted by it.

"It's just a dream now," he says, "but some day I'd like to build a course on that scale around Philadelphia. We don't have the terrain for it, of course, but if we could just duplicate some of its features ..."

Unfortunately, as Barness' influence in golf flourished, his time for it and his skill playing it has decreased ... Friends say he once played in the 80s. "I only played about 15 rounds last year," he says. "I'm just another hundred-shooter."

LIBERTY BELL SETS FAST EARLY PACE
The Bulletin
September 10, 1965
By John Dell of the *Inquirer* Staff

The people at Liberty Bell Park are mere colts in the harness racing business. Trotters and pacers have been in competition in America since Colonial times, but these guys just latched onto them less than three years ago. And already they're in the thick of the race.

With a bare two years behind them, they boldly announced last winter they would seek the Hambletonian, harness racing's holy of holies, for their modernistic plant.

The people at Liberty Bell are babies in their sport, and they know it. But they expect to grow steadily. These people with high sights include the guys who operate there as tenants under the name of the William Penn Racing Association.

The William Penn people, who will be ready to greet you with open mutuel windows for at least 25 nights, starting Saturday, are bustling men who have scored quickly in their field. They were the first to engineer $1 million betting nights hereabouts. They had three $1 million openings in their spring meet, which shows what a tremendous public interest has been generated at a track that's still waiting for all its access roads to be opened.

In the meantime, William Penn president Herb Barness predicts business will be better than ever. "I think we'll have a better meet in the fall than we had in the spring because we have come of age," he says.

The man who forecast not one "but several" $1 million nights before the start of the spring meet makes the same prediction for the Fall. He feels fan interest built up all through the summer, that a great number of non-fans discovered the track when they turned out to see Arthur Godfrey at the recent Country Fair there, and many more newcomers will be attracted by stepped-up promotions such as community group nights.

That's the way these Liberty Bell people are—always a little different, a little bolder in their thinking. They're little babies in their game, but not little people.

G.G. AMSTERDAM HEADS NCCJ DINNER
Source unknown
1965

Gustave G. Amsterdam, board chairman and president of Bankers Securities Corp, will be chairman for the 1965 anniversary banquet of the National Conference of Christians and Jews in the Bellevue Stratford Dec. 2.

Herbert Barness was named a vice chairman of the banquet.

1966

BARNESS & SON HONORED
Bucks County Board of Realtors Presents Historic Bucks County (Magazine)
Winter 1966

Joseph Barness & Son, Warrington, Pa., was honored by the Montgomery County Planning Commission on Monday, November 14th, with its 1965 certificate for "The Best Land Subdivision of the year."

The Jewish Exponent
January 21, 1966

Herbert Barness, president of Joseph Barness and Son and Engineering and Planning Associates, both of Warrington, Pa. and president of the William Penn Racing Association, has been elected to membership in the International Real Estate Federation. The federation, formed nearly 20 years ago, has members in most of the developed Free World countries, with headquarters in Paris.

Barness, one of Bucks County's most active builders and developers, has taken a similar position in the Caribbean and West Indies regions. He currently has two major home and apartment developments nearly completed on St. Thomas and St. Croix in the Virgin Islands and is planning a major project in Puerto Rico and on several of the islands in the West Indies group.

BUCKS CONSTRUCTION GROWTH CONTINUING TO MAKE GAINS;
Sparked by Industrial Expansion
The Daily Intelligencer
February 3, 1966
By Herbert Barness
President, Joseph Barness & Son, Warrington

The growth of Bucks County in the past year was very heartening in every way, and I am confident that in 1966 construction in the county will continue to show considerable progress in every element.

From our own experience, the number of home starts in the county should pick up noticeably during the coming year. This will be true especially in high-priced, quality homes in keeping with the historic atmosphere of the area.

On the industrial construction front, an increase of 20 to 25 percent is expected in 1966. This will stem from new construction by companies coming into Bucks County and from expansions on the part of those presently located in the county.

BUCKS BUILDER—HERB BARNESS: A Hand in Most Everything
Trenton Sunday Times: Bucks County
March 6, 1966
By George Ingram, *Times* Advertiser Staff Writer

My dad had so many interests, and he was involved in an amazing number of ventures, but it seemed like he was always home for dinner! I remember him waking me (and my sister) up for school in the morning through an intercom, followed by sprinkles of water if we didn't get up quickly. And he often drove us to school on the way to work. This article describes my father as I knew him: Loving life, loving his family, and loving all of the work—and charitable, and political—activities he was involved in. One of his favorite sayings was, "Every day is a good day. Some are just better than others." And that's how he lived his life.

Warrington—At first glance Herb Barness doesn't look like Bucks County's number one wheeling and dealing businessman.

His soft voice and scholarly black horn-rimmed glasses seem somewhat incongruous in a man who has built countless homes, shopping centers and apartment developments in Greater Philadelphia and the Caribbean, a man who is president of the William Penn Racing Association and the Miss Pennsylvania Pageant, a man who is a member of the Bucks County Planning Commission and many civic agencies.

His name isn't even on the sign outside the nerve center of the Barness empire founded by his father, Joseph Barness, at 1352 Easton Road.

But outward appearances are not an infallible index to an individual.

The truth is that Herb Barness at 42 is a dynamo who'll tell you he doesn't work a single hour a day. It just isn't work to him.

"I enjoy everything I do," Barness said the other day, "and I don't consider it work. If I did, I wouldn't spend as much time as I do at it."

Barness arrives at his office each day about 7 a.m. Since he lives close by, he can go home for dinner. But he still packs a lot of active hours into every 24.

"Sixteen hours, maybe," he said when pressed for specifics. "Eighteen ... Twenty. Time really means very little to me."

Herb Barness has been involved in so many business ventures and community projects that it would almost take nine newspaper columns of type to list them all.

In 1963 he tried, unsuccessfully, to buy the Philadelphia Eagles, for example. At the same time he and his friends were dickering to bring a pro basketball team to the City of Brotherly Love after the Warriors left for San Francisco.

The headquarters for the Miss Pennsylvania Pageant was recently moved from West Chester to Warminster because Barness is president of the competition.

"I wanted to get it close by where I could keep my eye on it," Barness quietly explains.

Although he's far from being an Arnold Palmer on the green and doesn't bet at the track at all, Barness is president of both the Philadelphia Golf Classic and the William Penn Racing Association at the Liberty Bell harness track.

"I never place a bet," said the Bucks builder. "It would be the worst thing in the world if I were a bettor. I'd be there every night of the week. I must go broke."

"Besides if I were to bet down there and someone would watch me walk up to the winner's window and collect a bet, it would look bad. I don't think in my position it would be good."

The Barness firm has done hundreds of millions of dollars in building projects throughout the Greater Bucks area, and within the last five years has turned its attention to construction in the Caribbean.

"It's a moving area," commented Barness significantly.

Examples of the Barness Caribbean touch include a 37-unit garden apartment development on St. Croix and other projects on St. Thomas. Both islands are in the Virgin Islands. Housing developments are now underway in Jamaica. Barness once estimated his goal for this area is about $200 million in building within a five- to eight-year period.

Barness doesn't get down to brass tacks when he's asked by outsiders how much he's worth.

"I've never counted," he says casually, echoing J. Paul Getty. "I wouldn't have any idea."

One would expect that Barness, with his considerable influence in the community, would be a behind-the-scenes man in Bucks politics. Although his close friends may think he's being too modest, Barness does not accept such a mantel.

"I'm interested in politics," he said, "but I'm not actively interested in it. I don't know what's going on from day to day, really. I'm interested, but I do not consider myself a man behind the scenes.

"I'm not in the 'in' group," continued Barness. "I'm extremely interested in politics in Bucks County, but I'm as good a friend with John Welsh [Democratic Party Leader] as I am with Chick Afflerback [Republican Party Leader]."

Barness considers business a hobby. Another one is being with his wife and two daughters.

"I guess one hobby is spending time with my family—I don't say that in a grandiose fashion—but I feel I don't spend enough time with my family."

A graduate of Doylestown High School and Bucknell University, Barness has lived in Warrington all his life. He has never stopped going to school, either. When things started looking well in the Caribbean in the early 1960s, he started learning Spanish.

Barness is no slouch when it comes to participating in community and civic organizations. He is a past president of the Bucks County Industrial Development and of the county planning commission, of which he is still a member. For the past four years he has been president of Welcome House, an adoption agency for Asian Children, founded by Pearl Buck.

He's been associated with the Boy Scouts, the Park Foundation, Big Brothers, and many other endeavors. The Golf Classic and the Miss Pennsylvania Pageant are non-profit undertakings, too.

A logical question to ask a man like Barness is what motivates him.

"I like people," he answered. "And I just really enjoy everything I do."

OPENING NIGHT AT LIBERTY BELL FOR JUNE FETE
Times Chronicle
May 19, 1966

A gala "Opening Night at the Races" is set for tomorrow at Liberty Bell Park as one of the pre-Fete Activities of the June Fete. Sponsored by the Fort Washington Auxiliary of Abington Memorial Hospital, the event will include a gourmet dinner on the Turfside Terrace and a special "June Fete" race with the hospital group presenting the winning trophies.

Herb Barness, president of the William Penn Racing Association, has also made an unlimited number of grandstand passes, which will be given to the public in return for a dollar donation to the hospital.

BARNESS SEEKS TEAM IN SOCCER
The Bulletin
June 16, 1966

A third group, including Herb Barness of this city, will apply for the right to operate a professional soccer league in this country. Barness is president of the William Penn Racing Association.

Pat Rooney, general manager at the Association, last night said: "Mr. Barness has all the information about the league and is out of town at present. I do know there is a meeting planned in New York today. If we do land a franchise, it is hoped that we can play our games in Franklin Field."

BARNESS BACKS SOCCER TEAM HERE: New Pro League Formed
The Philadelphia Inquirer
June 17, 1966

Philadelphia will be represented in the second nationwide major professional soccer league to be organized in two months.

Herb Barness, Bucks county builder and president of the William Penn Racing Association, was revealed as backer of the Philadelphia franchise in the new National Professional Soccer League. Formation of the National League was announced Thursday in New York.

Program from the 1966 Miss Pennsylvania Pageant
Convention Hall, Philadelphia
July 7, 8 and 9, 1966

The winner of this pageant represents the Commonwealth of Pennsylvania in the Miss America Pageant ... Talent, personality, poise, intelligence and social grace are prerequisites for these contestants; and there are approximately $6,000 in educational scholarships and awards awarded at the Miss Pennsylvania Pageant, including a four-year gubernatorial scholarship for the winner.

Miss Pennsylvania Proclamation

The reigning Miss Pennsylvania, Judith McConnell, and Pageant President Herbert Barness look on as Governor William W. Scranton signs the 1966 Miss Pennsylvania Proclamation.

The Philadelphia Inquirer
August 2, 1966

Herbert Barness, Philadelphia Golf Classic president (center), gives a tailor-made jacket to General Dwight D. Eisenhower, who will present prizes in pro-amateur event Wednesday at Whitemarsh Valley CC where the Classic begins Thursday. Looking on is Whitney Kerchner, United Cerebral Palsy head.

SHAFER IN TOURNEY: GOP Represented
The Daily Intelligencer
August 18, 1966

Lt. Gov. Raymond P. Shafer will take time out of his schedule campaigning for governor to play in the Philadelphia Golf Classic's Pro-Am tournament next Wednesday, August 24, it was announced by Herbert Barness, president of the national tourney.

Barness said today he received Lt. Gov. Shafer's entry fee of $200, and he will take pot luck with all other entrants on his professional partner.

The Warminster Spirit
August 24, 1966

BARNESS LAUDED. Herbert Barness, Warrington, President of the annual Philadelphia Golf Classic, scheduled this week at the Whitemarsh Country Club, and President of the William Penn Racing Assn., accepts the Schmidt's Sports Award of the Week on WCAU-TV from Tom Brookshier, Sports Director of the Station. The award was made for Barness's part in keeping the national golf tourney in Philadelphia.

JANUARY EQUAL TO CLASSIC PRESSURE: Relieves Jack Nicklaus of Crown

Source unknown
September 1, 1966
By Jack Smith, Sports Editor

... One of the highlights of the tournament was the appearance of General Dwight D. Eisenhower to present Pro-Am Awards on Wednesday. Eisenhower added class to the Classic.

JANUARY IN AUGUST. Don January accepts Philadelphia Golf Classic trophy from Lieutenant Governor Ray Shafer and tournament president Herbert Barness. January shot four-round 278 to win.

HARNESS FOLKS BET ON SOCCER CLUB
The Bulletin
October 19, 1966
By Sandy Grady

In the heart of the depression 33 years ago, Art Rooney was persuaded by his pal, Bert Bell, to invest $2,500 of his race-track winnings in an NFL team for Pittsburgh. Even with the Steelers' sad record, the franchise is worth millions. Money from the nags may strike again in 1966—the new soccer deal will be owned by Rooney, Herb Barness, and others in the William Penn Racing Association.

BARNESS FIRM PLANS $49 MILLION DEVELOPMENT FOR WARRINGTON
The Daily Intelligencer
Undated

A tract of 55 acres at Street and Valley roads, Warrington, in historic Paul Valley, Bucks County, has been acquired by Joseph Barness & Son, who will develop it with apartments and an industrial park for light industry.

The apartments will contain 194 garden units and will border Neshaminy Creek. The development of Paul Valley Apartments and Paul Valley Industrial Park will cost about $9 million.

Engineering & Planning Associates Inc., of Warrington, will make all improvements. Joseph Cascardo, assistant to Barness, will direct construction.

"While our developments mean progress for this area of Bucks County," Barness, said, "we fully intend to maintain the historic and colonial atmosphere of the area, including much of the same landscaping and trees."

In 1727 Joseph Paul paid an English shilling per 100 acres for a 500-acre tract. Half of this original tract remains in the hands of Joseph

H. Penrose and Mrs. William Penrose, direct descendants of the original founder of Paul Valley. The original Joseph Paul home still stands.

JUSTA FARM WINS PRAISE FOR BARNESS
The Daily Intelligencer
November 18, 1966

Each community and development that my dad built was done under a separate corporate identity. Chapel Hill Development Corporation was just one of many over the years.

Articles about this award also appeared in the Philadelphia Jewish Times *and in* The Bulletin.

Herbert Barness, Warrington realtor, developer, builder and sportsman, a former Bucks County Planning Commission chairman, practices what he preaches when it comes to planning and developing.

Barness, the son of Joseph Barness, who has been active in building, developing and expanding real estate projects since 1927, was honored by the Montgomery County Planning Commission for the best land subdivision for 1965, which is under Chapel Hill Development Corp., 1352 Easton Road, Warrington, one of the Barness's many subsidiaries.

The citation, signed by Robert E. Meloy, chairman, and Arthur F. Loeben, director, lauds the Barnesses for their good subdivision design and good development in planning and developing Justa Farm in Lower Moreland Township.

It is the Montgomery County Planning Commission's first annual award and appreciation of service commendation.

Justa Farm consists of 277 single-family homes on a 207-acre tract. The planning commission praised the Barnesses for their putting all utilities underground, seven acres of open space has been dedicated to the township for recreational purposes, a 20-acre school has been provided, all homes have public water and sanitary sewer, the variety of house types that lend charm and beauty, the street pattern that is functional and attractive, all of which make Justa Farm an asset to Lower Moreland Township and Montgomery County.

QUIET WAY TO AWAKEN A COUNTY
The Daily Intelligencer
November 20, 1966
By W. Lester Trauch

Have you seen the attractive brochure, "The Expanding World Of ... Joseph Barness and Son, Route 611, Warrington, Pennsylvania?" Isn't it wonderful their development, Justa Farm, won the Montgomery County award for the finest and best subdivision planning?

Under history and profile, it says, "In 1923, Joseph Barness left Philadelphia, bought 80 acres of land in Bucks County and entered upon his first subdivision effort.

"Before electricity lines could be extended to this property, he had to guarantee a minimum monthly usage of power. This was done and with it, the Barness firm was in business. Joseph Barness woke Warrington and Bucks County up in his own quiet way. "During the more than 40 years in which our firm has engaged in land development and building, tremendous gains in technology and facilities have been made," says Joseph Barness, the founder-father.

"Whereas electricity was not readily available in our first venture into rural development, now hundreds of projects later, we are on the threshold of having atomic energy available to use."

His son, Herbert, is president of Barness and Son. He is a mechanical engineer by profession. He presides over the 12 subsidiary companies of the firm, yet finds time to be active in the community and business world.

He is a past president of the Bucks County Planning Commission, past president of the Bucks County Home Builders Association, past president of the Bucks County Industrial Development Corp. and past president of the Bucks County Park Foundation. He is a member of the Bucks County Society of Professional Engineers.

As an avocation, he is president of the William Penn Racing Association, one of the four authorized harness racing associations in the Commonwealth of Pennsylvania.

If you think you are too busy some time, remember that Father and Son Barness are busy too. The Barness subsidiaries are: Warwick Water Co., Palomino Farms, Palomino Water Co., New Britain Water and Sewer Co., Chapel Hill Dev. Co. and Sewer Co., Barnsel Inc., Water and Sewer Utilities Services Inc., Earth Movers Inc., Recreational Pools, and Valley Sewer and Water Co.

Their overseas operations are: St. Croix, Virgin Islands, Golden Roc and Orange Grove Apartments; St. Thomas, V.I., St. Thomas House and Plantation Manor Apts.; Jamaica, British West Indies, Enson City Limited, and Seaton Hurst, Limited.

Apartment Projects are: Lincoln Arms, Morrisville; Spruce Court, Doylestown; Penndel, Penndel; Spring Garden, Ambler; Jamestown Village, Willow Grove; Paul Valley, Warrington; Lambertville, N.J.; Egg Harbor, N.J.; Warminster, Valley Park East, Bethlehem; Spring Manor, Lancaster; Elmwood Park, Bensalem; Middletown Apts., Plymouth Township.

Residential development sites are: Fairfield and Storybrook Homes, Warminster; Palomino Farms, Warrington; Lenape Village, New Britain; Sandy Ridge Acres, Doylestown; Rydal Estates, Abington; Hartsville Park, Warminster; Justa Farm, Lower Moreland, and Lamplighter Village, Warminster.

Warrington Industrial Park, created in 1960, has more than 300,000 square feet of industrial space. Fifteen firms are located there. Ground has been broken for a second industrial park of 50 acres.

Program from 25th Anniversary of Warrington Lions Club
Celebration December 8, 1966.

This was noted in the program's "History" article by Bill Lueckel.

Past President Joseph Barness [served 1955-56], an angel of the Lions and the building, is sojourning in Florida with his good wife, Mae, and in typical Barness fashion only wishes the best for everyone and wishes all of us a Happy Twenty-fifth.

WARRINGTON PRESENTED PROPERTY BY BARNESS
The Daily Intelligencer
December 1966

A 22.6 acre tract of land was given last night in Warrington Township by Mr. and Mrs. Joseph Barness, who donated the land valued at $100,000 as a public recreation area.

Barness is a well-known realtor, developer, and contractor who has had his business in Warrington since 1924.

The gift was graciously accepted by Gustav Petry, chairman of the township Board of Supervisors, while other township officials looked on in the township building.

Petry thanked the Barnesses for their gift and praised their public-minded spirit in the presentation. A symbolic $1 bill was exchanged by the township to the Barnesses to consummate the deal and a deed transferring the tract was also passed.

Barness said today that the only condition the tract was granted upon was the clause in the deed stating the township must use the site as a public recreation area—not for commercial purposes.

The tract is located on Bristol Road, one mile west of Route 611. It has been used for a number of years as a Little League field. The township immediately changed the name of the field to Barness Field.

The property had been in the hands of the Barness family for 20 years, Mr. Barness said today.

The township agreed to maintain the tract and to keep it open for public recreational use. Barness said the township may build on the tract, as long as it is for recreational and educational purposes.

Among those present for the presentation of the land to the township, in addition to Mr. and Mrs. Barness and Petry, were Arthur Harris, township solicitor; Supervisor Warren Roth, secretary and treasurer of the board; and Gordon Rudolph, chairman of the township park and recreation commission.

LAND GIFT. A symbolic $1 bill is exchanged last night in Warrington Township as Mr. and Mrs. Joseph Barness turned over the deed to a tract of land to the township. The gift was made to Gustav Petry, chairman of the township Board of Supervisors. The Barnesses' made the gift to the township of a 22.6 acre tract located on Bristol Road, one mile west of Route 611, to be used as a township public recreation area. The site is now a Little League baseball field. (Staff Photo by Don Renner)

NEW TEAM HARNESSED
The Daily Intelligencer
December 21, 1966

I knew all the men in this photo (they were YOUNG men!) and I remember going to soccer games. The team was called the Spartans.

Officers of the William Penn Racing Association, which conducts its racing at Liberty Bell Park, are backers of the Philadelphia entry in the newly formed National Professional Soccer League. The local kickers will play a 32-game home and away schedule, with their 1967 kickoff on Sunday, April 16, in Temple Stadium being televised in color. From left are: Jerry Lawrence, promotional director; John Rooney, secretary-treasurer; Herb Barness of Warrington, President; Walt Chyzowych, soccer star and personnel director; and Pat Rooney, general manager.

OFFICERS AND DIRECTORS

JOHN J. ROONEY
President

GERALD LAWRENCE
Vice President

PATRICK J. ROONEY
Treasurer

JOHN T. MACARTNEY
Secretary

ARTHUR J. ROONEY
Director

HERBERT BARNESS
Director

FRANCIS FOGARTY
Director

TIMOTHY J. ROONEY
Director

STAFF

JOHN SZEP
Coach

WALTER CHYZOWYCH
Director Player Personnel

JOHN A. LAUGHLIN, JR.
Business Manager

WALTER AIKEN
Public Relations

MAYER BRANDSCHAIN
Publicity

TED QUEDENFELD
Trainer

TOM GREEVY
Equipment Manager

JOHN WOLF, M.D.
Team Physician

JOSEPH TORG, M.D.
Team Physician

In this and the future issues of Goal, the Official National Professional Soccer League program, we will endeavor to introduce you to the members of the Philadelphia Spartan Soccer Club. We begin, in our first issue, with the team's management, Coach Szep and Walter Chyzowych, our Director of Player Personnel and star forward of the Spartans. In the 15 remaining issues, we will introduce to you all the members of the team, as well as the coaches, stars and management personnel of our visiting opponents. We hope that you will enjoy meeting the Spartans and that the information we include in the program will help you better understand soccer and that this will be the beginning of a long and pleasant friendship between the Philadelphia Spartans and Philadelphia professional soccer fans.

1967

BARNESS NAMED POP WARNER YOUTH CHAIRMAN
Source unknown
April 1967

Herb Barness, who has been active in youth work for years, has been named an honorary chairman by Pop Warner Little Scholars for their annual "All-American Eleven" award dinner, to be held on April 3 at the Bellevue Stratford Hotel.

Barness, who is president of a building and engineering firm and president of the William Penn Racing Association, makes his home on Easton Rd., in Warrington.

The Pop Warner Little Scholars movement is a scholastic betterment program for more than 600,000 boys throughout the United States and in several foreign countries, who play Pop Warner Junior League football. It seeks to instill in each of the youngsters the same desire to excel in the classroom that he has to be outstanding on the football field.

OPENING DAY
Press release for Bucks County Association for the Blind Capital Development Campaign
May 17, 1967

Hampton C. Randolph, Executive Vice President of Doylestown National Bank and Trust Company, welcomes John T. Welsh and Herbert Barness to mark the official opening of headquarters offices for $215,000 Bucks County Association for the Blind Capital Development Campaign. Campaign offices, at 30 East Court Street in Doylestown, were made available by the bank. Welsh is President of the Association's Board of Directors. Barness is the campaign's General Chairman. The Association plans a $475,000 expansion program, including a new building in Newtown.

HE'S A MAN OF MANY FACES—SPORTSMAN, REALTOR, CITIZEN

Bucks County Courier Times
June 3, 1967
By Ron Avery, *Courier Times* Staff Writer

At first glance Herb Barness might appear to be just a shrewd wheeler-dealer who has amassed quite a fortune.

After all, anybody who plans $200 million worth of building in the Caribbean, heads a harness racing association and once tried to buy the Philadelphia Eagles professional football team must be a pretty sharp cookie.

But examining only his business dealings shows very little of the man. There's much more to Herb Barness than just someone who likes to make money.

In fact, at this point in his career money means little. "I have enough money. Now it's more the challenge of something new, not the profit, that attracts me to a new business venture," he said.

The smart businessman is one side of Barness. The other side is Bucks County's most civic-minded citizen. To list all of his affiliations with charitable and public institutions would be impossible. There are so many he's not sure of the number either.

Well, you say, all wealthy people like to attach their name to some worthy cause. It's good for public relations.

But this is not the case with Barness. Public service is not just a pastime to improve his public image. It's his hobby, his great joy and a full-time job.

If public service was just a façade, he wouldn't take the job of fund-raising chairman as he has with almost all his organizations. There's too much work and too many hours in these jobs for the "sunshine citizen."

"I have at least one luncheon and [*I think he meant OR*] one dinner engagement with my civic work every day, five days a week," said Barness. "But I enjoy doing it. It's part of my recreation."

As Barness made these comments in his Warrington office, a group of people from his alma mater, Bucknell University, waited to speak with him about another fund-raising campaign. "I don't know why people always ask me to be campaign chairman. I have no real knack for raising money," he said.

But he always takes the job, and his reason is—"Somebody has to do it."

Barness is a soft-spoken 44-year-old native of Warrington. He's a veteran of World War II. He has a degree in engineering from Bucknell and a master's degree in political science from the University of Pennsylvania. [*Actually he attended some classes at Penn but didn't receive a master's degree.*]

He used to fly his own airplane. [*That's not true. He WISHED he could fly an airplane and loved flying!*] He likes politics but says he has no political ambitions.

He's married, has two teenaged daughters and travels all over the world. [*An exaggeration!*] The six-foot balding executive got his start after the war by joining his father's real estate business.

For 44 years Joseph Barness has been a realtor and builder in Bucks County. The county's growth has been phenomenal during these years, and the Barness name has been behind hundreds of thousands of dollars worth of that development.

Since 1961 the Barnesses' eyes have been on the Caribbean area. Their first garden apartment projects in the Virgin Islands are already complete, and they have plans for Jamaica and other islands.

Even closer than building to the Barness heart is sports. Barness is a fan of all sports and an avid golfer. He was one of the founders of the Warrington Country Club, and every year Barness promotes and runs the Philadelphia Golf Classic at Whitemarsh Country Club. The classic attracts some of golfing's finest pros. Proceeds of the tournament go to charity.

His most profitable sporting venture is the William Penn Harness Racing Association, which promotes about half the races at Liberty Bell

Park. Barness has been president of the association since 1964. The president is at the track almost every night during the season but has never placed a bet. "He's a true sportsman and a wonderful boss," said Ed Hogan, public relations director at Liberty Bell.

Recently the William Penn group brought professional soccer to the Philadelphia area when they created the Philadelphia Spartans. Barness is optimistic about the team's future. He has never had a financial failure in any business venture so far.

His desire to own a professional sports team goes back to 1963 when Barness and a syndicate tried to bring the Detroit Pistons basketball team to Philadelphia after the Warriors departed. But the group dropped the idea to go after bigger game. It made an offer for the Eagles football team, which apparently wasn't high enough and was turned down.

Barness said he has no new business deals in the fire right now, but he is always interested in a new challenge.

PEARL BUCK TOASTED AT BELATED BIRTHDAY: The Philadelphia Story
The Philadelphia Inquirer
July 20, 1967
By Ruth Seltzer, *Inquirer* Society Editor

A belated 75th birthday party was given in honor of Pearl Buck the other night—cocktails and dinner at "Pleasant Valley," the Newtown, Bucks County, home of Mr. and Mrs. Nathaniel Brewer.

The party was given by the board of Welcome House, the adoptive agency which Miss Buck helped found almost two decades ago. Mr. Brewer is president. Miss Buck is chairman of the board.

There were 23 at the Welcome House "welcome home" birthday party for the only woman to have won both the Nobel Prize and Pulitzer Prize for literature.

Herbert Barness, former president of Welcome House, and William Hammerstein, of New York and Doylestown, attend Pearl Buck's 75th birthday party in Newtown.

BARNESS FIRM GETS 2D RENEWAL JOB
The Philadelphia Daily News
August 18, 1967

The Chester Redevelopment Authority announced it has selected Joseph Barness & Son, Warrington, for its Smedley Urban Renewal Project.

This project, according to John J. Fitzgerald, comprises approximately 80 to 86 homes in the modest income range.

Herbert Barness, president of J. Barness & Son, said the project will cost approximately $1 million.

This marks the second redevelopment award for the Warrington firm. Several months ago, it was selected for the redevelopment project in Royersford, Pa.

Times Chronicle
October 5, 1967

SOCIETY HEAD. Herbert Barness, Rydal, has been elected president of the Philadelphia Chapter of the American Technion Society. He will assume office Jan 1.

INTERNATIONAL BLIND GOLFERS' TOURNEY SCORES AN ACE: Hope for Blind No Joke

The Suburban and *Wayne Times*
October 12, 1967
By Tim McHale

The third International Blind Golfers Tournament was played last week at the Edgmont Golf Club. If you were fortunate enough to see any of the action, and you are a golfer, chances are you won't complain about double bogies anymore.

Honorary Chairman of the Tournament, Governor Raymond Shafer, and his wife take a breather as they pull [their cart] alongside of Mr. and Mrs. Barness. Mr. Barness was the active Chairman of the tourney.

Bucks County Board of Realtors Presents Historic Bucks County (Magazine)
Winter 1967

Realtor Herbert Barness of Warrington, Pa., civic and philanthropic leader, smiles at a joke by Bob Hope at a reception for Hope and Governor Raymond Shafer and Mrs. Shafer at the Edgemont County Club during the Third International Blind Golfer Tournament. Barness is international chairman of the event.

HERBERT BARNESS RESIGNS AS HEAD OF RACING GROUP
The Philadelphia Inquirer
December 6, 1967

Herbert Barness, Bucks County builder and real estate developer, has resigned as president of the William Penn Racing Association, he said Tuesday night.

He denied, however, that he quit the night harness racing group, which conducts its meetings at Liberty Bell, in order to get into flat racing.

"There was talk of it, but that's not why I resigned," he said. "My reason was that it was just too much for me. I am in business in the daytime and I was spending all my nights at the track. I'm a family man and I never got to see my family."

Barness, who remarked, "I never did have much (financial) interest" in the track, said no successor had been named as far as he knew. Pat

Rooney, vice president and general manager, was out of town and could not be reached. Art Rooney, owner of the Pittsburgh Steelers, is chairman of the William Penn Racing Association and its principal stakeholder.

Barness said no disagreements or conflicts of any kind prompted the move. In fact, he said, "They didn't want me to quit."

SHAFER SIGNS FLAT RACING BILL, FIRST FOR PENNA.
The Philadelphia Inquirer
December 12, 1967

Thoroughbred racing with pari-mutuel betting was legalized in Pennsylvania Monday afternoon.

A new law permitting thoroughbred (flat) racing in the State—for the first time in Pennsylvania's history—became effective immediately when Gov. Raymond P. Shafer signed a bill passed by the Legislature to legalize this sport.

A mad scramble for the four flat track licenses is anticipated after Shafer appoints the three members of the [*State Horse Racing*] commission.

One syndicate expected to apply will be headed by Herbert Barness, Bucks County developer, and Art Rooney, owner of the Pittsburgh Steelers Football Club.

Barness was president of the William Penn Racing Association, which conducts harness racing meetings at the Northeast Philadelphia track owned by the Liberty Bell Racing Association. Rooney owned the controlling interest in William Penn.

However, Barness resigned as head of the William Penn track, and Rooney was reported to have transferred his stock control to his sons.

It is likely that if the Barness-Rooney syndicate is awarded a license—many believe it will be—it will seek to lease the Liberty Bell track for flat racing.

Liberty Bell sources say that its racing oval can be converted into a flat track within a period of several months.

1968

RACETRACK NOT THE ROAD TO RICHES, BARNESS SAYS, BUT IT HAS ROMANCE
The Sunday Bulletin
January 21, 1968
By Bayard Brunt of the *Bulletin* Staff

Herb Barness, Bucks County real estate developer, is a friendly joiner who doesn't like crowds, but he enjoys people, sports, and horses.

Barness, 44, quit last October as president of the William Penn Racing Association, which conducts harness racing at Liberty Bell race track, because he said the job was interfering with his family "togetherness" and his real estate business. Barness, a strapping six-footer who has never bet on a horse race, said the other day he cannot say at this time whether he would be interested in getting into a flat-racing track.

"I have no real plans to get into flat racing," Barness said. "I've been approached by people. But it's too early to decide; so far, the only thing is that has happened is that flat racing has been legalized in Pennsylvania. A commission hasn't even been appointed. I want to see what is going to happen.

"We may be a year away from thoroughbred racing here, especially if someone is going to build a track. Liberty Bell could be converted. But that depends on who gets the license. And there would be conversion problems.

"There would be no trouble getting land for a new race track with many locations within 45 minutes of downtown Philadelphia. Of course, you would have to pay for it.

"It could be in many places, including Montgomery and Chester counties. I have heard rumors that a track would be built at Bristol, at Valley Forge, in Delaware County, even at 30th and Market St., Philadelphia.

"People don't realize that a racetrack is not the greatest investment in the world, the sure road to riches, the pot of gold at the end of the rainbow, but there's a lot of romance to it."

Barness was interviewed in his paneled office from behind an almost bare desk in the building on Easton Road (Route 611) Warrington, occupied by Joseph Barness and Son and the Doylestown sub-station of the State Police. Barness explained how he became involved in William Penn.

"It was just like buying stock in General Motors," Barness said. "It was an investment. I knew no one involved, not Dan Parish or Art Rooney, who were from Pittsburgh, and not Jim Clark or Bill Green." (The late James C. Clark, the trucking magnate and finance chairman of the Democratic City Committee, built Liberty Bell for late U.S. Rep. William J. Green, Jr. The Democratic city chairman, had an option to buy a block of Liberty Bell stock. This was exercised after his death by his widow, Mary.)

Barness, a Republican who disclaims any political activities, said he is a close personal friend of John Welsh, Bucks County Democratic chairman. "John offered me some William Penn Stock. I bought 10,000 of 1 million shares, at $2 a share. I now hold about 20,000 shares, worth around $4.5 each.

"I met Parish and Rooney at a stockholders' meeting in Philadelphia. They were putting together a board of directors. They put John Welsh on the board; they asked me if I would like to be on the board.

"Dan Parish was president the first year. Then I served as president for four years. I did not accept any salary, although I was offered any amount I wanted.

"I was there at the racetrack 62 nights a year—10 weeks a year. I didn't have time to go home for dinner. I felt I was giving up too much of my family, that I had to choose between real estate and racing and the challenge was gone."

Over the past four years, Barness said, betting at William Penn meets increased from $450,000 a day to more than $700,000.

He said he did not think that William Penn stock had turned out to be a good investment.

Barness said he not only never bet on horse races but never gambled, even in a place like Las Vegas, which he has visited several times.

"This real estate business is so much of a gamble, maybe that's why I don't bet. I gamble in business every day."

Barness said he wanted to be an athlete in school—he was graduated from Doylestown High School in 1940 and Bucknell University in 1948 after World War II Air Force service—but never had the ability. "But I tried out for all the teams," he said.

It seemed natural to ask him whether he had any interest in trying to acquire the Philadelphia Eagles professional football team from financially beset Jerry Wolman, another real estate developer.

Barness said emphatically that he did not.

"Poor Jerry," he added. "He's a fine fellow. But he went too fast and overextended himself. I don't think he has anyone else to blame, but I often think, 'There but for the grace of God go I.'"

Barness said his building operations total $8 to $10 million a year, with $2.5 million of this in the Virgin Islands on St. Thomas and St. Croix.

He estimated the firm founded by his father also does about $1 million in ordinary real estate transactions, mostly in Bucks County, during the year. He said he has no Philadelphia business connections.

"My personal end of the business is real estate development through Barness Construction Co.," Barness said. "I also have an interest in an engineering firm I established, Engineering and Planning Associates, which does our engineering work. I was graduated from college as a mechanical engineer. I thought I might go into aeronautics before I went in business with my dad. He doesn't spend much time with the business now. He and my mother, who are in their mid-70s, live six months a year in Florida."

Barness said he is building in New Jersey, Lancaster, Pittsburgh and the Allentown-Bethlehem area, as well as in the Virgin Islands, and he has a $5 million commitment with the Agency for International Development to construct 900 low-cost houses in Jamaica, the West Indies. He said he may be asked to build in Africa.

He declines to classify himself as a millionaire.

"It probably sounds corny," he said, "but I really don't know my actual net worth in dollars and cents. But we're comfortable."

He said the firm went into large-scale building operations in 1952, "after the Korean War just as a natural growth and desire to expand."

Barness was born in Philadelphia on Dec. 1, 1923, where his father, a Polish Jewish immigrant, had a small clothing manufacturing business. But when Barness was only four months old, his father moved the family to a 98-acre farm in Warrington.

Barness has an older brother, Lewis, a graduate of Harvard University and its medical school, and now a professor of pediatrics at the University of Pennsylvania.

The elder Barness turned to the real estate business when he found himself starving to death as a farmer, according to his son.

Barness said his father started in 1928 by building one house on a portion of his farm separated from their farm house by a road, sold that house, "built a second one, and so on."

Barness, his wife, the former Irma Shorin, daughter of a New York City bubblegum manufacturer, and their two daughters, Lynda, 18, a freshman at Jackson College [*Tufts University*] and Nancy, 16, a junior at Central Bucks High School [*this is an error—my sister and I both went to Abington High School*], live in Warrington. [*This is also an error. We moved to Rydal, in nearby Montgomery County, when I was entering 7th grade.*] But Barness in

December bought a 150-acre farm in Buckingham Township, where they are going to move because Warrington has become "too crowded." [*They did buy a farm in Buckingham Township, and my parents moved there when my sister and I were both in college.*]

Barness said he's the "beachcomber type" who hates crowds, and that's why he and his family have never taken a vacation at the seashore. For the past seven years, they've spent the winter holidays in the Virgin Islands. He and his wife, an amateur painter and sculptor, will have been married 20 years on June 27. They met at Bucknell, where she was a psychology major. "She graduated into matrimony," Barness said.

Barness said he would never go into any business venture "just for the profit." He said he has to enjoy it, as he did watching harness races and meeting people at the track. He said he never got tired of watching harness races, with which he first became familiar as a boy at the Doylestown Fair.

He said he enjoys belonging to many civic organizations, including a number in Philadelphia, such as the Chamber of Commerce, the Crime Commission, the Fellowship Commission, and the World Affairs Council. He said he belongs to about everything you can belong to in Bucks County, and almost every day he attends a civic luncheon somewhere—seldom a business luncheon.

He has given up both smoking and drinking as a "waste of time," watches his weight, but is on no special diet, enjoys good health, and needs only three or four hours [*of sleep*] a night. He usually is at his office by 7:30 a.m.

He likes to spend his evenings at home, and seldom goes out to dinner. "You lose your children too quickly," he said. "We have great times together." Even when he goes to the Virgin Islands on business he usually makes it a one-day trip, so he won't be away from home overnight.

One of the activities of which he seems proudest is his presidency for five years (up to a year ago) of Welcome House, the adoption agency founded by fellow Bucks Countians Pearl Buck and Oscar Hammerstein, for children of racially mixed parentage, primarily those fathered in the Far East by American GIs. He is still on the agency board.

BARNESS SEEKS BUCK ... [page torn]
The Bulletin
February 7, 1968?
By Fred Selby of the *Bulletin* Staff.

The on-stage political debut of one of Bucks County's most influential behind-the-stage leaders will feature the battling for endorsements by the Bucks County Republicans in the next week.

The behind-the-stage leader is Herbert Barness of Warrington, a real estate developer and sportsman who is known throughout the state.

He is in a four-way race for two posts as Bucks County delegates to the GOP National Convention, which will be held in Miami Beach, Fla., in August.

The others seeking these glamorous non-paying posts are Republican County Chairman C.V. Afflerback; W. Donald Heinemann, recorder of deeds; and Mrs. Janet Acker, party leader in Upper Southampton Township.

Afflerback seems certain to get one of the endorsements.

Barness is favored to get the other one, if for no other reason than he has been one of the largest contributors to the Bucks GOP, and it's a national tradition that such contributors become delegates.

BARNESS DONATES 15 ACRES FOR PARK
The Evening Bulletin
February 29, 1968

Developer Herbert Barness has donated 15 acres to Warminster Township for use as a park.

He turned the deed for the land on Bristol Road near Log College Drive over to the Board of Supervisors at a meeting Monday night.

This brings to 75 acres the township's park and playground areas.

Technion Magazine
March 1968

There was a handwritten note by my dad at the top of the cover of this issue that said, "Mail to Lynda." I was a freshman at Tufts University.

Lt. Colonel Yerachmiel Dori, chief engineer of the Israeli army, spoke at the recent installation of new officers and Board members for the Philadelphia Chapter. Here, Col. Dori is seen talking with Herbert Barness, President of the chapter, and Benjamin Fox, the chapter's Vice President for 1968.

The Daily Intelligencer
March 14, 1968

FOURTH SECTION. Enjoying U.S. Virgin Island food at a reception in Le Bistro, on St. Thomas, following groundbreaking for the fourth section of Plantation Manor on St. Thomas are Herbert Barness of Warrington, an owner of the apartment development; Yvon, of Le Bistro; Gov. Ralph M. Paiewonsky of the Virgin Islands, and Claude L. Benner Jr., president of Bankers Bond & Mortgage Co., also a co-owner of the apartment development.

COMMONWEALTH OF PENNSYLVANIA OFFICIAL DOCUMENT—VOTES FOR DELEGATE
Election April 23, 1968

I, Joseph J. Kelley Jr., secretary of the Commonwealth, do hereby certify that at the Election held on the twenty-third day of April, 1968, Herbert Barness having received Twenty thousand six hundred ninety-eight votes, was duly elected to the office of DELEGATE to REPUBLICAN NATIONAL CONVENTION in the Eighth Congressional District of Pennsylvania.

Witness my hand and the seal of my office this twentieth day of May 1968,

                Joseph J. Kelley, Jr., Secretary of the Commonwealth

Program from the Pop Warner Little Scholars 1968 All-American Eleven: Service to Youth Dinner
April 29, 1968
Bellevue Stratford Hotel
Philadelphia, Pennsylvania

Herbert Barness, 40th Anniversary Celebration Committee Chairman

MID CITY FEDERAL ELECTS BARNESS
The Dispatch
May 5, 1968

A similar article appeared in The Jewish Exponent.

Herbert Barness, Bucks County real estate developer, was elected to the Board of Directors of Mid City Federal Savings and Loan Association, as announced by Edwin S. Malmed, president.

Barness, a past president of the William Penn Racing Association, which conducts racing at Liberty Bell Race Track, lives in Buckingham Township with his wife and two daughters.

He is a registered professional engineer who graduated from Bucknell University after serving four years as a Captain in the U.S. Army [*the Army Air Force*], during World War II.

In announcing the election of Barness, Malmed said: "We're terribly pleased to have Herb Barness on our Board. He brings to it a wealth of personal experience in Real Estate Development, both in the Philadelphia area and in the Virgin Islands. And, in addition to his professional acumen as a financier, he brings to Mid City his notable civic accomplishments such as a directorship in Welcome House and membership in the Crime Commission and the Fellowship Commission. It's not often I can take as much personal pride in the election of a fellow board member as I can in that of Herb Barness."

BARNESS PARK DEDICATED TO KIDS OF WARRINGTON; FOR BETTER CITIZENS

The Daily Intelligencer
May 13, 1968

"THIS WILL BE MY REWARD," PHILANTHROPIST SAYS

The dedication of Barness Park at noon on Saturday in Warrington was filled with emotion as Joseph Barness, 72, addressed the crowd gathered for the event.

Barness said that he hoped that his donation to the community will help make the children of Warrington better citizens. "This will be my reward!"

The ceremony followed a parade which began at Bristol and York roads and ended at the field on Bristol Road opposite Warrington Airport. Taking part were numerous community organizations, including the Tamanend Junior High School Band and the Warrington Volunteer Fire Company.

Among the dignitaries in attendance were State Senator Marvin Keller, Frank Purcell, who is secretary of the Bucks County Board of Commissioners, and William Graham, Doylestown Township Supervisor.

Walter Hayes, Chairman of the Warrington Board of Supervisors, read a telegram of congratulations from Representative Benjamin Wilson.

Also attending were Dr. and Mrs. Lewis Barness and Mr. and Mrs. Herbert Barness and their children.

The finale of the event was the dedication of a stone and plaque with the inscription, "Gift of Mary and Joseph Barness." [*A photograph of this plaque appears on page 257.*]

Following the ceremony, many local residents came to Mr. and Mrs. Barness to offer personal appreciation. Mrs. George Klein was one of those who came forward. The Klein home, built in 1928, was the first constructed in the area by Barness, who moved to Warrington from Philadelphia in 1924.

Both Mary and Joseph Barness stated in a personal interview that they have always wanted to show their love for the community and its people in a significant way, while they could both enjoy it. Barness said that he has had more time to do some of the things for the community now that he is less active in the business.

During the Little League baseball season, 25 teams from various Central Bucks communities will use the field.

The park is the result of two years' planning. In addition to the ball field, there are facilities for other sports.

[*There was a photo, in poor condition, with the following caption*: BARNESS PARK—Joseph and Mary Barness examine the stone and plaque presented in honor of their donation of Barness Park on Saturday afternoon in Warrington Township. The ceremony followed a parade composed of community organizations. Area governmental leaders attended the event in addition to hundreds of residents. (Staff Photo by Don Renner)]

REAL ESTATE: CONSTRUCTION CARIBBEAN STYLE—A LOCAL BUILDER DEVELOPS THE ISLANDS
Philadelphia Magazine
May 1968
By Greg Walter

I remember my father talking about all of the problems that were mentioned in this article, and I assume that's why he didn't continue to build in the islands. I can recall watching a retaining wall go up ... very, very, very slowly. A few blocks per day!

... St. Thomas is changing, and the hills are the basis of that change. Where plantation owners found it impossible to grow sugar cane, builders are planting new houses on building lots that each year double in value.

Despite the honky-tonk that is Charlotte Amalie below, the view from those hills is very lovely. The boom is on in St. Thomas, and a number of enterprising Philadelphians are finding it both challenging and profitable to be in on the change.

Virtually the entire economy of St. Thomas is based on what will be in 1968 a $75 million tourist industry. The really big problems are the ones caused by mushrooming economic expansion ...

The islands operate semi-colonially under what is known as the Revised Organic Act passed by Congress in 1954. The act allows for a U.S.-appointed governor, a legislature and a judiciary. The present governor, Ralph Paiewonsky, was appointed by President Kennedy at the urging of the late Bill Green, whose family still retains property on St. Thomas ...

In this highly charged atmosphere, U.S. businessmen often find themselves baffled by the way decisions are made. Probably the greatest potential in the islands is low-cost housing for the growing number of residents. There is also a good deal of promise, according to Paiewonsky, in middle- and upper-income homes since the island needs to house the professionals it hopes to lure there with an increase in local industries.

Gearing up to no small degree in this field is Herbert Barness, partner in his father's firm of Joseph Barness & Son, and former president of the William Penn Racing Association, among other things. Barness has built a healthy reputation as a construction man in various levels of home building in and around Philadelphia.

Quiet, most often enigmatic, Barness exudes a kind of confidence that is most helpful in encouraging the capital he needs for his various projects.

He says the Virgin Islands started to interest him several years ago after friends who'd vacationed there started talking about the gross lack of housing. He made one or two trips, then in 1962 bought 28 acres on a hillside on St. Thomas, some 900 feet above Charlotte Amalie.

Although the Virgin Island government did not then—and still does not—offer any tax inducements to builders, local property taxes are attractively low. At the same time, water costs are quite high.

Since St. Thomas has relatively little in the way of public water, the first problem Barness and his men had to cope with was getting water up the steep hill and into cisterns. By law, homes built on the island must have rooftop rain collectors. An arrangement was made to tap the government water supply, stocked by an ever-increasing number of desalinization plants, at a cost of $1 for 500 gallons. Pumping stations were set up at various points on the hillside, and an elaborate electrical system keeps tabs on their operation 24 hours a day. This relatively small amount of water, plus what is accumulated on rooftops, is enough to provide for the 60 apartment units Barness currently operates there. Ninety-six more are planned by him, in addition to a 100-unit hotel, the Golden Falcon, for which funds have already been committed.

"The water system cost us around a quarter of a million dollars," says Barness, "and it's probably the only time I've built something without knowing what it would ultimately cost. We had to have water, and there was no one around to tell us how to get it up."

Barness must also provide sea water for sanitation in his building ventures. This, of course, must also be piped up the hill and provides an occasional headache when it begins to corrode tanks and pipe-fittings.

Barness frequently makes one-day flying trips from Philadelphia to the islands. It is strictly business, a time for talks with local bankers, a check with his Stateside building crew and with local managers on St. Thomas and St. Croix. Managing Plantation Manor on St. Thomas is a former auto agency owner and one-time executive with Bankers Bond & Mortgage, Guy Hayden. William Brooks is a retired Navy man from Philadelphia and manages two St. Croix operations, Golden Roc and Orange Grove.

Although it's usually business, Barness has devoted the past seven Christmas holidays to taking his wife and two teenage daughters to the islands. A small part of his 28-acre spread will eventually be turned into a vacation home.

Apartments on the island are built of concrete block and poured concrete. At Plantation Manor, lots of louvered windows and sliding doors look down the sweeping hillside to the sea. Units stay rented at prices ranging from $175 for a single bedroom to $250 for a double.

... Besides the proposed apartments and Golden Falcon Hotel, Barness and his Pennsylvania Overseas Development Corporation have other plans for that 28 acres on St. Thomas. The company has received preliminary FHA approval to build 600 more modestly priced apartments under the 221-D-3 rent subsidy program. [*This was never built.*]

There are pitfalls. First, the labor problem in the islands is incredible. Native St. Thomians are normally pleasant people, but they consistently resist the Stateside way of doing things. More than one builder has gone down the financial drain because he miscalculated the amount of time necessary to complete a project. There are almost no local industries so that everything from coarse sand for mixing cement to doorknobs has to be shipped from the States ... A St. Thomian will not be rushed, and to add to management's problems, official holidays in the island total 24—combining traditional native holidays and Stateside celebration ... One of the big reasons why there is a low supply of local laborers is that on St. Thomas, at least, almost everyone and his brother works for the government, the biggest single employer on the island ... To keep construction going at Plantation Manor, Barness keeps a full-time crew of about 45 people. To do this, [*general manager*] Guy Hayden must run through about 250 bodies a year.

Some of the immediate problems also have to be taken into consideration by would-be investors in the islands. One of the most essential ingredients to the modern operation of a successful business is woefully bad: communications.

GOP 'GROUP' SET UP FOR CONVENTION ROLE
The Philadelphia Inquirer
June 9, 1968
Inquirer Harrisburg Bureau

A group known simply as "the group" has been established here to provide inside information on other delegations and to keep Pennsylvania's contingent united as this State prepares for a major role at the August Republican National Convention.

"The Group" was triggered by Secretary of Administration and Budget Arthur F. Samson, and has met regularly though not too frequently for the last seven months. The pace is expected to be stepped up as the convention approaches.

In addition to Sampson, Jordan, Maxwell, and Kunzig, the members include:

Attorney General William C. Sennett; Hugh E. Flaherty, Shafer's Secretary for Legislative and Public Affairs; Lt. Gov. Raymond J. Broderick; Herbert Barness, Bucks County builder, businessman and former harness racetrack executive; J.L. Davies, of Meadville, an automobile dealer and close friend and supporter of Shafer; and Ralph Johnson, of Pittsburgh, an executive of the H.J. Heinz Co. and of the Pennsylvanians for Rockefeller organization ... and others.

Fund Raising—Assigned to Davies, Barness, Breen and Burnham, they are to prepare a budget of $75,000 for pre-convention activity and $300,000 for convention expenses; they are to raise the necessary funds. A bank account was to be opened under the name "United Pennsylvania Delegation—1968" with Sennett as treasurer.

SUBURBAN GOP LEADERS, DELEGATES PLAY IT SAFE IN NIXON-ROCKEFELLER FIGHT FOR NOMINATION
The Evening Bulletin
June 20, 1968
By Forrest L. Black of the *Bulletin* Staff

Republican suburban county leaders and national convention delegates were playing it safe today in the fight for the GOP presidential nomination.

Gov. Shafer abandoned his "favorite son" status in favor of New York Gov. Nelson A. Rockefeller over the weekend.

In Bucks County, a party spokesman said Republican Chairman C.V. Afflerback and the other convention delegate, Herbert Barness, are still awaiting the outcome of a survey of rank-and-file Republicans before taking their stand.

A week ago, Afflerback said early results indicated Republicans were giving Rockefeller and Nixon about equal support.

'SCHOLARS' VACANCY FOR BARNESS
The Jewish Exponent
June 21, 1968

A similar article appeared in The Philadelphia Dispatch *and* The Philadelphia Jewish Times.

Herbert Barness, the builder and civic leader, will become board chairman of the Pop Warner Little Scholars tomorrow evening when the annual meeting of the trustees is held on the Wayne estate of George M. Ewing, Jr., the architect. The post has been vacant for the past year as a tribute to the late Samuel H. Daroff, who held the position for many years. This agency also sponsors Pop Warner Junior League Football among 600,000 youngsters in this and several foreign countries.

POP WARNER

The Philadelphia Inquirer
June 28, 1968
By C. Allen Keith

Joseph J. Tomlin, founding president of Pop Warner Little Scholars, an organization sponsoring a Junior Football League for 600,000 boys in the United States and abroad, has been reelected for his 40th term. Herbert Barness, builder, was named board chairman, a post left vacant for a year in respect to the late Samuel A. Daroff, clothing manufacturer, who served many years.

The Daily Intelligencer
July 17, 1968
Staff Photo by Rudy Millarg

CONVENTION CONVERSATIONS. Pausing in their day-long conference in Philadelphia are Herbert Barness, Republican Presidential hopeful Richard M. Nixon, and Bucks County Republican Committee Chairman C. V. Afflerback. Barness, a land developer, and Afflerback, are uncommitted delegations to the Republican National Convention from the 8th Congressional District of Bucks County.

GOP DELEGATES UNCOMMITTED

The Daily Intelligencer
August 1, 1968 [*This was right before the 1968 Republican National Convention in Miami Beach. I went to the Convention with my dad!*]

Bucks County Republican chairman C. V. (Chick) Afflerback and Herbert Barness, delegates to the GOP National Convention from the 8th Congressional District said Wednesday they remain uncommitted as they prepare to go to Miami Beach.

Afflerback said the decision was reached "because I think that gives us the best options at the convention where the real, hard decisions are made."

If he and Barness had announced in favor of one candidate or another, it would have been harder to pull factions together for the fall campaign, Afflerback said.

Both men are willing to settle on a number of combinations, Afflerback said, but indicated their main responsibility during balloting would be to reflect the sentiments of Republicans in the district, which includes southern Lehigh and Eastern Montgomery counties as well as Bucks.

Afflerback and Barness, a county contractor and developer, will be leading a 60-member workforce. Only State delegations from Philadelphia and Pittsburgh are larger.

Though Afflerback and Barness expect to remain neutral, a private poll conducted among some 300 GOP workers showed Richard M. Nixon edging Nelson Rockefeller 43 to 40 percent. [*My dad became a Rockefeller delegate.*]

Afflerback said the Bucks representatives would be operating out of a fifth floor suite of the Diplomat East Hotel in Miami Beach. The 700 members of the State delegation will also be in the same hotel.

The main job, he said, would be to assist the State staff contact delegations from other states to keep up with minute-by-minute changes in sentiments.

Barness will be leaving for Miami Beach on Thursday, while Afflerback will depart Friday morning.

PHILA. GROUP SPEARHEADS CAMPAGIN FOR $4 MILLION TECHNION BUILDING
The Philadelphia Jewish Times
August 29, 1968

Israel has no interest in going to the moon, Alexander Goldberg, president of Technion, Israel Institute of Technology since 1965, told a luncheon conference at the Locust Club this week.

"We stress," Goldberg elaborated, "the practical side of technology for Israel ... desalinization, solid state physics and mathematics, to specify a few."

In that pragmatic facet, Goldberg said, a $4 million structure devoted to solid state physics will soon be built with the aid of two Philadelphia industrialists, brothers Maurice M. and Ruben P. Rosen. The former is national president of the American Society for Technion. Half of the funds necessary for the solid state physics building, Goldberg said, will be appropriated by the Israel government; the remaining portion will be obtained through a campaign spearheaded by local realtor Herbert Barness and the Rosen brothers. A cocktail reception honoring the Rosens will be held Sept. 9, 4:30 p.m., at the home of Jack Wolgin, 250 S. 18th Street. Guest speaker will be Israeli columnist and executive vice-president of Technion Carl Alpert.

POP WARNER PROGRAM THRIVES AT AGE 40; INTERNATIONAL MEMBERSHIP EXCEEDS 600,000

The Football News
September 14, 1968

The Pop Warner Junior League Football Program is now 40 years old, with an international membership of more than 600,000 boys from 7-15 years of age. Nobody is happier about its growth than Herbert Barness, chairman of the program.

"It's safety-first football that we endorse," Barness said. "We frown on building football heroes, with All-Star games, the trophies and the glory.

'The pre-teen years should be spent learning the fundamentals and how to avoid injury.

"Moreover, we don't want any boy spoiled by glory so that he can't go into the ninth grade football team as a 'scrub,' starting all over.

"What we want to see is a boy building a hunger for high school football and a hunger for success in the classroom."

Barness emphasized that the Pop Warner League cooperates with high school coaches. They confer with the coaches, ask how the program would best benefit the high schools, then set standards to adhere to the coaches' judgments.

TWO FLAT RACING LICENSES OK'D FOR BUCKS COUNTY

The Philadelphia Inquirer
November 21, 1968
By Joseph H. Miller of the *Inquirer* Staff

The State Horse Racing Commission on Wednesday granted flat track licenses to two Philadelphia area syndicates—Continental Thoroughbred Racing Association and Eagle Downs Race Track, Inc.—which plan to conduct separate meets at a new $34 million plant in Bucks County.

The commission bypassed two groups seeking franchises to operate flat racing at Liberty Bell Park in northeast Philadelphia, under lease arrangements.

One was Man O' War Racing Association, operating on behalf of a hospital benefit trust, which would provide several millions annually for nonprofit hospitals in southeastern Pennsylvania. The other was the Valley Forge Thoroughbred Racing Association headed by Walter M. Jeffords, horse owner and breeder.

Mayor James. H. J. Tate was upset by the city's failure to obtain one of the revenue-producing licenses and threatened court action. He termed the action "an arbitrary decision" and apparent political "discrimination."

The commission also granted license to Shamrock Racing Association for flat meets at a converted harness track at Pocono Downs, near Scranton, and to Pennsylvania National Turf Club, Inc., which plans a new $9 million track at Grantham, eight miles from Harrisburg.

Granting two licenses to operate at a Bucks County track ultimately will result in a loss of several millions annually to the Philadelphia Board of Education, and an equal amount to the city.

The leading figure in organizing the Continental syndicate was Herbert Barness, Bucks County builder and a personal friend of Gov. Raymond P. Shafer. President of the syndicate is Peter D. Carlino, Blue Bell insurance man.

[A box at the bottom of the article said, "All the syndicates applying for licenses to operate flat racing tacks in Pennsylvania were required to list all persons with financial interests" and then named the four syndicates and listed such persons.]

Continental Thoroughbred Racing Association:
Peter D. Carlino, Blue Bell insurance man, president; Leonard Tose, Norristown trucking company official, vice president; Dr. A. A. Hobson of Wayne, secretary and treasurer; Gustave G. Amsterdam, banker, lawyer, and chairman of the city's Redevelopment Authority; Dr. F. Bruce Baldwin, board chairman of Horn & Hardart Baking Co.; Hal L. Bemis, Philadelphia industrialist and former president of the Greater Philadelphia Chamber of Commerce; John Murphy, a Philadelphia broker; J. Permar Richards, president of the Union League and a business leader; William T. Elliott, a life insurance executive; Walter Gay Jr., a Philadelphia attorney; James D. Morrissey Jr., a Philadelphia contractor; Roger Firestone of Bryn Mawr; Arlin M. Adams, a Philadelphia attorney and former state Secretary of Welfare; and Herbert Barness, a Bucks County developer.

1969

TOSE TO BUY EAGLES IF WOLMAN PLAN FAILS
The Philadelphia Inquirer
January 18, 1969
By Gordon Forbes of the *Inquirer* Staff

Leonard Tose, the trucking executive, has agreed to purchase the Eagles for more than $15 million if troubled owner Jerry Wolman is declared bankrupt, it was learned Friday. Wolman, contacted at his Silver Spring, Md., home, would name no names, but said he had a prospective buyer, "a gentleman, a Philadelphian and a great sports fan."

Tose later was identified as the prospective purchaser by Earl Foreman, the attorney who controls 48 percent of the Eagles stock. Wolman owns the other 52 percent.

"It is a contract between the Eagles and Mr. Tose," Foreman said in a telephone interview. "It is still being considered but probably will be presented to the Eagles board of directors in the near future, probably one day next week."

Club directors include Wolman, Foreman and attorney Kenneth W. Gemmill.

Foreman said he received a copy of the contract Friday morning. "As far as I can see it's a complete contract," he said.

Wolman, however, said there were a number of "technicalities" to be cleared up.

Under an agreement filed in U.S. District Court in Baltimore, Wolman has to come up with a buyer before Jan. 21. Wolman still owes about $35 million, including $5.5 million to Morgan Guaranty Trust Co. of New York and $2.5 million to the Fidelity Bank of Philadelphia.

Should Wolman meet his debts, the contract with Tose would be null and void.

"This guy"—referring to the purchaser he "wouldn't identify" as Tose—"is really a gentleman," Wolman said. "He will tell you he would rather have me make it than end up owning the team. He will be rooting for me."

Tose, 51, is an executive of a motor freight company in Bridgeport that does an annual business of $10 million. He is a graduate of Notre Dame and a football, baseball and horseracing enthusiast.

In 1956 Tose headed a syndicate that tried to buy the Eagles for $1 million from Frank L. McNamee and the late James P. Clark. At that time Tose was an Eagles stockholder. He was also interested in purchasing the Eagles in 1963 when Wolman bought the club for $5,505,500.

Tose also owned 40 percent of the now defunct Ramblers hockey team. In addition, he is a stockholder in Continental Thoroughbred Racing Association, one of the four groups licensed to conduct flat racing in Pennsylvania this year.

"He always has been interested in buying the Eagles," a close associate said. "And he is wealthy enough to do it. He has a number of wealthy friends, too."

One of Tose's associates, builder Herb Barness, said he wasn't involved in any proposition to buy the Eagles. Tose himself was unavailable for comment.

16 MEN WILL DIRECT PHILA. GOLF CLASSIC
The Philadelphia Inquirer
February 16, 1969

A 16-man board of business, civic and golf leaders has been named to direct the 1969 Philadelphia Golf Classic. In announcing the appointments, tournament General Chairman Donald B. Houder said, "Our goal is to create greater involvement of the community in the Classic ... We're confident we'll accomplish this through the board leadership present on this board of directors."

The tournament, sponsored by Industrial Valley Bank and Trust Company, will be played at Whitemarsh Valley Country Club July 17-20. The following were named to the Classic board of directors: Herbert Barness, real estate developer and former Classic sponsor ...

JEFF KEEN SAYS
The Jewish Exponent
February 21, 1969

Herbert Barness, the suburban builder, and Maurie H. Orodenker, advertising exec., are listed among the incorporators of the Pop Warner Little Scholars, for which U.S. Sen. Hugh Scott will introduce a bill to grant a federal charter. A similar bill will be introduced in the house. Both members of the local community are active in the youth movement, which sponsors Pop Warner Junior League Football throughout the nation. The last federal charter granted was for the Boy Scouts. If granted to the Little Scholars, it will be signed by President Nixon, and that will make him the titular head of the group.

TOSE TOPS MCCLOSKEY'S BID, GETS EAGLES FOR $16 MILLION; OPTION USED TO INCREASE OFFER BY $5000
The Philadelphia Inquirer
March 12, 1969
By E.J. Hussie of the *Inquirer* Staff

I included this article here to follow the Eagles story-line. My dad was finally a (minority, he had 29%) partner in a football team, and for a while it was great fun. Our whole family had been going to Eagles games since 1959, and this really took being a fan to a whole new level ... we met players, sat in the owner's box, and in general had a blast. My father thoroughly enjoyed it ... for a time. But the partnership soured, as you will see further on.

Trucking executive Leonard Tose outbid his nearest competitor at a public hearing Tuesday to win conditional ownership of the Philadelphia Eagles for $16,055,000—a record price for a professional football club.

Tose exercised his right to top the highest sealed bid submitted to Federal bankruptcy refer Joseph O. Kaiser by going $5,000 higher than builder Thomas D. McCloskey's $16,050,000.

The price was not only a record, it nearly doubled the previous record. It also represented a sum three times what Wolman paid for the Eagles, and then some.

PENNSYLVANIA FLAT SPORT STARTS TODAY AT LIBERTY BELL
9 RACES; 1.30 POST; MR. WASHINGTON HEADS $29,350 KEYSTONE 'CAP

The Morning Telegraph
May 31, 1969
By Nick Sanabria

Thoroughbred racing will be introduced in Pennsylvania at 1:30 p.m. Saturday as the Continental Thoroughbred Racing Association presents the first card of its 34-day meeting.

This will mark the first pari-mutuel thoroughbred meeting ever conducted in the Keystone State. There are nine races slated daily and there will be a daily double, as well as an exacta, on the fifth and ninth races.

A field of 13, headed by Pin Oak Stable's Mr. Washington, has been named to the $29,350 Keystone Handicap, the first of seven added-money events to be contested during the meeting.

President Herbert Barness and general manager Phil Baker both are optimistic that Pennsylvanians will warmly support the three Continental meetings at Liberty Bell. The association will conduct an 11-day session from December 9 through December 20 and a five-day meeting from December 26 through December 30.

Plans are also underway for the construction of a $35,000,000 plant, Neshaminy Downs, adjacent to the Pennsylvania Turnpike about three and a half miles from Liberty Bell.

BARNESS IN RACING IN A BIG WAY NOW; CONTINENTAL HEAD OWNS PA. FARM

The Morning Telegraph
May 31, 1969

"I'm really a farm boy," Herbert Barness, president of the Continental Thoroughbred Racing Association, said with a smile. The chief executive of the first pari-mutuel track in Pennsylvania's history, which opens Saturday for a 34-day meeting at Liberty Bell Park, said, "Actually, I never became seriously involved in racing until four or five years ago. Now I've purchased a farm in Buckingham Township, where I hope to breed thoroughbreds. As a matter of fact, I have been conferring with Carl Hanford about having him train my horses. I'm certain that we will work out something in the near future." [*He did buy a farm, Nanlyn Farms, but he never bred horses there.*]

An industrialist and land developer, Barness was one of the founders of Continental, although at the time he did not expect to become president of the group.

Being president of a sports organization is nothing new to Barness, however. He has always been keenly interested in sports. Barness "rescued" the Philadelphia Golf Classic and remained as president until the fixture was on solid ground.

As for the coming meeting, Barness, said, "I'm looking forward to a great session. You know how openings sometimes are. I imagine there will be a few kinks, but nothing that we can't handle.

"The roads to the track are good, and they'll get better, so we should have little problem in getting the folks out here. I guess it will be up to us to make them want to come back.

"I feel certain that Philadelphia and the vicinity will support thoroughbred racing. We have every indication that there are many fans in the area, and we feel that if we give them good racing, they will respond."

Barness and his wife Irma are both graduates of Bucknell University. They have two daughters, Lynda and Nancy.

Before departing on a last-minute tour of the Liberty Bell plant, Barness added, "You know, it will be nice having people from New Jersey and Delaware supporting Pennsylvania racing instead of vice-versa."

CONTINENTAL TRIES TO STEM LOSSES; AMOUNT IS SECRET
The Philadelphia Inquirer
June 18, 1969
By Jack Fried

At first, there was harness racing AND flat racing at Liberty Bell Park, and somehow they competed with each other even though they ran at different times during the year. When the flat racing associations, Continental and Eagle Downs, moved to Neshaminy Park, they had many more days of racing and were more successful.

They're losing money by the bucketful at Liberty Bell Park these days—or so people are saying about the first thoroughbred race meeting with mutuel betting in Pennsylvania.

Continental Racing Association president Herbert Barness admits outgo is outstripping income. By exactly how much, he doesn't know.

"But it isn't anywhere near what those people are saying," Barness said. "I'm sure we'll get it all back—and more—before the end of the year."

Where's the money coming from to make up the deficits?

"They're being defrayed from the fund put up by Continental's incorporators for their shares of stock," Barness said. "We haven't gone public, but plan to do so later on."

When and if Continental begins to show a genuine profit, he meant. Not until then could an offering of stock attract buyers.

The association's management, from Barness and Baker down, mirrors disappointment.

"It's amazing," Barness said, "that so many people around Philadelphia never heard of Liberty Bell Park. Since we started this meeting we've had numerous calls for information about where the park is located and how to get here.

"Imagine such questions about a place that has been in operation since 1963 and has drawn far over a million in attendance in that time?"

Better days are coming, Barness said, when Continental and the Eagle Downs Racing Association have "the only wheel in town."

The two groups are scheduled for 50 days of racing each at Liberty Bell this year and next, but will run 100 days each when Neshaminy Park is completed by 1971.

After the harness racing season ends in October, Continental and Eagle Downs will return to action at Liberty Bell, to continue operating until Dec. 21—with a brief interruption during the Christmas holiday.

That's when they look to cash in and make up for the summertime losses.

BARNESS IS EAGER TO OPEN NEW TRACK: BECAUSE OF LIBERTY BELL LOSSES
The Philadelphia Inquirer
July 9, 1969
By John Dell of the *Inquirer* Staff

Silver-hued shovels were wielded Wednesday by Philadelphia's leading functioning horse race impresarios, who momentarily left their red ink bottles at Liberty Bell Park to break ground for their brand-new track in Bensalem Township.

Land developer Herb Barness, who is president of the budding Continental Thoroughbred Racing Association, and dairy head John J. Finley Jr., president of committed tenant association Eagle Downs, turned earth with broad smiles for the cameras.

They were joined in the ceremony at the 400-acre Neshaminy Park site by Mrs. Ruth I. Rees, chairman of the Bensalem Township Board of Supervisors, and two members of the State Horse Racing Commission, A. Marlyn Moyer Jr. and Thomas A. Livingston.

Ground was broken for the stable area, which will be ready to house horses in November when the Continental-Eagle winter meetings begin at Liberty Bell. Construction of the grandstand will begin when architects' plans are approved. The target date for completion is February 1971.

After the ceremony, the shovelers and some 200 onlookers moved about three miles to watch the races at Liberty Bell. Barness admitted he'd just as soon not see another horse race in Pennsylvania until the $35 million-plus plant is completed.

Continental and Eagle Downs have been taking a bath at Liberty Bell. Estimates of losses for the 34-day Continental meeting (concluded Wednesday) run about $20,000 a day, and Eagle Downs, which starts a 33-day meeting Thursday, also figures to drop a bundle.

The word around horse circles has been that the two smartest moves the two Philadelphia associations could make would be to end summer racing at Liberty Bell and wait until they got their new plant up. Winter racing hopefully will give them a rich field, clear of competition.

"That would be the best thing," Barness admitted. "But we can't do it. The State Commission would not let us. The State wants the revenue."

PERSISTENCY [sic] FULFILLS A DREAM FOR TOSE; HE GETS HIS TEAM
The Philadelphia Inquirer
September 18, 1969

… Out of them all, Jerry Wolman picked Leonard Tose.

The football-happy millionaire from Shenandoah, Pa., met the football-happy millionaire from Bridgeport, Pa., in Miami a few days before the Super Bowl.

They were introduced by a mutual friend, Herb Barness, a football-happy millionaire from Warrington, Bucks County.

In 1963, when Wolman took over, Barness was another rival buyer—he offered McNamee $4.5 million for the team ... Barness is president of Continental Racing Association, which is building a racetrack in Bensalem Township. Tose is a Continental stockholder. Barness also has been active in harness racing and golf tournament promotion, and once tried to buy a professional basketball franchise and a pro soccer team. [*My dad's interest in soccer was way ahead of its time. Attendance at the games was poor at best, and the decision was made not to continue operating the club into the 1968 season.*]

BARNESS TO RECEIVE 17TH TECHNION AWARD
The Evening Bulletin
November 13, 1969

Herbert Barness, Warrington land and real estate developer, will receive the 17th annual award of the Philadelphia Chapter of the American Technion Society at a black-tie dinner-dance Saturday at the Bellevue-Stratford Hotel. Gov. Shafter will present the award.

The society was founded in Germany in 1912 to establish a technical institute in Palestine, now the Israel Institute of Technology. Technion recruits academic members of top universities around the world for and provides financial assistance to the technical institute in Israel.

Barness, a partner in the firm of Joseph Barness and Son, is a mechanical engineer and president of the Philadelphia chapter of Technion.

He is also a director and past president of Welcome House, the Pearl Buck adoption agency; director and past president of Bucks County

Industrial Development Corp; Executive Committee member of the Bucks County Council, Boy Scouts of America; and director of the Pop Warner Little Scholars, Inc.

In addition, he is a member of the American Military Engineers, the Locust Club of Philadelphia, the Pennsylvania Society, and the Lions Club.

You are cordially invited
to a
Dinner-Dance
in honor of
HERBERT BARNESS
sponsored by the
Philadelphia Chapter
American Technion Society
Saturday Evening, November Fifteenth
Nineteen Hundred and Sixty-nine
Seven-thirty o'clock
Bellevue-Stratford Hotel
Cocktail Reception Six-thirty o'clock

Black Tie, R.S.V.P.   Minimum Contribution $110 per couple

TECHNION HONORS HERBERT BARNESS
The Jewish Exponent
November 14, 1969

Another article about the award that appeared in The Daily Intelligencer *on November 17, 1969, mentions that, "His wife and children were present to witness presentation of the award." I have only a faint memory of the event itself, but definitely remember that it happened! Also on November 17, Hy Brody, the Executive Director of the Philadelphia Chapter, sent a letter to Herb's parents informing them that there would be a Barness Building at the Technion that would be for computer teaching.*

More than 500 civic and communal leaders will attend a testimonial dinner honoring Herbert Barness, president of the Philadelphia Chapter, American Technion Society, tomorrow, 6:30 p.m., at the Bellevue Stratford. The dinner is sponsored by the Philadelphia chapter of the society.

Barness is being cited for his contributions and dedication to the causes of higher education and to the development of scientific and technological advancement in the State of Israel and especially for his support of the Technion-Israel Institute of Technology.

Gov. Raymond P. Shafer will present the award to Barness, on behalf of the American Technion Society. Dr. Leon Riebman, of Colmar, Pa., will be the guest speaker.

Marvin Orleans is dinner chairman. Honorary sponsors include Judge Arlin M. Adams, Lt. Gov. Raymond J. Broderick, State Rep. Herbert Fineman, U.S. Rep. William J. Green, Councilman John B. Kelly, Jr., former Gov. George M. Leader, U.S. Sen. Richard S. Schweiker, U.S. Sen. Hugh Scott, former Gov. William W. Scranton and Gov. Shafer.

HIGHEST AWARD. Herbert Barness (right), Warrington real estate and land developer, receives highest award of the Philadelphia Chapter of American Technion Society from Gov. Raymond P. Shafer, while the recipient's wife, Irma, smiles approvingly. Barness was honored for his contributions to advancement of science and technology in Israel.

ROUND CITY HALL SQUARE
The Philadelphia Dispatch
November 23, 1969
By Pat Pending

TRIBUTE: Governor and Mrs. RAYMOND SHAFER, and Lt. Gov. and Mrs. RAYMOND BRODERICK not only came to pay tribute to HERBERT BARNESS when he was honored by the American Technion Society at an overflow dinner last week, but stayed throughout the evening. The Governor not only praised BARNESS for his work with Technion, but surprised a lot of people with his intimate knowledge of the Israel Institution. BARNESS is president of the Philadelphia Chapter.

The 1970s

In the summer of 1970, my parents moved back to Bucks County. They had purchased a farm of about 350 acres some years before, and in the late 1960s they decided to build a new house that looked like a farmhouse on the property rather than renovate one of the existing buildings. When my parents originally thought about moving back to the "country," they thought they were just building a summer home. So they didn't build the new house with many closets, because they thought it was only going to be a part-time residence! They sold our house in Rydal and rented an apartment in Jenkintown, a few miles away, so they could have an easy time visiting Rydal friends and my mother, an artist, could be close to her art classes. As it turned out, once they moved into the new house, they almost never went to the apartment and never renewed their lease. They both absolutely loved the farm, called Nanlyn Farms (NAN for my sister and LYN for me), and they never looked back. And my mother simply used my closet and my sister's since we were both grown and out of the house.

Nanlyn Farms continued to evolve for many years. Over time, my parents renovated a small carriage house to use as a guest house, the cow barn was renovated to create a clubhouse with bathrooms, a swimming pool was built, and a 9-hole golf course was created in the "back yard." My sister and I had a double-wedding there in June of 1971, and that was the impetus for an indoor tennis court; it was constructed for our rather large reception and, of course, was used for tennis going forward. Both of my parents played golf and tennis regularly for years. There were still silos and another barn, which were used for a small herd of beef cattle. And soy beans were grown on the farm by a neighboring farmer, I think, and then sold.

My father was then 48 years old and he lived to be 74, and I truly think he enjoyed every single day on the farm. Although the property became a real area for play, my father raised cattle (polled—meaning hornless—Herefords) and would also climb on the tractor to till the soil. There was only one other person who worked on the farm full-time, and my dad loved to pitch in. You can take the boy out of the country, but clearly you can't take the country out of the boy! He loved it.

My father used to say that he didn't care about whom my sister and I married—race and religion didn't matter to him—as long as we didn't live more than 20 minutes away from our parents. I don't know how he did it, but my sister and I lived within about 45 minutes of our parents for the rest of their lives. My first daughter was born on my

Barness grandparents' 52nd wedding anniversary, and they were alive and thrilled beyond words. My grandfather had had a stroke the prior year, so he really wasn't himself, and he died less than a year later. My second daughter and one of my sister's two daughters were also born in this decade, and my dad was a loving and doting grandfather. His fourth granddaughter was born in 1981, and he was surrounded by four little girls who loved—and were so loved by—their Popee.

A word about my dad's parents: They were just amazing. They defined unconditional love. Family and community were central to their lives. I always knew that if I had grandchildren someday, I wanted to be called Mom-mom Barness, in loving memory of my own Mom-mom, and that is, indeed, what my grandchildren now call me. I feel so grateful. And so very lucky.

During this decade the name Joseph Barness & Son was still used for construction, but the name of the overarching company became The Barness Organization. My dad also continued to be very involved in politics and many local organizations.

1970

Program for the The Mary Bailey Institute for Heart Research
1970 Golden Heart Achievement Awards
Presentation at the April Ball, April 11, 1970
Bellevue Stratford Hotel, Philadelphia, Pa.

The Mary Bailey Institute
for
Heart Research
proudly
announces
1970
Golden Heart Achievement Awards

Presentation
The April Ball
April 11, 1970
Bellevue Stratford Hotel
Philadelphia, Pa.

Herbert Barness
    President, Joseph Barness & Son

Dr. Charles Cameron
    President, Hahnemann Medical College and Hospital

Marvin Comisky, Esquire
    President, Pennsylvania Bar Association

Walter Matthau
    Internationally Famous Academy Award Recipient

Roy T. Peraino
    President, Continental Bank & Trust Company

WIND ONLY SIGN OF MOVEMENT AT NESHAMINY PARK
The Philadelphia Inquirer
April 29, 1970
First of two articles by Gordon Forbes of the *Inquirer* Staff

The wind whips across the sprawling site in Bensalem Township where ground was broken 10 months ago for Neshaminy Park, Pennsylvania's $35 million thoroughbred spa.

There are no other signs of movement.

Construction equipment on the 409-acre grounds consisted last week of a single trailer and one unmanned bulldozer.

The first project at Neshaminy, erection of 20 barns to house 1,200 horses, was scheduled to be completed last November. The barn site is marked only by dozens of grading stakes plunged into soggy ground.

"It's a big, muddy mess," admitted Herb Barness, a wealthy land developer who is chairman of the board of the Continental Racing Association. "But we're under construction there. We just can't move any equipment around."

Continental and its tenant, Eagle Downs Racing Association, expect to conduct 200 days of racing at Neshaminy in the winter of 1971-72.

But there are signs that the three-tiered, glass-enclosed plant may then still be a dream. And some skeptics insist Neshaminy will never be built.

Acquiring the financing for the track has been a painfully slow process. A year ago, the Sonnenblick-Goldman Corp. of New York agreed to put up the $35 million at an interest rate of 8-½ percent over 20 years.

But Barness diverted to other banks, seeking lower rates.

"Contrary to what people thought," said Barness, "we never had any trouble getting financing. It was a matter of what we wanted to pay for it. We have all the construction financing amounting to between $25 and $28 million committed to us."

Barness conceded it would be July before visual construction would begin at Neshaminy.

TOMLIN HEADS YOUTH GROUP FOR 42ND YEAR
The Philadelphia Inquirer
July 30, 1970

For the 42nd successive year, Joseph J. Tomlin, who founded the Pop Warner Little Scholars, has been re-elected president of the youth services agency.

Reelected for a third term as chairman of the board of directors was Herbert Barness, builder and civic leader.

Technion Magazine
February 1970

Dr. Leon Riebman, new president of the Philadelphia Chapter, is being congratulated at the installation ceremony. From left to right, Dr. Riebman, Herbert Barness, who became board chairman, Benjamin Fox, national board member, and Joseph J. Harris, also on the national board.

1971

The Daily Intelligencer
May 20, 1971

SCHOLARSHIP BOOSTERS. Kicking off the Pennsylvania American Legion Endowment and Scholarship fund are Herbert Barness, Warrington Realtor, developer and business leader, who is giving a check of $1,000 in the statewide drive, to Legionnaires Theodore R. Foedisch and Robert W. Valimont, founders of the project.

1972

TALK AROUND TOWN: BARNESS QUITS RACING FOR POLITICS
The Evening Bulletin
February 25, 1972
By Frank Brookhouser

Strangely, it was never noted, but Herbert Barness resigned weeks ago as board chairman of the Continental Racing Association to accept a post with the National Republican Finance Committee. Had to—under state law.

TOSE BEEFS UP HIS (TAX) DEFENSE FOR COURT TILT AS IRS BLOWS WHISTLE
The Evening Bulletin
December 4, 1972
By Lou Antosh and David Taylor

The Internal Revenue Service thinks it has caught Eagles owner Leonard H. Tose offside and has blown the whistle.

The agency has told Tose that he has gone overboard in using his football players for tax write-offs, and has ordered a 50 percent cut in the value, which he originally pinned on his player contracts.

The IRS has been taking a look at the Eagles' books ever since Tose bought the team in 1969 and pinned a $12.9 million value on the players. By contrast, the franchise itself was valued at a mere $50,000.

The $12.9 million depreciation figure was to be written off over six years at $2,157,500 annually. Since the Eagles are making a net profit of $1 million a year, the depreciation deduction creates a paper loss of more than $1 million.

Because the Eagles are set up as a partnership, rather than a corporation, Tose, who owns 75 percent of the Eagles, is able to utilize 75 percent of this paper loss to offset any outside income he may have.

The other partners are Herbert Barness, John Firestone and Anne I. Firestone, trustee for the estate of Roger Firestone.

1973

APARTMENTS FOR THE AGED OK'D IN DOYLESTOWN
The Evening Bulletin
June 19, 1973

Doylestown Borough Council last night approved final plans for a $7 million apartment building for the elderly. The developer and property owner is Herbert Barness of Warrington. He plans to build the six-story building on a 32-acre tract on Broad Street near Chapman Lane.

The building will contain 354 one-bedroom units. In order to qualify for a lease, applicants will have to be at least 62 years of age or older.

Barness said a survey by Bucks County disclosed there were about 25,000 residents at least 62 years old. He said hundreds of applications are filed for this type of housing every year.

Rentals will be subsidized by the U.S. Department of Housing and Urban Development. Barness declined to estimate the rent.

He said construction of Centre Square Towers will begin within 60 days. He estimated construction time at 18 months.

The developer has made a "sizable" donation to the Doylestown Fire Company. While the company is free to use the money anyway it sees fit, it was noted in previous hearings that present equipment might not be adequate to deal with a fire on higher floors.

In addition, Barness has promised to give the borough a 50-foot-wide right-of-way along the bank of Cook's Run Creek. This will allow the borough to connect Broad Street with Chapman Lane, although there are no plans to do so now.

Barness' apartment proposal previously was approved by the borough planning commission.

JOSEPH BARNESS, 82, DIES

The Daily Intelligencer
September 17, 1973

Obituaries also appeared in The Philadelphia Inquirer *and in* The Evening Bulletin.

Joseph Barness, pioneer real estate broker, developer and Warrington Community benefactor, died Saturday in Doylestown Hospital. He was 82.

He lived at 1334 Easton Road, Warrington, and was the founder and president of Joseph Barness Real Estate Broker, builder and developer organization. He founded his own business 50 years ago.

Mr. Barness was born in Russia and has lived in Warrington Township for more than 50 years. He is credited, his friends say, with "getting Warrington out of the mud" and transforming it into a modern business, housing, and community center. His friendship with William H. Satterthwaite Jr., banker-lawyer, as his mentor, confidant and counsel, was legendary.

About a decade ago he was feted at a testimonial dinner at Warrington Golf and Country Club, attended by nearly 1,000 persons who honored him and his wife for their generosity and community leadership.

Housing colonies, shopping centers, apartment houses, playgrounds and recreational sites are the results of Mr. Barness's leadership and gifts.

He used to like to recall in his quiet gentle and humorous manner that five families—the Cadwalladers, MacNairs, Cornells, Clymers and Nashes—were in control of the township's community progress when he settled there.

He was one of the founders and charter members of the Bucks County Board of Realtors.

He was a director of Doylestown Federal Savings & Loan Association; a director of Doylestown National Bank and Trust Company, now Continental Bank; a director of Doylestown Title & Abstract Co.; a former member of the Bucks County Planning Commission, Big Brothers, Warrington Community Building; and a member of the Board of Delaware Valley College of Science and Agriculture and other organizations.

He was responsible for the construction of Warrington Shopping center, with its new post office building; the community building; Warrington Golf and Country Club; Spruce Court Apartments, Doylestown and the expansion and development of Warrington Township, providing hundreds of homes, water and sewer facilities.

He is survived by his widow, the former Mary Silverstein, Warrington; two sons, Herbert, who is carrying on his father's business, Rydal, and Dr. Lewis A. Barness, a children's specialist, Tampa, Fla. There are five grandchildren and a great-granddaughter. [*My first child, Jennifer, was born on my grandparents' 52nd wedding anniversary, in October 1972.*]

A sister, Mrs. Goldie Armel, Brooklyn, N.Y., also survives.

Services will be held at 11 a.m. Tuesday at Temple Judea Synagogue, Swamp Road, Doylestown.

The Warrington office will be closed today and Tuesday because of the death of the founder.

Warrington Shopping Center will be closed Tuesday from 11 a.m. to 1 p.m. because of Mr. Barness' funeral services.

Editorial: JOSEPH BARNESS

The Daily Intelligencer
September 18, 1973

Joseph Barness, Warrington Township resident, developer and benefactor, who died Saturday at 82, was the epitome of the American success story.

He came to the United States as a young boy from Russia. He moved from Philadelphia to Warrington a half century ago. Mr. Barness, quiet, firm but never arrogant, dreamed, worked, planned, imagined and trusted until he achieved success, wealth, friends, and goals of satisfaction.

He worked with the system as it existed in lean, undeveloped, rural Warrington Township. He not only helped improve it from the inside, but had vision enough to go beyond, far beyond, its limitations 50 years ago.

He has been credited with "getting Warrington out of the mud."

His goals were good roads, good housing, good water and sewer facilities, good township government and eventually good, rich, full community living.

His generosity in many ways and for many things is known to only those he helped. Children will long enjoy the playgrounds, athletic fields and recreational areas he made possible.

He passed on his ambition, cooperation, integrity and success to his two sons, one carrying on his dynasty, and the other a physician.

Joseph Barness gave to his home in America endless gifts, to display his joy at being an American.

BARNESSES DONATE $100,000 TO HOSPITAL
The Daily Intelligencer
Undated—late 1973?
By Lawrence C. Hall, *Intelligencer* Staff Writer

A $100,000 donation to the Doylestown Hospital Relocation Fund campaign was announced this morning.

The donors are Herbert Barness of Buckingham, a prominent land developer, and Barness's brother, Lewis, a medical doctor living in Davis Island, Fla.

The gift was made in memory of their father, Joseph Barness, who died in 1973, and William H. Satterthwaite Jr., a Doylestown banker, lawyer and close friend and adviser of Joseph Barness. Satterthwaite died nine years ago [1883-1964].

It was also given in honor of Mrs. Mary Barness, the wife of Joseph.

The gift, the largest single donation by an individual, is in the form of an interest in landholdings of Barness. He said details are yet to be worked out.

Herbert Barness this morning said that the donation, which will pay for the hospital lobby, memorialized Satterthwaite, because "he was really my father's patron saint."

He said he and his brother decided to make the gift, as they had been lifelong residents of the community, he and his father had made their livelihoods here and "this part of the county is of great interest to us."

He said, "It's something my father wanted to do, and had he lived, he would have made the donation himself."

This afternoon, the final total raised in the campaign will be announced at a victory tea at the James-Lorah House in Doylestown.

The $11.7 million, 160-bed hospital is under construction on Route 202 near Memorial Drive, Doylestown Township.

1974

WARRINGTON AMBULANCE UNIT DEDICATES NEW HEADQUARTERS
The Daily Intelligencer
January 26, 1974

Dedication ceremonies were held Saturday at the new headquarters of the Warrington Community Ambulance Corps.

The building, situated on Easton Road, behind the Warrington Community Building, was dedicated in honor of the late Joseph Barness, "a long-time community benefactor." A plaque was unveiled in his memory by Barness's son, Herbert. Local and county dignitaries were in attendance at the ceremony.

DEDICATED. The new headquarters of the Warrington Community Ambulance Corps, Easton Road, was dedicated Saturday in memory of the late Joseph Barness, a Bucks County developer and benefactor of the Warrington community. The new building houses two ambulances and provides office space for the corps.

MODULAR HOMES: AN IDEA WHOSE TIME IS PAST
The Philadelphia Inquirer
March 10, 1974
By Oscar B. Teller, *Inquirer* Real Estate Editor

As explained by George Romney, auto manufacturer-turned-housing czar, the idea made a lot of sense.

In the decade of the '70s, the United States was going to need some 26 million new houses and apartments just to keep up with population growth.

And this country has a positive genius for producing everything from toasters to automobiles on the assembly line.

So all we had to do was couple our needs with our abilities—and we could be turning out houses just like Romney did when he was head of American Motors back in Detroit.

It sounded good ... but there are a lot of huge, empty buildings around the country to attest to the fact that "Operation Breakthrough," as Romney called his ambitious program, promised a lot more than it delivered.

Any number of companies, big and small, got into the act ... What happened? First of all, the production economies promised by Operation Breakthrough never came about.

General Electric was lucky in the one project it built modules for in this area, the Richlieu Gardens Apartments in Bensalem Township, Bucks County.

Richlieu Gardens, the Bucks County project, was developed by Joseph Barness & Son under Section 236 of the 1969 Housing Act. This program encouraged builders to develop low-rent housing by subsidizing their mortgage interest payments.

One-bedroom apartments at Richlieu Gardens rent for $143 per month; two bedrooms for $163. There are maximum income limits, ranging from $6,250 per year for a single person occupying a one-bedroom unit to $8,900 for a family of three or four occupying a two-bedroom unit. Twenty percent of the apartments and town houses in the development are under a blanket lease to the Bucks County Housing Authority, which provides rent subsidies to families with even smaller incomes than the above limits.

Since November, when the first building was occupied, more than 270 of the 352 units have been leased. Unlike the usual low-rent housing project, apartments come equipped with wall-to-wall carpeting, automatic garbage disposals, and similar features associated with "luxury" rental units. On the grounds, too, are tot lots, a basketball court, laundry rooms and a swimming pool scheduled to open at the end of May.

Tony Lemisch, an executive of the Barness firm, indicated that Richlieu Gardens never would have been built as a modular project had not Romney [*George Romney, auto manufacturer turned "housing czar" who was promoting modular housing*] been so enthusiastic about "Operation Breakthrough." The Richlieu Gardens project was one of the last approved under Section 236 before President Nixon shut off funds for the program in January 1973.

"Nobody was really pushing us, but let's say we were encouraged to go modular," said Lemisch. "I think we could have saved money by using conventional building methods."

Still, he said, the Barness firm is going to try a different type of modular construction in a midrise housing-for-the-elderly project scheduled to be built in Doylestown.

This project will utilize concrete shells produced by a factory in the Midwest and shipped to the site by rail or truck. Once there, they will be stacked by a crane to six-story height.

1975

Invitation to *Give 'Em Hell Harry*, a benefit performance for the Bucks County Playhouse in honor of the Barness Family
March 16, 1975

My dad was a partner in the Bucks County Playhouse for about five years. My parents took me and my sister to the theater often, and I have great memories of it. I have a collection of programs, including the 1963 production of The Crossing *starring Howard Keel;* The Hostage *with Julie Harris (1965);* The Private Ear *with Dick Shawn (1966);* Lyrics *by Oscar Hammerstein II with Imogene Coca (1967); Woody Allen's* Don't Drink the Water *(1969);* Hello Dolly *(1981);* Bye Bye Birdie *(1982);* Show Boat *with Pat Paulsen (1983); and* How to Succeed in Business Without Really Trying *with Ron Palillo (1984). Broadway productions would start out at this theater in New Hope and end up in New York City, and major stars of the day would perform. The show* Come Blow Your Horn *started here too, and went on to have a major run in New York and then on the big screen. To my recollection, there wasn't any other live theater of this caliber anywhere near Bucks County at the time.*

My father and grandfather both supported the playhouse throughout their lives, and in 1975, a special theater performance was held for the benefit of BCP, and to honor their contributions and present a plaque. Tickets to the evening were $25 a person, and the invitation contained a special brochure that read:

Bucks County Playhouse has been perpetuated through the generosity of the Barness Family in memory of Joseph Barness, 1974.

The Bucks County Playhouse can be construed as one of the many living memorials to Joseph and Mary Barness. Bucks County can be truly proud that Joseph and Mary selected the Warrington area to be their home in 1923. His vision, confidence, and dedication to the County and its people was evidenced early, and those who reside there will be forever touched and enriched by his endeavors.

Joseph passed his strength to his sons, Herbert and Lewis. Lewis is now Chief of Pediatrics at The University of South Florida at Tampa. It was Herbert's good fortune to have worked side by side with his father daily for many years. Being a product of their environment, it would only be natural for his sons to share his enthusiasm and continue his efforts for enrichment of all residents in Bucks County.

It was Joseph that insisted that Herbert acquire the Bucks County Playhouse and keep it available to all the people. After all, he reasoned, the Playhouse was a cultural experience that could be shared by everyone, theater goers and artists alike.

To this end, his scion sustained the Playhouse for many years at great personal expense.

When BCP was finally turned over to a group of interested and concerned citizens for continuation, it was once again done by the Barness Family at no personal gain—quietly, in the true Joseph Barness manner.

In honoring the Barness Family, all of us joyfully feel a kinship to them and a regeneration of spirit, direction and purpose, and yes, a tremendous sense of pride that this family chose our beautiful Bucks County as their home and work.

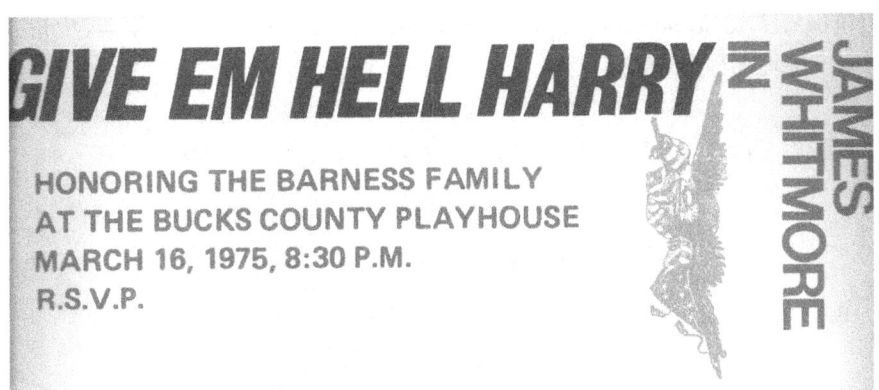

Part of the invitation to *Give 'Em Hell Harry*, a benefit for the Bucks County Playhouse that also honored the Barness Family.

The Bucks County Playhouse *Give 'Em Hell Harry* Program
March 16, 1975

The program for the special benefit performance of Give 'Em Hell Harry *included a letter from the Theater's president, Arthur Gerold:*

Dear Friends:

Tonight is a happy occasion on which we say thank you to our good friend Herbert Barness and his family for making it possible for the Bucks County Playhouse to pass from the private to the public sector. Without his help and consideration, it would never have been possible ...

There were also ads in the program saluting the Barness family, including this one:

THE REPUBLICAN AND DEMOCRATIC PARTIES

of

Bucks County

Extend

Warm Greetings

to

THE BARNESS FAMILY

for its

Cultural Contribution

to Bucks County

Milton Berkes, Democratic Chairman

Harry Fawkes, Republican Chairman

There was also a page with the following tribute:

In 1923 when Joseph Barness brought his family to Warrington, Bucks County, to take up their new life—quite different from that which they had known previously—this is what they looked like.

Love and devotion to family, purpose in his lifestyle and a genuine interest in the land and the people who lived and worked on it were his watchwords.

Several years ago a testimonial dinner was accorded Joseph Barness when more than 300 people were in attendance. The chairman at the tail end of the evening asked if there was anything that anyone in attendance wanted to say. Dozens of hands shot up and thereafter for a solid hour, until the chairman called a halt, person after person rose and paid tribute to this gentle man. Tales of how he helped them in their daily lives—with food, clothing, shelter, business, personal concern and charity—filled the room! The individual manner in which the Barness family has touched the lives of many is perhaps not known—because each person thought it was only himself who had been helped.

The Officers and members of BCP have also been privy to the Barness family's generosity.

Truly the Barness family is very special!

We are proud to honor them this evening.

Letter from Herbert Barness to his mother [*who was in Florida*]
March 17, 1975

Last evening at the Bucks County Playhouse, a plaque was presented on which was inscribed "The Bucks County Playhouse has been perpetuated through the generosity of the Barness Family in memory of Joseph Barness."

It was a very nice evening and an absolutely excellent performance by James Whitmore in his portrayal of Harry S. Truman. Whitmore is going to be touring the country with this one-man show, and if you ever get an opportunity to see it, the show is certainly worthwhile. It was a very pleasant evening and looked like a complete sell-out of the theater. The ad book was the largest that the theater has ever had in its 38-year history.

In thanking the President of the Playhouse for this honor, I said something like the following: "On behalf of my family, my mother and my brother, who unfortunately could not be with us this evening, we want to thank you for this honor and thank all of you here for sharing it with us. My parents loved this theater and they were always attending performances since the theater opened until my father passed away. My father loved this county, and he would have loved all of you to be here this evening."

Radio Station WBUX photo
1975

My father and some friends formed a partnership and headed WBUX, a local radio station, in 1975. The general manager, George Pleasants, wanted to put together a group of local influential people to help the station reflect what was happening in the area. Seated at the table (left to right): Partners Herbert Barness, Don Meredith, James Michener (the novelist, and fellow Bucks County resident), Robert Valimont. Back row: George Pleasants, who worked at the station, and Partner Walter Conti. The station was sold to Network Communications in 1988.

487 WARWICK TOWNHOUSES PLANNED: INSTEAD OF 720 APARTMENTS

The Daily Intelligencer
April 30, 1975
By Anita Alberts, *Intelligencer* Staff writer

On this day, the front page headline of this paper announced VIETNAM: FIGHTING IS FINISHED. This new plan for townhouses became the Stover Mill community by Barness, still in existence today.

A plan for 487 townhomes was reviewed Tuesday night by the Warwick Township Planning Commission for construction on the former Harcourt Wells tract at Jamison and York Road.

The plan was submitted instead of 720 apartment units originally planned, that would be permitted on the 65-acre tract under a decision by the Pennsylvania Supreme Court.

1976

SUCCESSFUL APARTMENT DEVELOPERS HEAD FOR THE FAR REACHES

The Philadelphia Inquirer
November 14, 1976
By Oscar B. Teller, *Inquirer* Real Estate Editor

Some real estate developers have made their fortunes by building in the path of development, figuring that the traffic generated by their competitors will spill into their own backyards.

Others have done equally well—or perhaps better—in areas shunned by competition.

During its 50-year history, the organization founded by the late Joseph Barness and continued by his son, Herbert, has played it both ways. But this year and next, the bulk of the company's construction will be in the far reaches of suburbia and upstate Pennsylvania.

"There isn't another apartment development within four miles of here," Tony Lemisch was saying the other day as he escorted visitors through Barness's new Wyntre Brooke project in Chester County, "but I think we've hit this market right; we're renting extremely well."

Although a 20-acre farm in sparsely populated West Bradford Township might seem an unlikely spot for 212 new apartments, the site, on Phoenixville Pike, is within a mile of Route 202's Boot Road exit. That means the job-rich Valley Forge-King of Prussia area is but 15 minutes away, while West Chester, Exton, and Paoli—all growing white-collar employment centers—are even closer.

"And water and sewers were available at the site—that's very important for an apartment development," added Lemisch, who is director of property operations for Joseph Barness & Son, Inc.

The Barness organization will manage the project for a limited partnership composed of members of the Barness family and a small group of outside investors. The investors' principal payoff will be an income-tax offset rather than cash generated by the rents.

Lemisch said the Barness organization had put together other syndicates to build housing-for-the-elderly projects in Mount Pocono and Mechanicsburg, Pa. The company also had options on multifamily sites in Towanda and Sayre as well as other upstate towns.

1977

Ad in *The Philadelphia Inquirer*
February 6, 1977

For 54 years, we've been known for what we've done.

Now we want to be known for who we are.

THE BARNESS ORGANIZATION
Developers • Realtors • Property Management

Apartments, townhomes, single homes. Shopping centers. Industrial parks and professional offices. A professional ice rink. Post offices. A country club.

Since 1923, we've been planning, developing, building and managing successful real estate communities, office parks, shopping centers, and recreational facilities in places as close as Bucks County and as far away as the Virgin Islands.

You may know some of our successes by name.

Now we think it's time you know the name behind them.

The Barness Organization. We've built a lot of pretty good things in our time, including a pretty good reputation.

Warrington, Pa. 18976/(215) 343-0700

This ad was one of the first to reflect the business's change in name, from Joseph Barness & Son to The Barness Organization.

Certificate of Appreciation from Bayse Newcomb Lodge
1977

My father became a member of this Lodge in 1952.

To Herbert Barness: For his past 25 years of loyal and sincere efforts on behalf of his Lodge and to the principles and ideals of Free Masonry.

PALOMINO GLEN HAS TWO STYLES
The Evening Bulletin
October 21, 1977
By Raymond A. Berens, Real Estate Editor

Most housing developments are built entirely by one builder, but sometimes the original builder does not finish his community—so other builders complete the work.

This happened in Palomino Glen, a small community on Bristol Road at Easton Road (Route 611) in Warrington Township, Bucks County.

Herbert Barness, head of the Barness Organization in Warrington and one of the biggest homebuilders in Bucks County, began construction of the 112-house development in March, 1976, through his Palomino Homes Inc. subsidiary.

He built all but 38 of the houses and sold the remaining lots to two other area builders: 13 lots to the Three A Co., of Horsham, and 25 lots to Thomas J. Kelly Sons, a firm that has built many houses in Bucks County and Northeast Philadelphia.

Barness shifted his construction crews next door to the 123-house Fox Hollow—the entrance is a short distance away on Bristol Road, but the development connects with Palomino Glen toward the rear of both developments—and across Easton Road to Warrington Mews.

The average home hunter would not even notice that more than one builder was involved in Palomino Glen, except for the model house signs posted outside the sales offices of Three A and the Kelly firm. The houses are basically the same.

TOSE RIPS HIS FORMER BANKER
The Evening Bulletin
August 10, 1977
By Ray Didinger of the *Bulletin* Staff

Staging a fourth-quarter rally worthy of a Super Bowl champion, Leonard Tose today announced he has paid off a $5.3 million loan to the First Pennsylvania Bank.

The Eagles owner made the payment less than a week after the bank, outraged by Tose's extravagant spending, appointed a "financial consultant," Sidney Forstater, to govern the team's budget.

Fuming, Tose borrowed enough money to pay off the bank and rid himself of its watchdog—Forstater. Like a quarterback who has just thrown a touchdown pass on fourth-and-20, Tose comes out of his latest predicament in style.

"Leonard is back in the driver's seat," a club employee said last night.

If Tose is delighted with the settlement, so is First Pennsylvania Bank—which financed the trucking executive's purchase of the Eagles for $16.1 million in May 1969.

"He (Tose) has been behaving in such a way that loan covenants were violated," a bank source said yesterday. "We've been paid off. We're ecstatic. He was such a spendthrift that many of his partners were so alarmed they began turning on us and asking us to do something about it."

At a press conference today, Tose denounced the First Pennsylvania Bank and Chairman John R. Bunting.

Under Tose, the Eagles gained a reputation as one of the National Football League's most free-spending teams. Last year, the Birds lost over $1.2 million while selling out Veterans Stadium for all seven regular season home games.

The bank grew impatient with such losses, as did Herb Barness, a minority stockholder in the Eagles. According to club sources, it was Barness who encouraged First Pennsylvania to crack down on Tose and urge him to reduce spending in all areas, including player salaries, travel and training camp expenses.

When the warnings were repeatedly ignored, the bank appointed Forstater to control the club's cash flow. Tose didn't like the idea of having an employee—Forstater was the Eagles' vice-president in charge of finance—telling him how to spend his money.

Thanks to today's settlement, Leonard Tose is his own boss again.

There are indications that today's announcement, made at a Veterans Stadium press conference, will be followed by a shakeup in the Eagles front office. Forstater, who publicly questioned Tose's fiscal judgment, is sure to go. Other high-ranking employees are reportedly in jeopardy too.

Talk of imminent financial collapse has haunted Tose for several years. The whispers grew almost deafening last season, forcing Tose to seize the intercom on an Eagles' charter flight from Cleveland and declare: "This team is not for sale." His announcement, though dramatic, did not end the speculation.

STRONG FEELINGS FOR LEONARD TOSE
Source unknown
August 1977

I only have part of this article.

... Apparently, the league and many of the league owners were a little nervous about the emergence of First Pennsylvania to a power position in the Eagles and to the bank's appointing of former Tose financial adviser Sidney Forstater to run the franchise.

Forstater was known to have irritated Commissioner Rozelle when, during his 10-day takeover of the franchise, he began cutting and slashing expenses. One of Forstater's first moves was to quit paying on the final two years of Joe Kuharich's 15-year contract. Forstater said he could find a legal loophole that would save the Eagles $100,000 over the next two years. Rozelle, who is fond of Kuharich, felt he had to intervene.

That was only one of the many sore spots that developed during Forstater's brief regime. Another involved the near resignation of head coach Dick Vermeil. In fact, if Forstater stayed on, Vermeil was known to be set to pack up and head back to California.

For the past two weeks, the Eagles front office has been in an upheaval. Forstater, who had been with Tose since 1958, defected to First Pennsylvania. "My loyalty," he told Tose, "is with the bank. Not you."

When a lot of the club's confidential doings became known by First Pennsylvania Chairman John Bunting and Vice Chairman Pemberton, and then was leaked to *Philadelphia Inquirer* reporter Gordon Forbes, Tose became suspicious that there was a plot to get him.

He suspects also that Herb Barness, a 27 percent owner and "silent partner" is probably involved. Barness, a First Pennsylvania source said yesterday, has the right of first refusal should Tose ever sell (or lose) the team. Barness would have been the next owner (if he so desired) had Tose not surfaced with the bank loan from Detroit.

Barness could not be reached immediately for comment.

Aligning himself with Forstater was Eagles' business manager Leo Carlin. They formed an interoffice adversary to Tose and Murray, and for 10 days the operation of the franchise was in chaos.

Yesterday, Tose gave Forstater the boot.

1978

DOYLESTOWN HOUSING
The Evening Bulletin
January 6, 1978

By 1978, Warrington Country Club continued to exist, but other clubs had opened their doors, and I think that there was a greater business opportunity in developing the club's land for housing. My dad began trying to develop the land in 1977. Due to zoning laws, his efforts were constrained; some years later, he sold part of the ground to another builder who developed it, and the members took over ownership of the Club until another buyer purchased it. It is still in operation today.

Herbert Barness, a leading Bucks County developer, asked the county court to set aside the rejection by the supervisors here of his preliminary plan for a 429-unit development of housing on the site of the Warrington Golf & Country Club along Almshouse road at Route 611. Barness said the township's notice of rejections was improperly vague.

WARRINGTON COUNTRY CLUB GOING SEMI-PUBLIC
The Daily Intelligencer
March 8, 1978
By William G. Shuster, *Intelligencer* Staff Writer

The Warrington Golf and County Club in Doylestown Township will be a semi-public course this summer.

The move came as negotiations are still underway to change the land into a 429-unit housing development.

Two weeks ago, *The Daily Intelligencer* has learned, the entire board of directors of the club resigned and asked The Barness Organization to reorganize the club and its membership fee schedule.

In another development Tuesday night, the supervisors gave unanimous support to the possible purchase of the club from owner Herbert Barness by Bucks County.

BARNESS SELLS HIS 29% OF EAGLES TEAM TO TOSE
The Philadelphia Inquirer
1978

Philadelphia Eagles owner Leonard Tose has bought the 29 percent share owned by Herbert Barness to settle part of a $12 million lawsuit filed last month.

On May 5 Tose announced suits against Barness, John Bunting, chairman of First Pennsylvania Bank, and John Pemberton, vice chairman, charging them with masterminding a conspiracy to oust him from control of the Eagles in favor of Barness.

Barness, a Buckingham Township resident, is president of The Barness Organization and Joseph Barness and Son, Inc., his Warrington-based real estate management and property development companies.

In a joint announcement by Joseph Alioto, former San Francisco mayor acting as attorney for Tose, and Bernard Borish, attorney for Barness, the purchase price was not disclosed.

Tose said he was continuing his suit against the others, including former partner John D. Firestone, Chase Manhattan Bank of New York, Girard Bank, Provident National Bank and the Philadelphia National Bank.

Bunting and Tose have been at odds since Bunting called in a $5.3 million loan on Tose last August. Tose was forced to negotiate a $7 million loan from Manufacturers National Bank of Detroit to pay off First Pennsylvania.

In April, Tose negotiated an $8 million refinancing loan from a three-bank syndicate, including Citibank of New York, Central Penn National Bank of Philadelphia and MidAtlantic Bank of New Jersey.

In his May suit, Tose sought $6 million in actual damages and $6 million in punitive damages.

The Barness companies have built commercial, residential and governmental buildings throughout eastern Pennsylvania, New Jersey, and the Caribbean.

1979

VASSAR SQUARE APTS. SOLD TO PA. PARTNERS
The Atlantic City Press
January 10, 1979
By Sonny Schwartz

The multi-million dollar, 32-story luxury Vassar Square Arms apartment building on Ventnor's Boardwalk has been sold to a partnership headed by two prominent Philadelphia area developers for an estimated $10 million, *The Press* learned Tuesday.

Heading the partnership are Herbert Barness of Warrington, Pa., and Jeffrey Orleans of Huntingdon Valley, Pa.

An associate of Barness said the high-rise was purchased "as an investment" and maintained "no future plans for (for the Vassar) have yet been finalized."

He also related that the realization of casino gaming in Atlantic City helped serve as a catalyst which sparked the partnership to buy the beachfront high-rise.

Both Barness and Orleans are well-known builders and real estate developers in Pennsylvania and in New Jersey's Cherry Hill area.

Final settlement on the Ventnor high-rise has been made.

Barness is the founder and principal operator of The Barness Organization, while Orleans is a partner in the A.P. Orleans Construction Co.

THE DYNAMOS

Who, What, Where, When Magazine: A Central Bucks Chamber of Commerce Publication
March-April 1979

On the wall of the reception room of The Barness Organization, there is a hand-lettered memorial plaque with a statement about Joseph Barness, its founder, and a founding member of the Chamber of Commerce in Central Bucks.

It says, in part, "Joseph Barness, Warrington Township resident, developer and benefactor, who died Saturday, September 15, 1973, at 79, was the epitome of the American success story. He came to the United States as a young boy from Russia. He moved from Philadelphia to Warrington a half-century ago ... He was," the plaque reads, "quiet, firm, but never arrogant."

His son, Herbert Barness, now president of Joseph Barness & Son, Inc., and chairman of The Barness Organization, shares this philosophy of success.

"What measures success?" he asks. "If you consider money as a measure of success then my father was moderately successful. If you consider love, affection, and respect from his family and community, then he was a vast success. He came to this country as an immigrant, as a young man. He and my mother, also an immigrant, were financially comfortable in the latter years of his life. My father's business and financial success afforded me greater opportunities than he had. We can succeed and grow. You can't live tomorrow; you can't live yesterday or next week today.

"My father's contributions were all part of his background. In his time, there were very few public water and sewer facilities, which we subsequently built and owned. He had great foresight. Most of our more recent charitable contributions are anonymous."

Its holdings include real estate sales, real estate management, engineering and architectural companies and syndication. The latter is the purchase of income-producing real estate as apartments and office buildings where "we bring in limited partners. We are the general partner." Of this empire, Barness said, "We are really a very informal organization, country-bred and reared."

Business and family are not the end of activities for the middle-generation Barness. Much of his philanthropy is anonymous, however, he has volunteered much of his time to his home community. He has served as the chairman of the Bucks County Planning Commission. He was founder and chairman of the Bucks County Park Foundation, which is now the Bucks County Conservancy, and was instrumental in the founding of the Bucks County Industrial Development Corporation.

A former member of the Board of Delaware Valley College, he is on the executive board of the Bucks County Boy Scouts of America. He is a supporter of the county's symphony.

"I have been involved in harness racing and in thoroughbred racing, and did own horses," Barness said. He is also part of a group that has applied for a taxi franchise in Philadelphia. He has invested in the past in *The New Hope Gazette,* is a principal of radio station WBUX, and with Wally Perner owned the Bucks County Playhouse for about five years.

Behind Barness's desk in the Warrington office, there is a plaque from the Top Farmers of America Association—an award of honor for distinguished achievement in farming. "When people ask what I do," Barness said, "I say I'm a farmer—not a gentleman farmer. At this time of year there is not much to do on a farm; we work on the equipment. This year another man and myself will farm several hundred acres of ground. I spend as much of my time farming as I do in the business."

Barness's crop this year will include soybeans, corn, and wheat, and there are some beef cattle, Herefords, at his Nanlyn Farm in Buckingham. His father was a farmer who went into real estate, and Herbert Barness first went into real estate and then became a farmer. His wife Irma is an artist whose paintings and sculpture decorate the Barness office.

The importance of family is apparent in an enlargement of a photo of his father, mother, brother, and himself, standing on Bucks County soil in the days when his father was wearing overalls and "helping to get Warrington out of the mud."

To the anti-land development segment of Central Bucks, Herbert Barness says that "if it were not for the developers, housing would be so limited that the complainers would not even be here." At a time in the late '30s, when George Kaufman, Moss Hart, and Oscar Hammerstein were discovering Bucks County, the Barness name was well established. In the county where Washington once slept, a native son looks back and can say, "The county has been good to us, and we have tried to repay it."

The 1980s

Home sales slowed in the early 1980s, due to the recession that hit the nation. But the economy got a boost with the presidency of Ronald Reagan, and the real estate market improved.

In 1985, I joined my dad in the real estate development and homebuilding business. I spent about a year at a desk in his secretary's office, right outside my dad's always-open door, and it was a perfect way for me to learn while doing. The following year, I graduated to my own small office, and was feeling my way and learning all I could. I had a degree in Political Science from Tufts University and a Master's Degree in International Relations from the University of Pennsylvania, but the only real estate education I'd had before this time was from the class I took to earn a real estate license. But now, I had the best teacher. My dad kept the boundaries between father and boss, and we never had a problem. I am forever grateful for my dad's tutelage and for all of the opportunities he provided.

My dad had been involved with politics for some time, but during this decade and for the rest of his life, he took on an even more active role, mostly behind the scenes. His gift for connecting with people and rallying support for causes he cared about made him an invaluable friend and supporter. He loved people and enjoyed "working a room." Our family joke was that if you got on the elevator on the fifth floor and my dad was already on, by the time you reached the lobby he knew your name and your story, and he treated you like an old friend. If he saw you on the street a month later, he would ask about your job and your kids by name! He really had an incredible memory (and no, I didn't inherit that trait, but I think my daughters did!). When he hosted a function, political or otherwise, and guests were seated at tables, he would introduce each guest by name and mention the guest's business too. No note cards, no prompting, just spontaneous. It was impressive to watch.

My sister and I accompanied our parents to Washington, D.C., to attend both Reagan inaugurations, although at the second one, the weather was so bitterly cold that the parade was cancelled! My dad was appointed to the Presidential Commission on Housing in 1982, and worked hard throughout the '80s on behalf of Senators Arlen Specter and John Heinz and later for Governor Tom Ridge. We visited the White House on several occasions, and my father even hosted a campaign fundraiser for the first George Bush at Nanlyn Farms in the 1990s.

Larry Kane, an iconic broadcast journalist who appeared on TV news in Philadelphia for decades, was a friend of my dad's for many years. In 2000, he wrote a book called *Philadelphia* (University of Temple Press) and had this to say about my father:

"Few men can pick up a phone and get through to a President, but Herb Barness could do that with Ronald Reagan and George Bush ... [He] helped elect three governors, two presidents, and the senator with the longest tenure in Pennsylvania history, Arlen Specter." He was, Kane wrote, "the most respected Republican power broker in Pennsylvania," defined by his "early support for a candidate and absolute loyalty."

Loyalty and commitment—two hallmarks of the Barness name.

1980

MOST OF $3 MILLION DAMAGE SUIT AGAINST TOSE IS DISMISSED
The Philadelphia Inquirer
July 11, 1980

A federal jury yesterday dismissed most of a $3 million damage suit against Philadelphia Eagles owner Leonard Tose but directed that Tose pay $69,167 in lost wages to an aide he fired for alleged disloyalty.

The jury found that two other monetary claims by Tose's former financial adviser, Sidney Forstater, were invalid and that Tose had not defamed Forstater when he publicly accused him of being a "disloyal employee" who schemed with bankers to oust him from the football club in 1977.

The Forstater case, which kept the jury in deliberations for most of two days, was an outgrowth of Tose's $12 million damage suit claiming that three banks and several individuals conspired to deny him credit and force him to sell the Eagles to a former partner, Herbert Barness.

1981

MEREDITH, FEVER BOSS WANT PHILS
The Philadelphia Inquirer
March 9, 1981

My dad's friend, Walter Conti, owned Conti's Cross Keys Inn in Doylestown. The Conti and Barness families had known each other for two generations—the parents were all immigrants and had moved to Bucks County early in the 20th century. What we called "Conti's" was a fabulous restaurant that happened to be located within a mile or two of Nanlyn Farms. It drew diners from Philadelphia and beyond, and was truly ahead of its time. We celebrated all of our major and minor family occasions there.

Don Meredith, the former star quarterback for the Dallas Cowboys and an original member of ABC's *Monday Night Football* broadcast team (where he was known as "Dandy Don"), and his wife Susan had moved nearby, and they went to this outstanding restaurant and that's where my parents met them. They became fast friends, and Don, along with Ben Alexander (who is mentioned in the article below), were two of the speakers at my father's memorial service.

Philadelphia Fever president Ben Alexander said last night that he, former NFL quarterback Don Meredith and Bucks County real estate developer Herb Barness want to join Bill Giles in a group to purchase the Phillies.

Phillies' owner Ruly Carpenter announced Friday that the club was for sale because he had become dismayed by recent developments in baseball. The next day, Giles, the Phillies' executive vice president, revealed that he planned to put together a group to purchase the team.

Alexander, who said he occasionally played tennis with Giles, said Meredith is a friend of Barness, who at one time was a partner of Leonard Tose in the Philadelphia Eagles. He said Barness is "agent, or business adviser" for Meredith, now a television commentator and actor.

'GONG SHOW' HOST IS INTERESTED IN PHILLIES

The Philadelphia Inquirer
March 10, 1981
By Larry Reibstein, *Inquirer* Staff Writer

Bill Giles ultimately bought the Philadelphia Phillies baseball team from the Carpenter family. After Giles sold his part-ownership, the Phillies has been owned by John S. Middleton, Jim and Pete Buck, and David Montgomery.

Apparently after counting their cash over the weekend, nearly 20 individuals and groups, including television game show magnate Chuck Barris ("The Gong Show"), have expressed interest in buying the Phillies.

On another front, Bill Giles, the Phillies' executive vice president, plans to meet tomorrow with two people to discuss forming a syndicate to buy the team.

The two other men are Ben Alexander, president of the Philadelphia Fever, and Herb Barness, a Bucks County real estate developer.

"We're investigating this. We'll see what happens," Alexander said yesterday. "I don't think anyone is going to come up with any figures until they've really looked into it. We're trying to look at this in a sensible light. It's a business."

STRIKE THREAT HAS BARNESS BIDING HIS TIME

The Philadelphia Inquirer
May 12, 1981
By Gordon Forbes, *Inquirer* Staff Writer

The big league players are threatening to strike on May 29, and Herb Barness, who has dreamed of owning the Phillies since he left pro football, doesn't like the pessimistic lines coming from the negotiating rooms.

The scene is hauntingly familiar to Barness, who suffered through two player strikes when he was a minority partner of the Eagles. "There've been no developments on the sale," Barness said yesterday. "None whatsoever, nothing at all. And I don't think there will be, at least for another month or so.

"I don't think anybody will make any move while there is the threat of a strike. Nobody wants to buy anything that might not be in business for a year. And this might be the year, it just might be that the owners do something.

"The mood of the country is now a conservative mood. There's that to consider. So you could have the owners doing something. But we are still interested."

Barness's attorney, Charles G. Kopp, said he met last week with lawyers representing Phillies owner Ruly Carpenter. "We are continuing to talk to their lawyers," Kopp said. "At least I am, on behalf of Herb. We had a meeting last week, and we will have another one in a couple of weeks. We're moving ahead.

"I would say it's normal in a deal of this size. We're talking about a lot of money. And I don't care whether you're talking about sports franchises or widgets."

Widgets?

"Yeah, it's a word we as lawyers use for a product. You know, instead of saying screwdrivers, we say widgets. But I would say it's alive."

Kopp said he isn't sure how much a big league franchise such as the Phillies is actually worth. "I really don't know," he said. "We haven't seen the figures yet. Til I see them, I can't tell. You can speculate. We all know what the Mets sold for and what the White Sox sold for (about $20 million). And you've got to assume it would be somewhere in that neighborhood."

Barness, a wealthy real estate developer from Warrington, Bucks County, once owned 29 percent of the Eagles. He bowed out as a minority partner last year after a series of disputes with owner Leonard Tose that climaxed with an antitrust suit against several local banks. In a pre-trial agreement, Barness approved a settlement of $3,118,000 for his 29 percent interest, and Tose agreed to drop Barness as a defendant in the suit.

In his attempt to purchase the Phillies, Barness has been joined by two partners. They are Fever owner Ben Alexander, who also owns a paper company that manufactures school notebooks, and television's sportscaster-actor Don Meredith, a former Dallas Cowboys quarterback.

"I personally don't know of any other groups," Kopp said. "There may very well be. There could be a half-dozen or more. But I don't know of any." Kopp described his recent meeting with Carpenter's representatives as "very informal. And there could be 10 more meetings like that. In a deal of this size, whether it's a team or widgets, you don't do things overnight."

Meanwhile, Phillies vice president Bill Giles attributed the delay in negotiations with prospective owners to an ongoing financial audit of the club. Giles said the audit would enable potential buyers to get a "clear picture" of the team's financial situation. He also said the sale probably wouldn't be completed until anywhere from June 15 to some time next year.

A CONDO RISES FROM THE ASHES OF THE WINDSOR

The Philadelphia Inquirer
August 30, 1981
By Gene Austin, *Inquirer* Real Estate Writer

There has been a painful gap in Cape May's Victorian beachscape since the century-old Windsor Hotel burned down in 1979, but it is being filled with a new building that blends modern standards and marketing needs with some antique charm.

Regent Beach, a 52-unit condominium currently being built on the Windsor's site at Beach Drive and Windsor Avenue, facing Cape May's main beach area, won't look exactly like the famous old Windsor, but the resemblance will be close enough to satisfy many history buffs.

Regent Beach is being built by the Barness Organization, a Warrington, Pa., developer with other condo projects in Atlantic City and the Towne of Historic Smithville near Atlantic City.

Prices for the Regent Beach condos start at $124,000 for a one-bedroom apartment and range to $202,500 for a corner apartment with two bedrooms and a den.

... the sales pace isn't quite up to that of a previous Barness Organization condo project in Cape May—the 1980 conversion of the Seaport Motel at Beach Avenue and Jackson Street to condominiums. The 52 condos in that building, now called The Tides, were sold out in about 30 days last summer at prices ranging from $60,000 to $115,000.

CORINTHIAN CONDO PROVIDES LUXURY OCEANFRONT
The Jewish Exponent
October 2, 1981

The first major new oceanfront condominium to be built here [*Atlantic City, NJ*] in the past decade has taken its first big step to realization.

The Barness Organization has started accepting reservation deposits for apartments at the Corinthian, the $40 million, 34-story tower it plans to erect on the ocean between Elberon Ave. and Lincoln Place.

The Barness Organization is currently sponsoring two new communities in the area—Regent Beach, a luxury five-story oceanfront condominium in Cape May, and Hunting Run, a cluster of condominiums in the historic Smithville planned environmental developments.

A LUXURIOUS BUCKS COUNTY ESTATE IS ON THE BLOCK
The Philadelphia Inquirer
December 26, 1981

One of the major facets of the homebuilding business is, obviously, land acquisition. At Nanlyn Farms, my parents were living on a large tract of land, and in the 1980s it presented a business opportunity. The property didn't sell, and it was taken off the market. My parents continued to live there for more than a decade, and then, after a curative amendment that permitted new zoning, it was decided that The Barness Organization would build homes there. My parents ultimately moved a few miles away to neighboring Solebury, to a beautiful home on 10 acres with an indoor pool so my father could swim every morning.

Another of the Philadelphia area's dwindling supply of luxurious estates is up for sale, with an asking price of $2.1 million.

The new offering is Nanlyn Farms, a 90-acre Bucks County property with amenities including a nine-hole golf course, a 15-room main residence, a three-bedroom guest house and a four-bedroom caretaker's cottage. The estate is located in Buckingham Township about three miles east of Doylestown.

The zoning of the Nanlyn Farms tract, which would permit construction of 10 housing units per acre, means that housing developers logically might be among the prospective buyers. Marketing of the estate is being handled by Previews Inc. of Greenwich, Conn., which specializes in high-priced properties, in conjunction with David C. Kurfiss Real Estate Inc. of New Hope.

The current owner of the estate, who wants to remain anonymous during the sale, "is not a celebrity." Craig [*William L. Craig, vice president of Previews Inc.*] said. Craig said Nanlyn Farms is an outstanding estate for several reasons—not only is it a working-farm operation, but the recreation facilities can be compared only to those found at a resort or country club.

In addition to the golf course, there is an indoor tennis court plus an outdoor court with night lights, a heated swimming pool and a large recreation area in a barn.

The main house, built in 1970, has colonial styling and includes, along with five bedrooms, a solarium, library, family room and greenhouse.

About 12 of the 90 acres are wooded with maple and oaks. The rest of the estate is in farmable land or fruit orchards, and there is a full range of farm buildings.

1982

Several articles from this year had "Mutual Press Clipping Service Inc." tags on them. It looks like the service may have been hired to collect the articles, or else it was just done by a friend of my dad's. I have no idea.

BARNESS IS APPOINTED TO JUDGE MERIT BODY
The Daily Intelligencer
Undated. 1981 or 1982?

Herbert Barness of Warrington is one of seven persons appointed by Sen. Arlen Specter, R-Pa., to a statewide commission to recommend judges for U.S. District Courts.

The Judicial Merit Selection Commission is one of four independent bodies appointed by Specter and his fellow Republican senator, John Heinz. In addition to the judicial commission, the two senators appointed three U.S. attorney nominating commissions—one for each judicial district in the state.

In filling vacancies, the commissions usually will recommend three to five appointees for each post to Heinz and Specter, who will pass along the recommendations to the Justice Department.

Under the custom known as "senatorial courtesy," the president makes nominations to the official positions with the approval of senators from the majority party in the state where the nominee lives.

BARNESS NAMED FISCAL DIRECTOR FOR SCRANTON'S REELECTION BID

The Daily Intelligencer
January 1982

Bucks County businessman Herbert Barness is serving as finance chairman for the committee that has been formed for the reelection of Lt. Gov. William W. Scranton III, campaign director Marc Holtzman said Tuesday.

Barness, a land developer and professional sports entrepreneur, will head the effort to raise about $500,000 for Scranton's primary campaign.

Holtzman, a student at Lehigh University who has been a member of Scranton's staff, said Barness and Scranton became well acquainted during last year's presidential campaigns.

Barness, whose home is in Buckingham Township and whose businesses are based in Warrington Township, hosted a fund-raising event for Scranton at Keystone Racetrack in Bensalem Township last summer.

BARNESS NAMED TO PRESIDENTIAL HOUSING PANEL

The Philadelphia Inquirer
February 16, 1982

Herbert Barness, a prominent Philadelphia area land developer, has been named to the President's Commission on Housing.

The 30-member White House commission was created last spring to develop private-enterprise alternatives to publicly funded housing and mortgage-assistance programs. Barness was among eight members appointed last month.

The commission members include leaders in the banking and investment industries, nationally recognized builders and developers and a number of elected officials.

Barness, 58, of Buckingham, Bucks County, is chairman of the board of the Barness Organization, a real-estate development group based in Warminster [*actually Warrington*].

As part of his job with the mission, Barness will work on a task force to study mobile homes, rural housing and housing for the elderly.

The commission is to present its final report to President Reagan on April 20.

BARNESS NAMED TO WHITE HOUSE HOUSING PANEL
The Daily Intelligencer
February 18, 1982

Herbert Barness, a Bucks Mont builder and land developer, has been named by President Reagan as a member of the President's Commission on Housing.

Barness was one of five businessmen from across the country appointed by the president to his 30-member commission.

Barness is on the regional board of Continental Bank & Trust Company, a trustee of Bucknell University, on the Board of Trustees of San Francisco Real Estate Investors [*I never heard of this*], director of Unicorp American Corporation [*I don't know about this either*], and a director of the Pennsylvania Society.

Barness is a native of Pennsylvania and a resident of Buckingham, where he resides with his family.

BUCKS BUILDER NAMED TO PRESIDENTIAL PANEL
Source unknown
By Dave Chandler

Herbert Barness, a prominent Bucks County developer who is active in the Republican Party at county and state levels, has been named by President Reagan as a member of the President's Commission on Housing.

Barness is a resident of Buckingham Township, near Doylestown. He was one of five businessmen from across the nation to be appointed by Reagan to the 30-member panel.

He is president of The Barness Organization in Warrington Township. A major contributor to the county and state Republican organizations, he is also serving as finance chairman for the reelection committee of Lt. Gov. Bill Scranton.

Barness is a registered engineer and a licensed real estate broker and land developer in Pennsylvania and New Jersey. He is a charter member of the Bucks County Home Builders Association and has served in the national associations of both the Home Builders and Real Estate Boards.

Last May he was appointed to serve on the Federal Judicial Nominating Commission and the United States Attorney Selection Commission.

Barness is active in civic and community affairs. He has served as chairman of the Delaware Valley Philharmonic Orchestra Association and as a director of the Washington Crossing Foundation [*a non-profit that promotes the values of George Washington and provides student scholarships*].

He has also received civic awards from the American Legion, the Pop Warner Little Scholars, the Big Brothers of America, and the U.S. Blind Golfers. He is a graduate of Bucknell University, and serves on its board of trustees.

BARNESS APPOINTED TO HOUSING BOARD
The Jewish Times of the Greater Northeast
April 15, 1982
By Rita Perkin Charleston, *Jewish Times* Special Writer

Herbert Barness, president of The Barness Organization in Warrington, says he is unable to describe himself because he never even thought about doing so. So he lets his credits do the talking.

A registered engineer and licensed real estate broker and land developer in both Pennsylvania and New Jersey, Barness has recently been appointed to the President's Commission on Housing. This is a 30-member board that will, says Barness, "give recommendations to the President of the United States on all kinds of housing matters. He will then use this information as he sees fit to alleviate some of the problems facing the housing industry today to help it become a more stable industry."

Barness, of Buckingham, was one of five businessmen from around the country to be named by Reagan to join the panel. As a prominent land developer and active participant in a multitude of community and civic activities, Barness' appointment seems well placed.

But will the establishment of such a commission really benefit the population in today's decaying housing market?

"Let's just say there's a demand for housing," Barness points out. "How that demand will be handled and just when I don't know. But business works on the theory of supply and demand, and we do know there's a big demand for housing.

"One of the purposes of the President's commission," he continues, "is to try and de-regulate the housing industry, which is subject to all kinds of variables because of the economy. We are trying now to produce a more stable housing economy. The industry is over-regulated. That's one of our major concerns. Regulations amount, in some cases, to 30 percent of the cost of a house today.

"We must do away with our archaic housing codes. Not produce an inferior product," he adds quickly, "but builders just can't wait four years to have plans approved by the municipality. That costs a great deal of money, and it benefits no one. Just look how the costs are rising. A house that sold two years ago for $50,000, today costs $70,000."

President Reagan is to receive the commission's report by April 30. Then ... who knows?

But Barness seems optimistic. In the meantime he busies himself with dozens of other civic and community affairs. An active participant in the Republican Party at both county and state levels, last May he was named to the Federal Judicial Nominating Commission and the United States Attorney Selection Commission. He serves as finance chairman for the reelection committee of Lt. Gov. Bill Scranton.

A graduate of Bucknell University and a member of its board of trustees, he has also served as chairman of the Delaware Valley Philharmonic Orchestra Association and as a director of the Washington Crossing Foundation.

He has been honored with numerous awards in recognition of his civic involvements, namely from the U.S. Blind Golfers Association, the American Legion, the Pop Warner Little Scholars, and Big Brothers of America.

CARTER VISITS AREA TO SELECT CHINA
The Philadelphia Inquirer
September 24, 1982
By Ruth Seltzer, Society

When former President Jimmy Carter was in Philadelphia on Tuesday, he had dinner at the Huntingdon Valley home of his friends, Mr. and Mrs. Set C. Momjian. Mr. Carter also spent the night at the Momjian home and had breakfast with his hosts Wednesday morning.

The Momjians had 40 guests at the dinner for Mr. Carter, which we attended. Armenian foods were served, along with a cheese ring that was made from one of Rosalynn Carter's favorite recipes.

Set Momjian, who is himself a noted collector of presidential china, was a White House adviser to Jimmy Carter. He was appointed by President Carter to serve as a U.S. representative, with the rank of ambassador, to the U.N. General Assembly.

At the dinner party, the tables were set with presidential china from Set Momjian's fascinating collection—James K. Polk, Abraham Lincoln,

Rutherford B. Hayes, Woodrow Wilson, Franklin D. Roosevelt and Lyndon B. Johnson china.

The guest list included Philip J. Kendall, president of Packard Press, and his wife, Bunny; television personality Marciarose Shestack; Herbert and Irma Barness; Ned and Merle Santerian; Ronald and Millicent Asadoorian; Joseph Shanis … and more.

1983

Program from "An Evening in Honor of Herbert Barness"
The Bellevue Stratford Hotel Ballroom
Thursday, April 21, 1983

A plaque presented to my father said, "Herbert Barness... whose philanthropic contributions, communal leadership, and business expertise dedicated to the public interest have made the County of Bucks a better place to live and work." The seating chart lists my name and those of my daughters. I am also in possession of the original engraving plate from the invitation!

An Evening in Honor of
HERBERT BARNESS

The Bellevue Stratford Hotel
Ballroom

Thursday, April Twenty-first
Nineteen hundred and eighty-three

GROUP PAID NO CASH FOR CABLE SHARE
The Philadelphia Inquirer
October 11, 1983
By Ron Wolf, *Inquirer* Staff Writer

The four local partners in a company designated by the Green administration for a cable franchise, covering the Northeast, do not appear to have made any cash contribution in return for their interest in the venture—a share that eventually could be worth at least $14 million.

They have been granted their interest in Cablevision Systems Philadelphia Corp. primarily in return for introducing officials who organized the company to local bankers.

The partners are Herbert Barness, a Bucks County real estate developer; Robert Potamkin, the president of Potamkin Chevrolet; his brother Alan; and Benjamin Alexander of Jenkintown.

The four businessmen make up Philadelphia Cablevision Associates (PCA), which would be a special limited partner in the cable system proposed by Cablevision Systems if the company were given the franchise.

Barness is widely known in political, financial and sports circles. He is active in Republican affairs and contributes heavily to many of the party's candidates. He is a close friend of former Gov. Raymond Shafer's, and he served as finance chairman for Republican U.S. Sen. Arlen Specter's 1980 campaign.

In addition to his extensive real estate holdings in Bucks County and in the city, Barness has held interests in numerous professional sports ventures in the Philadelphia area.

He tried unsuccessfully to purchase the Philadelphia Eagles in 1963, then put up $1.8 million toward the $16 million price when Leonard Tose bought the team in 1969. In return, Barness obtained a 28.9 percent share of the club. He sold his interest to Tose in 1978 after a bitter court battle over management of the club.

Barness also tried to bring a professional basketball team to the city in 1963 and backed an ill-fated professional soccer team here in 1966. He was the principal force behind the William Penn Racing Association, which operates Liberty Bell Park, during the 1960s. In 1969, Barness organized Continental Thoroughbred Racing Association Inc., which built and operates Keystone Race Track in Bensalem Township, Bucks County.

Cablevision's response noted that "Mr. Barness is a businessman of considerable reputation and high standing in the Philadelphia business sector; his participation in Cablevision's activities enhances its credibility with local lending institutions and provides Cablevision the necessary working knowledge of Philadelphia's financial community.

"Further, because of Mr. Barness' experience with local sports ventures, there is a convergence of interest between Mr. Barness' group and Cablevision," the document said.

Though PCA has four partners, Barness would be the primary beneficiary. He holds a 76 percent interest in PCA, and each of his three partners holds 8 percent.

Ellen Roberts, Cablevision's Philadelphia project manager, said Barness and his group first attracted the company to the city and paid many of the fees incurred in preparing the 1979 application. She pointed out that Cablevision Systems Corp. was not nearly as large or as successful in 1979 as it is today, and that cable systems were not nearly as acceptable to potential lenders as they are now.

As a result, she said, PCA played an essential role in 1979 by making the company and its application more attractive to financial institutions.

Though Cablevision is better able to arrange its own financing today, "we don't walk away from pervious partners," she said.

1984

Warrington's 250th Anniversary Pictorial History Calendar

There is a page in this calendar that says, "On January first of 1962, Mary and Joseph Barness gave Warrington township a 22.8-acre recreational park. The dedication plaque from the presentation ceremony is pictured here. Young athletes of Warrington continue to participate in sporting events held at Barness field."

1985

SNIDER GROUP NEGOTIATING FOR EAGLES
The Philadelphia Inquirer
February 22, 1985

I don't have the first page of this article, only the continuation, but this article lists Ed Snider, Owner of the Flyers; Drew Lewis, Former Secretary of Transportation; Herbert Barness; Fitz Dixon; Robert Potamkin; and Jerry Wolman all as "attempting to organize in the aftermath of Tose's aborted plan to move to Phoenix ..."

1986

Eulogy for Mary Barness
Rabbi Robert Alper
May 12, 1986

Mom-Mom Barness was an amazing woman. Our house in Warrington was just a few miles from my grandparents' home on Easton Road, and we saw them regularly. When we moved to Rydal, we still stayed in close touch.

After my grandfather, her husband Joe, died in 1973, Mom-Mom moved from their house in Warrington to Center Square Towers, an apartment building in Doylestown that my father had built. My grandmother was always active, but she had never learned to drive, so my father provided her with a driver so that she could continue her activities. And continue she did. She went out every day ... to the supermarket, the race track (for lunch!), to the mall, and to visit friends and family. She loved to travel, and at age 80, went to Israel for the first time with her sister and a friend. And she complained that the "old ladies" held her back!

She was a major part of our lives and was healthy and very active until she was 92. Then she began to decline, but she stayed in her apartment with the assistance of an aide, and died on May 10, 1986, at the age of 94. Her memorial service was held two days later at Congregation Beth Or in Spring House, Pa.

I want to begin by telling you about a photograph that I have in my home, taken last Wednesday, developed on Thursday:

Two young girls in a Parent's Day program. Two young girls dressed in the costumes of the day—bright colors, oversized knit shirts, Swatch watches. It was a photograph taken on a day when the children recited poetry and sang songs for an appreciative audience of parents and teachers.

Two young girls—one my daughter, the other a great-granddaughter of Mary Barness. Both girls, Jessie and Melissa, are 10 years old.

I focus on this photograph of 10-year-old girls because it helps us understand and appreciate, through contrast, the life and character of Mary Barness. For when she was a 10-year-old girl, life was much different—we know a world of difference.

When Mary Barness was 10 years old, she left her mother in Russia and, by herself, set out to join her father in Philadelphia. This 10-year-old child was incarcerated in London for a month and sent home to her mother, and then she set out again for Philadelphia, this time successfully. A 10-year-old girl.

Mary Barness' life followed what many might call a classic American success story, a classic story of youthful energy, dreams and visions that developed and matured into a long and beautiful life.

As a young woman, Mary worked as a skilled seamstress. She married Joseph Barness at age 24. Independent and strong, Mary and Joe bought a farm way out in the country in Warrington and lived in that area for all of their married lives. Life was hard and, no doubt, character-building as well. No running water, two babies to care for, chickens to feed, butter to churn, clothes to wash and sew. Countless visitors—family from the city, suspicious neighborly farmers who soon became friends of this lone Jewish couple in their midst. Mary and Joe struggled as a team, and at one time she even ran a restaurant out of her home to help pay the bills.

Mary Barness' two sons, Lewis and Herbert, were the sources of continuing, limitless pride. In her eyes, they could do no wrong. How she savored their many accomplishments. How she rejoiced in their marriages, Irma living only a few miles away, becoming a wife and a daughter to Mary. Theirs was a deep and genuine special relationship. And how Mary delighted as, in turn, she became a grandmother and great-grandmother.

Indeed, one of the highlights of her life occurred on her 52nd wedding anniversary as she and Joe celebrated that momentous day by welcoming their first great-granddaughter, Jennifer.

Throughout her later years, Mary Barness lived for her grandchildren, their spouses, and her great-granddaughters.

She was a determined woman: just before her 91st birthday, she traveled to Houston and walked down the aisle in her granddaughter Laura's wedding, looking lovely in a dress she had made with her own hands.

She had a way of making everyone feel special. She always had a candy drawer in her apartment, originally for her grandchildren, then for her great-grandchildren.

She frequently wore purple because she knew that purple was her granddaughter Elizabeth's favorite color.

She was generous, she was loving, she was kind. She lived by the Golden Rule and in so doing provided a wonderful role model for all those whose lives she influenced.

She was also unselfish, thoughtful, concerned. There are many stories about Mary Barness that will be told in the days and years to come. Stories to be shared even with generations yet to be known. For here was a true modern pioneer, a woman of determination and fortitude, a woman who lived a beautiful life and left a challenging, inspiring legacy. She came to this country an immigrant, a greenhorn cut off from her roots. During her eight decades in this land, she built in her family a rootedness, a stability, all enveloped in love.

Yesterday was Mother's Day. I think it is important to recall that Mary Barness died on the day before Mother's Day, and her funeral is taking place on the day after Mother's Day.

What is the purpose of Mother's Day? It is a time to celebrate our mothers.

Yesterday, the Barness family assembled from all areas of the country to embrace, to cry, to comfort each other and most of all, to celebrate the remarkable life of their mother, mother-in-law, grandmother and great-grandmother, Mary Barness. And today we continue that painful yet reaffirming task.

We remember Mary Barness through these words by Robert Lewis Stevenson: "She has achieved much who has lived well, laughed often and loved with full heart; who has gained the respect of the wise and the trust of the young; who has filled a place, accomplished some task; who has left the world better than she found it; who has appreciated the true and beautiful; who has looked for the good in others and given of the good she had; whose life was an inspiration, whose memory is a benediction."

Let us pause for a moment of silent reflection on the life of Mary Barness ...

BARNESS IS LEADER OF PENNSYLVANIA SOCIETY
The Daily Intelligencer
June 11, 1986

Herbert Barness, chairman of the Barness Organization, has been elected president of the Pennsylvania Society, which holds a dinner once a year that has traditionally been a showcase for political candidates in the state.

The society was established in 1899 and has 2,000 members. Each year in December it holds a dinner at the Waldorf-Astoria in New York City.

In the past the dinner has been a largely Republican affair. Early in its history it is said to have been the place where Republican power brokers gathered to draw up the next slate of candidates or decide who will be named to a judgeship.

More recently it has become a bipartisan event. The dinner attracts the state's top political leaders, office holders and would-be candidates. It offers them a chance to see and be seen by some of the most influential business and professional people in Pennsylvania.

Barness operates a development business in Warrington Township and has long been active in Republican politics.

HOMETOWN BOYS MAKE GOOD; JEWISH ATHLETES HAVE PLAYED MAJOR POSITIONS IN PHILADELPHIA'S SPORTS HISTORY
Inside Magazine
Summer 1986
By Ron Avery

... While individual Jewish athletes still surface, the major role of the Jew in city sports today is that of owner and promoter. Many of their names are household words in the Quaker City: Leonard Tose, Harold Katz, Ed Snider, Irv Kosloff, Norman Braman, boxing's Peltz and racing's Herb Barness.

They are hard-driving, mostly self-made men. Many seem to be frustrated athletes. It is sometimes said that they couldn't make the team so they bought the team. They've been colorful and controversial. But one could also say that the new crop of Jewish team owners turned Philadelphia from a city of losers to a city of winners.

1987

CENTRAL BUCKS CHAMBER OF COMMERCE HONORS FIVE: SERVICE AWARDS SPARKLE WITH TRIBUTES AND WIT
The Daily Intelligencer
April 6, 1987

Herbert Barness admires Kenneth Wilfred Gemmill's exemplar medallion as Gemmill's wife Helen and Mrs. Irma Barness approve. Barness made the presentation to Gemmill on behalf of the Chamber [of Commerce]. The evening had an added interest for Barness. The Bucks County Playhouse received the Ambassador award. Barness was instrumental in saving the theatre in the '60s. He purchased it with Wally Perner so it would not be converted into a movie theatre, and they requested that former State Senator Marvin Keller introduce a motion in the state senate designating the Bucks County Playhouse as the "State Theatre."

MINOR LEAGUE BASEBALL CAN BE FUN
The Philadelphia Inquirer
June 19, 1987
Op-Ed page, By Tom Fox, *Inquirer* Editorial Board

... The Shamrock Society's return to Reading this summer was a special treat for McEwen and pols. One of the new owners of the Reading Phillies—one of their old crowd—is Herb Barness, the Bucks County developer who has made many a sizable campaign contribution to many a GOP campaign.

Actually, Herb Barness bought the club for his son-in-law, a likeable young man out of Penn State by the name of Craig Stein. And Craig Stein in turn leased the club back to its former owner who was a classmate of Herb Barness' when they were boys at Bucknell. [*Craig was married to my sister; they have since divorced.*]

The deal is rooted in the form of fiscal incest. Craig Stein and his father-in-law were looking for a tax break last fall. And so was Joe Buzas, who, over the years, has owned 66 minor league baseball franchises.

So they called in the lawyers, and Craig Stein bought the Reading franchise, but Joe Buzas still runs it. You figure that one out.

Joe Buzas is a real piece of work. He's Hungarian by blood and a moneymaker by nature. To give you an idea, in 1978 he bought the Reading franchise from the Phillies for $1. "They forced it on me," he says.

And last fall he sold the franchise to H. Barness and son-in-law for a cool $1 million.

PENNSYLVANIANS FIND PARTIES APLENTY IN N.Y.
The Philadelphia Inquirer
December 15, 1987
By Davis Iams, Society

The Waldorf waiters were pouring the champagne Saturday for more than 1,700 guests at the 89th annual dinner of the Pennsylvania Society. Originally hosted by executives of the Pennsylvania Railroad and other firms trapped in the Big Apple over the holidays, it has become an informal conclave of business people and politicians, according to Philadelphia Electric Co. vice president Clifford Brenner and his wife, Ros, who are longtime participants.

Around it have proliferated a whole series of parties—not only before and after the Saturday dinner itself, at which president Herbert Barness presented the Society's gold medal to the Penn State football coach—but for the whole weekend.

1988

Contribution to the Michener Museum in Doylestown
1988

My parents were friendly with James Michener, and when a new museum was built in Doylestown to honor his memory, they donated this room. The museum hosts traveling exhibitions and houses a permanent collection of works by local 19th and 20th century artists, but the Michener Room features the desk used by the famous author to write his novels, along with other bits of personal memorabilia.

PEOPLE: VIP
Philadelphia Business Journal
August 22-28, 1988

Charles G. Kopp began the year raising money for the Bob Dole presidential bid.

Last week, at the Republican National Convention in New Orleans, the Philadelphia attorney found himself applauding party rival George Bush.

Kopp, co-chairman of Wolf, Block, Schorr and Solis-Cohen, one of the largest law firms in the city, was not attending the convention as an inner circle member of a victorious campaign. But the GOP acknowledged Kopp's efforts by naming him as an honorary delegate, one of about 40 with the title from Pennsylvania. The title is for "someone who has unselfishly given of his time, talents and resources to Pennsylvania Republican causes," and Kopp said he got the honor through his Dole connection.

Among the others with the designation are former state Supreme Court Judge Bruce W. Kauffman, a name partner in Dilworth, Paxson, Kalish & Kauffman, another large Philadelphia law firm; and Herbert Barness, owner of the Barness Organization, a major Bucks County real estate developer.

BUCKINGHAM APPROVES PLANS FOR SEVEN NEW DEVELOPMENTS
The Daily Intelligencer
October 27, 1988
By Joseph J. McDermott, Staff Writer

Plans for seven developments totaling more than 200 new homes advanced during a five-hour Buckingham Township supervisors meeting Wednesday, including a 50-lot development on Cold Spring Creamery Road that was finally granted conditional approval after almost two hours of discussion.

Under the tentative approval granted by the board, the developers will also be able to temporarily receive sewer service from the Bucks County Water and Sewer Authority's Chalfont-New Britain plant, but will have the option to connect to a proposed spray irrigation sewage treatment plant scheduled to serve several curative amendment lots in the northern section of the township.

The plant, proposed by Herbert Barness, who owns one of the curative tracts, would eventually be owned and operated by the township under current plans.

NEW GOP GROUP TARGETS CENTER CITY RACE FOR FUNDS
The Philadelphia Inquirer
November 4, 1988
By Mark Fazlollah, *Inquirer* Harrisburg Bureau

A new Republican organization is tapping contributions from two of the region's wealthiest men to create a special fund that it hopes will help break the Democrats' domination of Philadelphia politics, a spokesman said yesterday.

The fund, the Philadelphia Leadership Council, has targeted the state House race of Rep. Babette Josephs as a test case and has pumped funds, albeit a relatively small amount, into the campaign of her opponent, Karen Chiseck, a former aide to U.S. Sen. John Heinz.

It also has as its goal protecting the city's preeminent Republican—District Attorney Ronald D. Castille—who is up for reelection next year.

Insurance executive Robert M. Flood, 3rd, treasurer for the newly formed group, said that F. Eugene Dixon Jr., heir to the Widener family fortune, and Bucks County developer Herbert Barness have already contributed to the group. Flood estimated that each of the men have personal fortunes well in excess of $100 million.

A NEW FEDERAL JUDGE IS SWORN IN WITH THE PROMINENT LOOKING ON

The Philadelphia Inquirer
December 17, 1988
By Katherine Seelye, *Inquirer* Staff Writer

In a formidable display of political power, the state's Republican elite and the cream of its legal society turned out yesterday to witness the swearing-in of Jay C. Waldman as judge of the U.S. District Court for the Eastern District of Pennsylvania.

Among the 300 guests crammed into the ceremonial courtroom in the Federal Building at Sixth and Market streets were U.S. Sen. Arlen Specter; state Attorney General LeRoy S. Zimmerman; former state Supreme Court Justice Bruce W. Kauffman; Philadelphia District Attorney Ronald D. Castille; Elsie Hillman, who oversaw President-elect Bush's Pennsylvania campaign; Bucks County developer Herb Barness; state GOP Chairman Earl Baker; Fred Anton of the Pennsylvania Manufacturers Association; a host of former and current Thornburgh aides; several members of the state judiciary; plus several federal and Common Pleas Court judges.

1989

Program from The Bucks County Council and Boy Scouts of America's Friends of Scouting Annual Dinner
March 14, 1989

At this dinner, the Bucks County Board of County Commissioners presented my dad with a Letter of Commendation that recognized him as a Distinguished Citizen. It read, "We recognize your commitment to the Boy Scouts of Bucks County. As Chairman of the Scout Service Center Building Committee and through your involvement with the Council Heritage Society, you provided the leadership necessary to help ensure the future of scouting in the county."

FRIENDS OF SCOUTING DINNER
honoring
HERBERT BARNESS
with the
DISTINGUISHED CITIZEN AWARD
March 14, 1989

The Fountainhead, New Hope

The Intelligencer/Record
March 15, 1989

Buckingham businessman Herbert Barness (center) is congratulated by Dale O. Smith (left), President, and Henry S. Climer, past president of the Bucks County Council of the Boy Scouts of America. Barness is a charter member of the council's Heritage Society, which has supported an endowment program to continue Scouting into the next century. He is also a member of the Council Advisory Board and chairman of the Scouting Service Building Committee. Staff photo by Richard M. Hendrickson of *The Intelligencer/Record*.

GOP IS OFF TO A SLOW START IN '90 GUBERNATORIAL RACE

The Philadelphia Inquirer
May 3, 1989
By Katherine Seelye, *Inquirer* Staff Writer

As the state GOP gropes for a candidate to challenge Democratic Gov. Casey next year, the clock is running on the length of time the eventual nominee has to raise money.

Herb Barness, a Bucks County developer and another key GOP fundaiser, is already involved in raising money for Sen. Arlen Specter's 1992 reelection campaign.

Program from the Dedication Ceremony for The Irma and Herbert Barness Endowed Chair in the Fine and Performing Arts
Germantown Academy
June 9, 1989

All four of the Barness granddaughters were graduated from Germantown Academy in Fort Washington, PA. My father became active in the school when the girls started there and became a member of the Board of Trustees. My parents made this contribution in the arts department because my mother was an artist. This ceremony also included the induction of the first Chairholder.

GEORGE ANTHONISEN SCULPTURE UNVEILED IN NATION'S CAPITAL
The Daily Intelligencer
September 11, 1989

George Anthonisen was a local and renowned artist. I am assuming that my parents knew him, although his name is not familiar to me.

George R. Anthonisen's sculpture honoring the men and women who risked their lives to rescue and protect Jews from Nazi persecution during World War II was unveiled during ceremonies last week in Washington, D.C.

"I Set Before You This Day ..." will be on display through Sept. 29 in the rotunda of the Cannon House Office Building, U.S. House of Representatives.

Left: Norman Leventhal and Herbert Barness. Right: Artist George Anthonisen, Lee L. Schlanger, and Irma Barness.

GOVERNOR TAPS BARNESS FOR PORT AUTHORITY:
Will represent Bucks
The Daily Intelligencer
September 1989
By James E. Stanton, Calkins Newspapers

Gov Robert P. Casey has appointed Bucks County developer Herbert Barness, a major fundraiser for the Republican Party, to represent the county on the newly created Philadelphia Regional Port Authority.

The name of Barness was one of three sent to the governor last month by the two majority Republican county commissioners.

Barness, a Buckingham resident, will be one of 11 members of the new authority, which will replace the Philadelphia Port Corp.

In announcing the submission of the three candidates, Commissioner Chairman Andrew L. Warren said the person chosen would be "Bucks County's voice, eyes and ears" on the authority and will have equal stature with the other members.

Last month, Warren described Barness as having had "a working relationship of many years with key elected officials at every level of government, including members of Congress and the Bush administration."

Of "equal importance" in the field of port development and international trade, Barness' firm has developed communities in the Caribbean and Mexico, Warren said.

SPECTER ALREADY FILLING WAR CHEST FOR '92 SENATE RACE
The Philadelphia Inquirer
October 9, 1989
By Katherine Seelye, *Inquirer* Staff Writer

His reelection campaign is more than three years away. But Pennsylvania's U.S. Sen. Arlen Specter is already raising money for his bid for a third term.

Specter began raising money for his 1992 campaign in January, just after paying off his debt from his 1986 campaign. In the first six months of this year, according to the Federal Election Commission, he pulled in more than $1 million.

His goal, according to Herb Barness, his finance chairman, is $10 million to $12 million.

Barness, a Bucks County developer and major GOP fund-raiser, explained Specter's activities this way: "Fund-raising is extremely important this far out from an election because of the limitations in the federal election law. We aren't allowed to take corporate checks.

The maximum that a person can give is $2,000 ... and some people are already maxed out; meaning they have already hit the $2,000 limit."

Early fundraising, he noted, is "standard all over the country."

HAFER MAY BE GETTING A RIVAL ON THE RIGHT
The Philadelphia Inquirer
October 22, 1989
By Katherine Seelye, *Inquirer* Staff Writer

James O. Picard, former commerce secretary in the Thornburgh administration, is preparing to challenge state Auditor General Barbara Hafer for the GOP endorsement for governor.

Hafer's finance chairman, Pittsburgh lawyer Evans Rose, came to Philadelphia last week looking for a top Republican to help host a Hafer fund-raising event Nov. 30 in Philadelphia as a kickoff to the Dec. 2 endorsement. Three people turned him down: Charles Kopp, a Philadelphia lawyer, and Herb Barness, a Bucks County developer, both major GOP fund-raisers, and Tim Carson, state GOP finance chairman.

Rose settled on Michael Smerconish, a Philadelphia developer and former aide to former Mayor Frank L. Rizzo. Smerconish said that Kopp, Barness and Carson would all participate in the fund-raising event. But his own appointment as co-chairman is raising eyebrows among local Republicans, who are well aware that his longtime feud with Rizzo could alienate the Rizzo camp from Hafer.

AROUND THE TOWN
The Jewish Times
December 14, 1989
By Leon Brown

Bucks County leaders Irma and Herbert Barness hosted the kickoff event for the charter year of the Heritage Society of the Bucks County Council of the Boy Scouts of America. They were also inducted as the first members of the Heritage Society.

The 1990s

In the 1990s, my parents moved to Solebury, and The Barness Organization began to build houses and townhomes on Nanlyn Farms. Those housing developments included Hearthstone, The Woods at Hearthstone, and Dalton Glen; and the townhome communities were called Fireside and The Woods at Fireside. We also started working on our first "active adult"—that is, over-55—community.

At the start of the decade, the big change in our workplace was new technology: we had desktop computers throughout the office, and the internet would soon come along and revolutionize the way we conducted business day-to-day. But the major shock was that my father was diagnosed with Non-Hodgkins Lymphoma in 1990. He would be treated for the disease—going in and out of remission several times—for seven and a half years. He had an amazing team of doctors at the Hospital of the University of Pennsylvania, headed by Dr. John Glick. Ever true to his nature, my dad maintained a high level of activity during these years except, of course, when he absolutely couldn't. Whenever anyone asked him how he felt, he always answered, "Great." And he meant it. He had the most positive outlook on life. My mother, sister, and I had been with my dad at his first appointment with Dr. Glick, and we were there at the last when John said that he didn't have any more tricks in his bag.

Even in his last years, my dad was fortunate to be the recipient of numerous recognitions and awards, and each and every one meant something to him. He was always humble and appreciative. He went to the many events knowing that the honor meant that he could bring recognition to an organization he cared about and believed in. He worked for the benefit of others until the very end.

My dad was in the office until 10 days before he died. I drove around the area with him that final day, a trip down memory lane in

Warrington, and I took a few photos of him and later made a poster from them. As I was driving, he told me who he wanted to speak at his memorial service. I can still see myself, driving and weeping, and remember how I felt in that moment. I drove him home, and he died 10 days later, surrounded by his family. He passed away on September 5, 1998, at age 74.

1990

TRANSCRIPT FROM KYW NEWSRADIO 1060 PRESENTS THE DELAWARE VALLEY: Backward Into The Future
In cooperation with the Regional Affairs Council
Part 10
March 1990
Written and Researched by Ed Kasuba, Bob Kotowski, Jay Lloyd, Richard Maloney

HOST: We're not talking about low-income housing, or even moderate-income housing. We're talking about a home that can be bought in the suburbs by someone earning $35,000 a year. Suburban employers want homes like that for their employees, and longtime suburban residents want them for their grown children. But experienced developers like Herbert Barness says it's not realistic, unless zoners provide for higher-density housing and local governments make other concessions.

BARNESS: They would have to streamline the approval process. They would have to help provide the public water, the public sewers. They would have to help in the street improvements.

HOST: But the question is, are any local governments rushing to create a climate for the development of affordable housing?

BARNESS: Absolutely not, absolutely not, there's no community saying, "Hey, we want affordable housing." I've never heard that expression used in all the years I've been in this business.

CAPITALIZING ON PROGRESS
The Daily Intelligencer
March 11, 1990
By Robert Benincasa, Staff Writer

The Barness Organization celebrates its 65th anniversary this year, and its chairman of the board—mid-Atlantic developer and avid politico Herbert Barness—holds a steady hand at the helm.

New York may lay claim to the flashy, flippant smirk of Donald Trump, but the greater Philadelphia region—and Buckingham Township in Bucks County specifically—has Herbert Barness.

The history of the company is forever interwoven with the economic and social history of the county, having flexed with the winds of the real estate market since the post-World War I years to earn its present status as a leading builder and developer of residential communities, commercial projects and apartments.

Herbert Barness, 66, remembers the simple vision that started the original Warrington Township-based company: that of his father, Joseph Barness, who emigrated to the United States from eastern Europe in 1912.

"He built a house and the house had a two-car garage, a chicken house, and five acres of land. That sold, so he built another." Since 1925, his father kept on building, Barness said, "one house at a time," for urban types who wanted to venture out "to the country."

Today, under his son's stewardship, headquartered in a Barness development on Easton Road, the company is a diversified veteran of many different ventures, including Keystone Race Track, Warrington Country Club and WBUX Radio in Doylestown.

For years, Herbert Barness was a partner in the Philadelphia Eagles football team, and today, he is a devoted fan of the Eastern League's Reading Phillies baseball team, which is owned by his son-in-law, Craig Stein.

Even the organization's conventional land development projects have made their marks—in locales ranging from the Caribbean to the Jersey shore—through its six corporate divisions.

Forceful in a business negotiation, Barness appears quiet and courteous in his other activities.

His roomy corner office in Warrington is outfitted with a wall unit containing several varieties of candy bars and other confections.

While many businesspeople decorate their offices with abstract pastels guaranteed not to disturb busy employees, Barness fills his walls with photos of his favorite (predominantly Republican) national political figures, sometimes including himself and his wife, Irma.

A large, attractive color shot of President Bush adorns the company's outer office, and bears the salutation "Irma and Herb—warmest personal regards, George Bush."

Parents of two daughters and grandparents of four girls, the Barnesses sponsor political functions and aid civic and charitable causes.

Herbert Barness is at the helm of The Barness Organization, a diversified veteran of many different ventures. Staff photos by Gian C. Luiso

Travelers along Route 422 in Royersford can't miss Barness's 400-unit condominium project, now in the second of three phases with about half the units built.

Capitalizing on the casino boom of the early '80s, Barness fielded several projects in Atlantic City, including a 3,000-car casino garage, condominiums and single family homes.

His company's commercial and residential building projects have taken shape in various parts of the world, but Barness is not one to be caught saying "not in my back yard."

His residence, the lush 90-acre Nanlyn Farms estate at Route 413 and Cold Spring Creamery Road in Buckingham, is next to his planned 850-home development. The home also is across from a county-owned field commonly known as the Lojeski tract, where a spray-irrigation sewage treatment operation is planned to serve his development and possibly some other planned homes.

Does it bother him that he'll soon have several hundred new neighbors?

"Not at all. Sooner or later, my property will be developed also. [*As noted earlier, my parents moved nearby after my father's cancer diagnosis.*]

Nanlyn Farms includes a nine-hole golf course, indoor and outdoor tennis courts, a swimming pool, 15-room residence and guest and servant houses. Barness put it on the market briefly in 1981, then asking $2.1 million. He decided to stay, however, after his children and grandchildren expressed renewed interest in the home's facilities.

In his bid to become a key developer of Buckingham, Barness was hardly welcomed with open arms. A long court fight with the township ended in 1979 with a U.S. Supreme Court refusal to hear a final appeal by the township.

Left standing was a 1978 Commonwealth Court ruling upholding "curative amendment" challenges to the township's zoning laws that Barness and six other developers filed in 1974.

Curative amendments are challenges by landowners who say flaws in a municipality's zoning laws must be "cured" to allow their development plans.

The court decision granted Barness the right to build 3,023 homes on his 346-acre Buckingham site, a number he cut to today's 850. So far, his company has submitted plans for 75 of those homes. The houses, he said, will sell for "$250,000 and $300,000 and up."

Barness is pushing the 850-home project forward by putting up $1 million for a 99-year lease of the Lojeski tract between the township and the county government, which owns it. He also will build a sewage treatment plant to serve his development.

Without the deal, his building plans could have been stalled pending expansion of the Chalfont-New Britain sewage treatment facility.

The spray irrigation plant, which "recharges" groundwater by spraying treated liquid sewage onto the ground, is under review by the state Department of Environmental Resources. Given proper approvals, it could treat 190,000 to 200,000 gallons of sewage each day, according to the township.

Regarding the company's future plans for Buckingham, Barness says he does not intend to start any projects in the township beyond the 850 and called the current real estate market "very slow."

"We have enough in Buckingham. It can take a long time to develop it.

"We do very little in Bucks County anymore. There are still a lot of areas that welcome development," he said, citing parts of New Jersey, Maryland and Delaware.

Barness did not name names when discussing the tension between developers and area governments, but said, "That did not exist in this area until perhaps 20 years ago." But, "as people moved into a community they didn't want other people to move in."

The greatest obstacle facing area developers is "a lack of understanding by the governing bodies. They don't understand that developments are need driven.

"A developer doesn't create a demand for a project. The demand is there, and he's there to help fill it," he says.

"One of the biggest problems," Barness believes, is that small municipalities all "want to be independent of each other. If they would pool their efforts, they could reduce costs." In areas that do not have many separate small governments, like Maryland, "they don't have the same problems we're facing here."

Municipal officials have been known to say at public meetings that development costs taxpayers more money than it provides, with long-term costs that far outweigh short-term windfalls.

"The reason that exists is that people who move in are demanding. They want newer and better schools, which they should have, and somebody has to pay for it."

Barness says rising taxes to accommodate development are "absolutely" just a normal part of "progress."

If that sounds a little political, it is no surprise. A key state and national Republican Party contributor, he has also been a financial backer and social contact of the Reagan and Bush administrations since the beginning of the Reagan era.

"A developer doesn't create a demand for the project. The demand is there and he's there to help fill it."—Herbert Barness

GOP ABORTION-RIGHTS GROUP NAMES BUCKS MAN A CO-CHAIR
The Philadelphia Inquirer
May 1, 1990

Bucks County developer Herb Barness yesterday was named national finance co-chairman of Republicans for Choice, a new political action committee dedicated to changing the GOP platform on abortion at the 1992 national convention.

Barness, a veteran GOP activist and fund-raiser, has been active in numerous Pennsylvania Senate and gubernatorial campaigns as well as the Republican presidential campaigns of 1980, 1984 and 1988. Republicans for Choice is an organization of about 300 legislators, fund-raisers and members of Congress trying to put abortion rights in the GOP platform, which currently calls for a constitutional amendment to ban abortion.

"Herb Barness can provide precisely the type of Republican leadership we will need to move our party to the pro-choice stance," said Ann Stone, national chairwoman of Republicans for Choice. The group hopes to raise about $3 million in the next three years to elect abortion-rights advocates to legislatures and party delegations in 50 states.

PRO-CHOICE REPUBLICAN GROUP SELECTS BARNESS AS FUND-RAISER; CHANGE IN GOP ABORTION STANCE SOUGHT

The Intelligencer/Record
May 2, 1990
By Edward Levenson, Staff Writer

Bucks County developer Herbert Barness will help raise $3 million on behalf of a newly formed nationwide organization of Republicans seeking to change the party's position against abortion.

Barness, head of the Barness Organization in Warrington, has been named national co-chairman of Republicans for Choice. It now has about 250 initial members, including state legislators, members of Congress and party officials.

Ann E.W. Stone of Alexandria, Va., national chairman, said Barness was asked to help because of his "track record" in raising money for Republican candidates, including Pennsylvania's U.S. Senators Arlen Specter and J. John Heinz and Presidents Reagan and Bush.

"(Barness) also has a talent for energizing people," said Stone, who owns an advertising agency and other businesses in Alexandria, a suburb of Washington, D.C.

An item in the April 30 issue of *Newsweek* magazine identified Barness and Cliff Sobel, a fund-raiser for former New Jersey Gov. Thomas Kean, as two of the "top moneymen" behind Republicans for Choice. Sobel is national finance chairman, Stone said.

Barness, a Buckingham resident, told *The Intelligencer* this week that he supports the pro-choice group's goal of changing the Republican platform, which advocates a constitutional amendment to ban abortion, at the 1992 national convention.

"We're opposing efforts to restrict what's in place," Barness said. Republicans could be hurt politically by the party's rigid stand against abortion, he added.

"Abortion is an emotional issue. It should not be a political issue," Barness said. "There should be a real attempt to take it out of the political arena. I hope we get a unified ruling once and for all by the Supreme Court that is the law of the land."

WASHINGTON FAX: PRO-CHOICE
Newsweek Magazine
Undated

Republicans for Choice, a new and ideologically diverse group, next month will launch a well-financed campaign to change the GOP's anti-abortion stance. Key leaders of the pro-choice group include Arizona Rep. Jim Kolbe and California Rep. Tom Campbell, both of whom have impeccable conservative credentials on economic issues, and moderate Rep. Nancy Johnson of Connecticut. Start-up funding will come from what's left of the GOP's liberal East-Coast wing. Two top moneymen lined up so far: Cliff Sobel, a fundraiser for former New Jersey governor Tom Kean, and Herbert Barness, finance chairman for Pennsylvania Sen. Arlen Specter.

BARNESS GIVEN STATE GOP POST

The Intelligencer/Record
June 8, 1990
By Edward Levenson, Staff Writer

Herbert Barness, a prominent Bucks County developer and GOP fundraiser, was named Thursday as one of Pennsylvania's two members of the Republican National Committee.

State party chairman Anne B. Anstine picked Barness to fill the remaining two years of the term of Drew Lewis on Montgomery County, who resigned this month after 14 years on the committee, which oversees the national GOP.

"Herb Barness will be a tremendous asset to the Pennsylvania Republican Party and the Republican National Committee," Anstine said in a statement.

She added, "I am confident that his leadership role in the Republican Party will generate a great deal of success in this critical election year."

Barness, president of The Barness Organization of Warrington, has raised money for numerous Republican candidates, including Pennsylvania's U. S. Senators Arlen Specter and J. John Heinz and Presidents Reagan and Bush.

Barness, a Buckingham resident, was named in May as national co-chairman of Republicans for Choice, a group of state legislators, members of Congress and party officials who want the GOP to adopt a pro-choice stand on abortion.

Finance committees on which Barness has served include those of the state and Bucks County GOP and the state Reagan for President campaign.

The developer has also been a delegate to the Republican national convention and cast one of Pennsylvania's electoral votes in the presidential election.

Anstine said that Barness had wide support among the 37 members of the state GOP leadership committee.

Party bylaws give the chairman the authority to fill a vacancy after consulting with Republican leaders.

The other national committee seat is held by Elsie H. Hillman of Pittsburgh.

BUCKS COUNTY DEVELOPER TO REPRESENT GOP
The Pittsburgh Post-Gazette
June 8, 1990
By Frank Reeves, *Post-Gazette* Staff Writer

A Bucks County developer has been chosen to replace Drew Lewis, a nationally prominent Republican who resigned his position as one of Pennsylvania's two national GOP committee members.

State GOP Chairwoman Anne B. Anstine yesterday selected Herbert Barness, 66, to succeed Lewis. Barness, who is president of the Barness Organization—a development and construction company—will serve the two years remaining in Lewis's term.

Anstine consulted with top Republican leaders—including U.S. Senators J. John Heinz and Arlen Specter—before making the decision, according to Tom Druce, state GOP executive director.

"She also talked to national committee woman Elsie Hillman, who said she would be very comfortable working with Herb," Druce said.

Hillman, a Pittsburgh resident, was first elected to the Republican National Committee in 1975.

Barness has served as a delegate to several Republican National Conventions and as a member of the state GOP's finance committee, Druce said. He also has been a member of the Electoral College, a largely honorary position, which technically elects a U.S. president every four years.

AROUND THE TOWN
The Jewish Times
June 14, 1990
By Leon Brown

Fred A. Shabel, chairman of the board of Spectacor, the Philadelphia-based sports, entertainment and marketing organization, will receive the annual Torch of Liberty Award from the Anti-Defamation League of B'nai B'rith. It'll be presented at the ADL award dinner at the Hotel Atop the Bellevue. Larry Kane, WCAU-TV anchorman, will be master of ceremonies. Co-chairing the dinner will be Herbert Barness, board chairman of The Barness Organization, and Jay Snider, prez of Spectacor and the Philadelphia Flyers.

HERB BARNESS—A QUIET FORCE IN GOP POLITICS
The Philadelphia Inquirer
June 17, 1990
By Jeffrey Fleishman, *Inquirer* Staff Writer

Herb Barness offered a gum drop from the gum drop bin. "Go ahead, take one, I have all kinds." Then he sat down behind his big desk—stark except for a date book and a telephone—and talked politics and how the abortion debate is overshadowing more "legitimate" issues.

Midway through his musings, the phone rang. "Uh, nope, not on Friday, can't. Busy ... But I'll send money ... Right ... OK ... Bye." Barness had just turned down an invitation to dinner with White House Chief of Staff John H. Sununu.

Back to abortion. And to a lesser extent, gum drops.

Barness, steadily, quietly and somewhat coyly, has become one of the most powerful Republicans in Pennsylvania and, some would argue, the country. A first-generation American, the son of Polish immigrants, he became a millionaire developer who has spun wealth into political clout.

That clout again was apparent June 7, when he was named to replace Drew Lewis, the former secretary of transportation, on the Republican

National Committee. Barness is also finance chairman for Sen. Arlen Specter's 1992 campaign, which seeks to raise $10 million. And on April 30, he was named co-chairman for Republicans for Choice, a group of 300 legislators and activists seeking to change the party platform on abortion.

"There are two ways to get real power in politics," said Charles Kopp, Barness' lawyer for the last 20 years and himself a powerful fund-raiser. "One, you can deliver the votes. Two, you can deliver money. Herb can deliver the money."

"My only agenda is to get good people into government," Barness said. "I am anxious to see that the right people do get elected." And he works hard to do that. Barness, 66, who lives in Buckingham, has helped raise millions of dollars for political candidates over the last 30 years. He recently contributed $10,000 to gubernatorial candidate Barbara Hafer.

"When I call people on the phone they know what I want," Barness said. "I guess I'm effective ... Money is the mother's milk of politics, and somebody's got to do it." Barness said the role is perfect for him because it allows him to stay close to politics without being a politician.

"I could never see him running for office," said Donald McCoy, a Bucks County Republican lawyer. "He's not one to go out kissing babies ... I call him Mr. Elder Statesman."

"He is very quiet, yet (he) has powerful influence," said Tom Druce, executive director of the Republican State Committee and a former aide to Sen. John Heinz. "There was a different way things were responded to when someone like Herb Barness called (Heinz's office) ... You could probably count those type of people on one hand."

But Barness' rustic office in Warrington—with its gum drops, Tootsie Rolls, autographed footballs and a tiny tractor—belies what Barness calls "the illusion of power" that surrounds him. According to himself and those who know him, Barness is a private man, searching more for how to get things done than notoriety. "I don't get impassioned. I get dedicated," he said.

Barness' political reach may extend to Washington, but his roots are in Bucks County. He was born and reared on the farmlands outside of Doylestown and was educated in a one-room schoolhouse, a replica of which sits in his office. He has a degree in mechanical engineering from Bucknell University, and during World War II he served three years in the Pacific with the Army Air Force.

When he returned to Bucks County, Barness worked his father's farm and later joined his father's real estate business, Joseph Barness and Son. "I tilled the soil. I was out there," he said, pointing out his window to Easton Road, where stores and blacktop smother the once rich farmlands.

Barness turned the successful real estate business into the Barness Corp., a development firm with present and past interests in Pennsylvania, the Caribbean islands and Atlantic City. But Barness did not confine himself to land deals. In the 1970s, he was a part-owner of the Philadelphia Eagles and was a member of the William Penn Racing Association, which had interests in different horse tracks. Barness was behind the building of what today is the Philadelphia Park race track in Bensalem. Friends of Barness said he had an uncanny ability to take what looked like a "hare-brained scheme" and make it good business. "He meets with everybody," said a close friend. "His date book is filled with people he knows and their birthdays and the birthdays of their families. And the cards go out. This a soothing low-key guy until a business deal ... then he's aggressive and he doesn't let up."

Barness sometimes found himself in controversy in the 1960s and '70s. There was his battle with Leonard Tose over control of the Eagles. And there were also allegations that Barness used his political connections to Gov. Raymond P. Shafter to get a license for a race track. Barness receded from the public eye in the late 1970s and went about his business endeavors and his political fund-raising.

Some Republican officials, however, say Barness' appointments to the National Committee and Republicans for Choice may force him to take on a more visible role. "He may have to shift gears a little," said one Republican official. Moreover, his quest to remove abortion issues from the political arena may put him at odds with GOP conservatives and President Bush.

"There will be a ripple, but it will be small," said a high-ranking Republican official. When asked if he was concerned about a possible backlash, Barness responded, "I don't really know yet." Barness said Republicans for Choice "is not a pro-abortion group; if it was, I would not be involved." He said abortion is an individual choice that has—mainly because of the press—turned into a large political conundrum.

"There's the S&L problem, the deficit, what are we going to do with the homeless and what about people getting laid off from defense contractors? These are the real issues, not (abortion)," Barness said.

To make his point, he told a story. "A few of us, my wife and I and another couple, were out to dinner recently," he said, leaning back in his high-back chair. The topic, he said, turned to politics and he found himself the odd-man-out in an argument about abortion's political importance.

Barness told his companions he could prove his position that Americans are uninformed about other more vital things. He turned to the waiter and asked him to name Pennsylvania's governor and two U.S. senators. There was silence. "He couldn't tell me," said Barness, his eyes widening behind his glasses. "All he said was, 'I should know. I'm a senior journalism major at Temple.' Honest to God."

The story about the waiter over, Barness turned to Eastern Europe and how the pace of change at home and abroad prevented him from predicting what will be the larger issues in the 1992 presidential campaign. He sat back, comfortable in the "illusion of power," knowing that whatever issues arise in 1992, he and the money he can raise will be key players. "I haven't gone very far. I've stayed here (Bucks County) all my life," he said. "I know this may sound philosophical, but I'm a country boy. I have been in the White House many, many times, and I am completely in awe and overwhelmed every time I get invited."

Republicans who know Barness' prowess are less surprised at the frequency of his trips to 1600 Pennsylvania Ave.

[*Interestingly, on October 27, 1990, there was a luncheon honoring Herbert Barness, "Our National Committeeman," at Bull Run Inn in Lewisburg, Pa., sponsored by The Union County Republican Committee, The Honorable Russell H. Fairchild, and Bob Garrett, Chairman of the Union County GOP. The above article was included in the invitation.*]

Program from Lunch with the President
Tuesday, June 24, 1990
Wyndham Franklin Plaza Hotel
Philadelphia, Pennsylvania

Master of Ceremonies: Herbert Barness, Republican National Committeeman of Pennsylvania
Address: George Bush, President, United States of America

Lunch

with the

President

Tuesday, June 24, 1990

Wyndham Franklin Plaza Hotel
Philadelphia, Pennsylvania

Herbert Barness and others meeting President Bush as he disembarks from Air Force One.

EXPERIENCE NETS BARNESS GOP COMMITTEE POSITION
Philadelphia Business Journal
July 23-29, 1990
By Gary Tuma, Special to the *Business Journal*

Asking other people for money is rarely pleasant.

But not many people do it better than Herb Barness, though he professes not to love the work.

"I don't think anybody enjoys it," Barness said. "But it is one of the necessities of political life."

That's exactly the roll-up-the sleeves attitude that has earned Barness a reputation among Republican insiders as a most effective fund-raiser. It resulted in his appointment recently to the prestigious and influential position of GOP national committee person, one of two from Pennsylvania. He replaced Drew Lewis of Montgomery County, who resigned effective June 23.

Barness was chosen partly to reward him for past services and partly in anticipation of continuing efforts to shake the money tree for Republican political candidates.

The 66-year-old Bucks County developer, who has previously shunned the limelight, said he did not aspire to the job.

"I never even gave it much thought," he said. "I just said if it would help, I would have an interest in doing it. I doubt that it will give me a higher profile. I'm just looking to be helpful."

State GOP chairwoman Anne Anstine, who made the appointment to fill Lewis' unexpired term, confirmed that Barness didn't campaign for the post. She had five potential replacement candidates on her list. When she contacted the 39 members of the leadership committee, she said, almost everyone agreed Barness would be an excellent choice.

The phrase one hears most frequently when asking about Barness is "behind the scenes."

"People either love or hate Herb Barness. Few people know him, though, even those who love him," said Andy Warren, chairman of the Bucks County commissioners. "He's a very behind-the-scenes guy. He's not interested in publicity for publicity's sake. He's not interested in being the show horse, but he is interested in being the groomer of the show horse."

The horse Barness is best known for backing lately is U.S. Sen. Arlen Specter (R-Philadelphia), for whom he has been campaign treasurer since 1980. Perhaps not coincidentally, Specter is regarded as a peerless builder of political war chests.

Barness has toiled for Republican candidates for 50 years, dating back to Wendell Wilkie's unsuccessful effort to unseat Franklin D. Roosevelt from the White House in 1940.

"I just didn't think any president should have a third term," Barness explained.

As his fortune and clout grew, he assumed more prominent roles in other campaigns. He was co-chair of the state finance committee for Ronald Reagan's presidential campaign and was William Scranton III's finance chairman when Scranton ran for lieutenant governor. He has also harvested money for the Bush presidential campaign in Pennsylvania, for U.S. Senator John Heinz, for former U.S Senator Richard Schweiker, and for Drew Lewis when Lewis ran for governor in 1974, among others.

Barness has lent his fund-raising skills to other causes as well, notably scouting and the arts. He was named Man of the Year last year by the Bucks County Boy Scouts of America.

A Bucks County native, Barness is a first-generation American whose Polish immigrant father, Joseph, started a real estate business. Barness served for 3-½ years in the Army Air Force, then earned a mechanical engineering degree from Bucknell.

He joined his father's business, expanding into development and becoming the wealthy head of what is now known as The Barness Corp. He still lives on a farm in Buckingham, in central Bucks County, and likes to refer to himself as a farmer. He works the land, raising primarily corn and soybeans.

Barness has engaged in other pursuits along the way. For a while he was part owner of the Philadelphia Eagles of the National Football League, and in horse-racing tracks.

He has been a delegate to the Republican National Convention and was a member of the Electoral College. He has also served for 10 years on a bipartisan panel that evaluates candidates for United States district judicial vacancies in Pennsylvania.

While Barness has opinions on issues, including a stance on abortion that has made him the subject of some controversy within the GOP, he claims he won't attempt to influence national policy just yet.

"He doesn't have his own agenda the way other people might," said Elsie Hillman of Pittsburgh, the state's other Republican national committee member. "He just wants to do a job."

Barness is a co-chairman of the national Republicans for Choice organization. That led unsuccessful GOP gubernatorial primary candidate Marguerite Luksik to protest his selection to the national committee last month. Luksik called Barness a liberal activist in a press release.

Barness describes himself as a moderate on social issues, but a longtime conservative on fiscal matters.

Mike Smerconish of the Main Street Group real estate firm in Bucks County, a close friend of Barness, describes him this way: His politics is like his golf game, conservative and consistent. He won't kill his drive, but it will always be in the fairway.

Barness hits the green too, in politics as well as golf.

The Philadelphia Inquirer
July 25, 1990
By Katherine Seelye, *Inquirer* Staff Writer

On a fund-raising trip yesterday to Philadelphia, President Bush declared his support for GOP gubernatorial candidate Barbara Hafer, who favors abortion rights, and at the same time heaped superlatives on his new U.S. Supreme Court nominee [David Souter], whose confirmation could tip the court's balance toward outlawing abortion.

Bush, Ronald D. Castille, and Herb Barness, Republican National Committee member, look perplexed over how to get Robbie Ziff, 8, to the microphone for the Pledge of Allegiance at the Franklin Plaza. Barness finally held Robbie up. [*This was so my dad!*]

GOP FUND-RAISERS LOOK TO KATZ AS ALTERNATIVE TO CASTILLE OR RIZZO

The Philadelphia Inquirer
August 1, 1990
By S.A. Paolantonio, *Inquirer* Staff Writer

Exasperated by District Attorney Ronald D. Castille's indecision over the 1991 mayoral race, top Republican fund-raisers are becoming increasingly serious about the prospects of municipal finance expert Samuel P. Katz and plan to meet with him today.

Fred Anton, one of the city's premier Republican fund-raisers, has invited Republican National Committeeman Herb Barness of Bucks County, state party finance chairman Mario Mele, former Rohm & Haas chief executive F. Otto Haas and others to meet Katz and discuss raising money for his fledgling campaign.

PRESENTING TORCH OF LIFE AWARD
The Jewish Exponent
August 31, 1990

The Anti-Defamation League of B'nai B'rith presented its Torch of Life Award to Fred A. Shabel, chairman of Spectacor, at a recent dinner event. Harmon Spolan, immediate past chairman of the ADL's Metropolitan Philadelphia Advisory Board, presents the award to Shabel, as looking on are Scott Feigelstein, regional director of ADL; Herbert Barness, chairman of The Barness Organization and co-chairman of the dinner committee; Jay Snider, president of the Philadelphia Flyers and co-chairman of the dinner committee; and Milton Schneider, chairman of the Metropolitan Philadelphia Advisory Board.

1991

Program from the United Way of Bucks County's Leadership Giving Circle Recognition
1991

At this event, a Commendation was presented to John F. McCaughan, CEO and Chairman of the Board of Betz Laboratories, Inc., by Bucks County Commissioner Mark Schweiker, and to Herbert Barness, by Bucks County Commissioner Andrew L. Warren. In the program, there was a page about McCaughan and also one about Herbert Barness.

Herbert Barness
Chairman of the Board
The Barness Organization

The philanthropy of Herb Barness has been felt strongly and for many years in Bucks County.

As a developer of real estate and one of the largest developers of senior citizen housing, he has helped to meet the needs of communities both locally and worldwide.

A leader in both professional, civic and philanthropic activities, his community service and leadership recognition includes: the American Legion Certificate of Meritorious Service; Big Brothers of America Outstanding Service Award; Boy Scouts Service Award; Technion Humanitarian Award; U.S. Blind Golfers Outstanding Service Award; Pop Warner Little Scholars Outstanding Service to Youth Award.

Herb Barness has been committed to serving as a good neighbor and a responsible corporate citizen. He has continually taken an active part in improving the quality of life in Bucks County.

As a member of the United Way's Alexis de Tocqueville Society he has demonstrated his leadership commitment to helping our community's most pressing human problems.

AT A CLEARING IN THE WOODS, 92 NEW TOWNHOUSES
The Philadelphia Inquirer
April 26, 1991
By Sheila Dyan, Special to the *Inquirer*

A community within a community, Ashford Glen is offering 92 new townhouses in a pocket of Terrestria, a wooded development built more than 10 years ago in Sicklerville.

The Barness Organization, based in Bucks County, is into its third generation of home builders. For 60 years, it has built primarily in Bucks and Montgomery counties but within the last 10 years has developed communities in Smithville and Cape May, N.J. Ashford Glen is the builder's first venture into Camden County.

Profile from the *Republican National Committee Directory*

PENNSYLVANIA
Herbert Barness

National Committeeman for Pennsylvania, appointed June 7, 1990.

Wife: Irma.

B.S., Bucknell Univ. Also attended: Barnes Art Foundation; Fels Institute; Wharton Grad School.

Member, PA Rep. State Fin. Cmte.

Mbr, Bucks Cnty Rep. Fin. Cmte.

Del., Rep. Natl. Conv., 1968.

Mbr., PA Electoral Coll, 1972

Co-Chrmn, PA Fin. Cmte, Reagan for Pres., 1980

Mbr., Natl. Society of Prof. Engineers

Mbr., American Society of Mechanical Engineers

Mbr., The Society of American Military Engineers

Mbr., National Association of Home Builders

Mbr. Bucks Cnty Bd. of Realtors

Appt. by Pres. Reagan to Pres. Comm. On Housing

Recipient, Outstanding Service Toward Community Award, Bucks County Council Boy Scouts of America

Recipient, Outstanding Service to Youth Award, Pop Warner Little Scholars

Recipient, Outstanding Service Award, Big Brothers of America

Recipient, American Legion Certificate of Meritorious Service

Chairman of the Board, The Barness Organization

Rev. 9/91

1992

The Philadelphia Inquirer
September 19, 1992

My dad is the fifth person from the right (the one wearing glasses).

President Bush is greeted by local officials at Willow Grove Naval Air Station. Photo by Sean Patrick Duffy of the *Inquirer*.

HERBERT BARNESS SELECTED VFC CITIZEN OF THE YEAR
Boy Scouts of America Today
January 1992

Chairman of the Board, The Barness Organization, Herbert Barness has been selected as Valley Forge Council's 1992 Citizen of the Year. Active in civic and professional organizations, Mr. Barness will be honored at a reception on February 19, 4:30 to 6:30 p.m., atop the ARA Tower in Philadelphia. This affair, designed to raise money for Valley Forge Scouting, is run by the Reception Committee chaired by Charles G. Kopp, Esq., Chairman of the Executive Committee of Wolf, Block, Schorr & Solis-Cohen. Andrew L. Lewis, IV, Valley Forge Council Executive Board member, is Sponsorship Chair for the event. Levels of sponsorships are $2,500, $1,000, and $500. Attendance is $250 for each person.

Mr. Barness' civic involvements, both past and present, include Bucks County Council, BSA; The Pennsylvania Society; The Delaware Valley Philharmonic Orchestra; Pop Warner Little Scholars; Welcome House; Washington Crossing Foundation; and Philadelphia's Annual Teenage Achievement Award. Deeply interested in government, Mr. Barness serves on the President's Commission on Housing; U.S. Attorney Selection Commission; and the Federal Judicial Nominating Commission. He is the National Republican Committeeman of Pennsylvania.

Program from CITIZEN OF THE YEAR Award Ceremony
Wednesday, February 19, 1992
Top of the ARA Tower
Philadelphia, PA

CITIZEN OF THE YEAR

Wednesday, February 19, 1992
Top of the ARA Tower
Philadelphia, PA

Herbert Barness: Citizen of the Year

In Herbert Barness, the Valley Forge Council [*of the Boy Scouts*] honors an individual who has had an extraordinary positive influence in our community.

Herbert Barness is a visible and active supporter of civic, community, and philanthropic causes. He serves on the Advisory Board of the Boy Scouts of America's Bucks County Council, and was Chairman of the Board of Pop Warner Little Scholars, Inc. He is a director of the Washington Crossing Foundation and Past Chairman of Pearl S. Buck's Welcome House. He is a director and former President of the Pennsylvania Society and a Director of the Annual Teenage Achievement Award. Mr. Barness is Past Chairman of the Bucks County Park Foundation and Bucks County Planning Commission. He is a Member of the American Legion and the Veterans of Foreign Wars.

Active in real estate financing, brokerage, development and property management, Mr. Barness is Chairman of the Board of The Barness Organization.

A former partner of the Philadelphia Eagles Football Club, Mr. Barness is Past President of the American Technion Society's Philadelphia Chapter, a Charter Member of the Bucks County Home Builders Association, and Past President and Director of the Bucks County Industrial Development Corporation. With all this he still has found time to serve on the Regional Board of Continental Bank, the President's Commission on Housing, and the Federal Judicial Selection Commission.

Mr. Barness' political activities include being Republican National Committeeman of Pennsylvania.

Mr. Barness and his wife, Irma, reside outside of Doylestown. They have two daughters and four granddaughters.

BOY SCOUTS HONOR BARNESS

The Daily Intelligencer
February 21, 1992

Citing his "extraordinary positive influence" on civic and community affairs throughout the region, state and nation, the Valley Forge Council of the Boy Scouts of America honored developer Herbert Barness as Citizen of the Year.

The award was presented to Barness, who lives in Buckingham, at a reception Wednesday in the Top of the ARA Tower, Philadelphia. Some 200 business leaders, Scouting executives and government officials, including state Auditor General Barbara Hafer, attended.

The council is comprised of Boy Scout troops in Montgomery, Delaware and Chester counties. Barness, chairman of The Barness Organization, Warrington, serves on the advisory board of the Bucks County Council.

The council noted that Barness is "a visible and active supporter" of numerous other causes with time, leadership, and philanthropy. He is a past chairman of Pop Warner Little Scholars and Pearl S. Buck's Welcome House.

He is Republican National Committeeman of Pennsylvania and serves on the President's Commission on Housing and the Federal Judicial Selection Commission.

State Rep. David W. Heckler, R143, presented Barness with a commendation resolution adopted by the Pennsylvania Legislature.

HERBERT BARNESS HONORED AS CITIZEN OF THE YEAR
Boy Scouts of America Today
April 1992

DUTY TO GOD & COUNTRY. At the core of the Boy Scouting is citizenship. Honoring Herbert Barness as the 1992 Citizen of the Year reinforced the belief in good citizenship and promoting the well being of everyone in the community throughout one's lifetime. Sharing in the celebration at ARA Towers were Joseph Paquette, Jr., CEP, Philadelphia Electric Company; Matthew Morak, Troop 260; Greg Cluver, Troop 151; Nick DeBenedictis, senior vice president, corporate and public affairs; Herbert Barness, honoree; Ed Fitzsimmons, vice president, ARA Services and president, Valley Forge Council.

WHAT WAS YOUR FAVORITE CHILDHOOD BOOK?
The Intelligencer/Record
Undated [*but the article mentions that Herbert Barness is 69, so the year must be 1992.*]
By Edward Levenson, Staff Writer

Long after the fads of childhood have been forgotten, the books of childhood will be remembered. Fourteen Bucks and Montgomery residents aged 20 to 84 were asked to recall their favorite book from their elementary school years.

Herbert Barness, 69, of Buckingham is chairman of The Barness Organization. Barness, who attended a one-room school in Doylestown Township in the 1930s, could not remember a specific favorite.

"In those days, we read books like Jack London's *The Call of the Wild*. They were always popular," he said.

He said he enjoyed adventure books and liked to use his imagination.

BUCKINGHAM EYES ZONING EXEMPTION
The Intelligencer/Record
July 8, 1992
By Robert Benincasa, *Intelligencer* Staff Writer

In an effort to improve their position in a turf war they are fighting with a private company over valuable public water service rights in the township, Buckingham supervisors tonight may move to exempt the municipal government from every provision of its own zoning ordinance.

The Buckingham Water Co., of which developer Herbert Barness is listed as chief executive officer in state government records, asked the Pennsylvania Public Utility Commission to serve about 1,600 acres in the Cold Spring Creamery Road corridor, Buckingham's chief residential development frontier

The township government, which has formed its own Cold Spring Water Co. to serve more than 1,200 anticipated homes, protested the October 1991 application.

After the protest was filed, the township had been negotiating with the private company in an attempt to resolve the dispute over the lucrative service rights, according to Buckingham Water Co. attorney Barnett Satinsky of Philadelphia.

Satinsky hinted the negotiations were unsuccessful and said the company is "reactivating" its application, which had been placed "on hold."

BUCKINGHAM APPROVES 378 HOMES
The Intelligencer
July 9, 1992
By Robert Benincasa, *Intelligencer* Staff Writer

Buckingham Township Supervisors gave final approval Wednesday to the initial 378-unit portion of Nanlyn Farms for what will be a 734-home development along Durham Road, bordered by Hansell and Cold Spring Creamery roads.

Construction of the detached homes will take about four years of what is expected to be a decade-long build-out for the entire project, according to representatives of the Warrington-based developer, The Barness Organization.

The project—which will include townhouses, condominiums and a 5-acre commercial section for which no use has been announced—is built around the estate of company chairman Herbert Barness.

Barness won the right to develop the multi-family housing on the land after settling a "curative amendment" lawsuit he and other landowners filed against Buckingham Township in 1974.

Barness' house and a 6-acre portion around it with 13 home lots will be marketed to prospective buyers as a single offering, according to planner Steven Gilmore.

Barness has agreed to serve Nanlyn Farms with public water provided by the municipally owned Cold Spring Water Co.

The developer was previously a principal in the privately owned Buckingham Water Co., but said Wednesday that contrary to state government corporate records he had not been involved in the private company "for at least a year."

The records, which have not been updated, were cited in a report in *The Intelligencer* on Wednesday.

Sewage from the development will be treated and sprayed on the nearby Lojeski Tract, which Barness leased from the Bucks County government for 99 years at a cost of $1 million.

With the approval comes an agreement by the developer to make more than $300,000 in "donations" to the township for road improvements, a traffic signal at Route 413 and Cold Spring Creamery Road, and other public facilities.

The agreement requires Barness to widen Cold Spring Creamery and Hansell roads along the development's property lines according to state Transportation Department regulations.

Pending resolution of some wetland crossing regulations, a paved, 4-foot-wide bicycle path will wind through the neighborhoods, from Cold Spring Creamery Road to Hansell Road.

By the time a development and escrow agreement is ready to be signed, the township government must decide whether to accept about 60 acres of open space and wetlands as public property, or leave it in the hands of a homeowners association.

The township planning commission, which conditionally recommended approval of the project on Monday, advised that the township not accept the land because of the cost of maintaining it and potential liability from its use.

The ad for the preview opening of Hearthstone, the first community built on what had been Nanlyn Farms.

Membership in the Philadelphia Association of Golf Course Superintendents
1992

My dad had so much fun with miscellaneous honors like these!

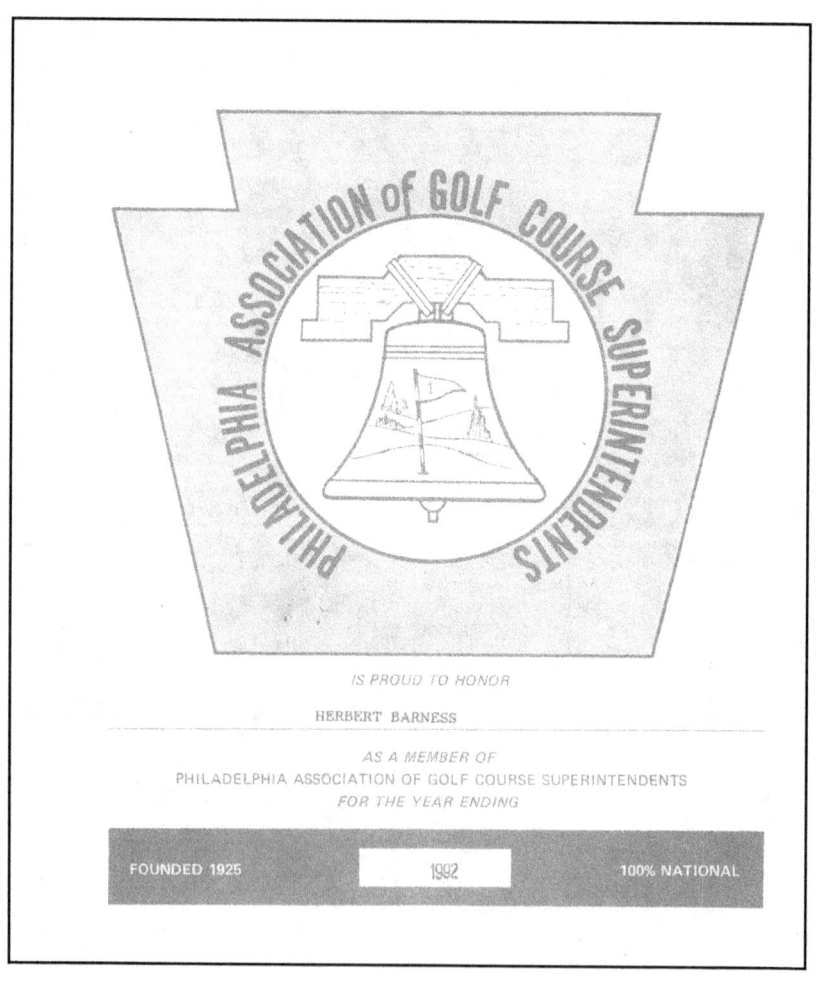

Award of Honor from Top Farmers of America Association
1992

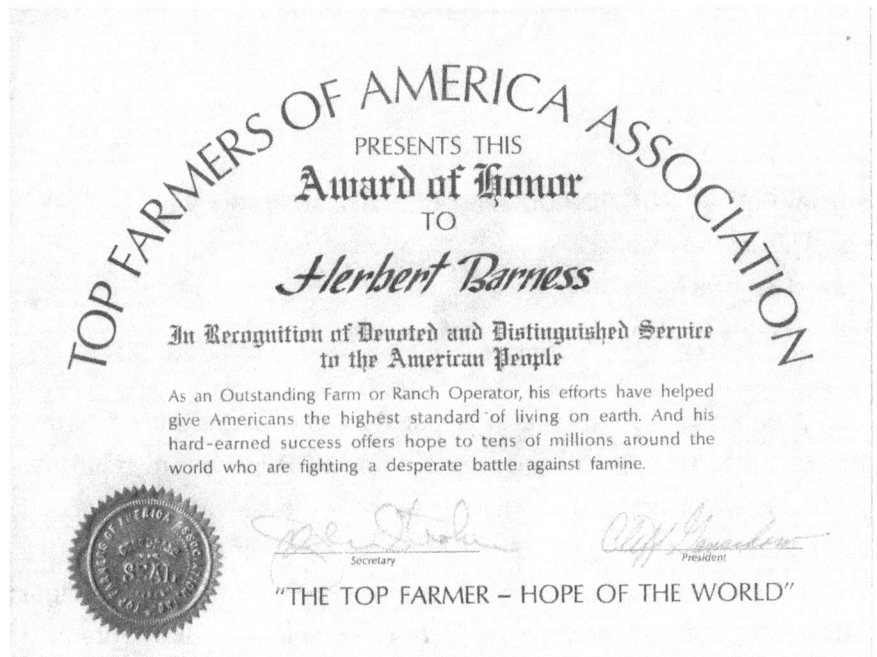

1993

A SHAKEDOWN RUN FOR GOP HOPEFULS: CAMPAIGN '94
The Philadelphia Inquirer
August 12, 1993
By Katherine Seelye, *Inquirer* Staff Writer

Faced with a virtual armada of Republican candidates for next year's governor and U.S. Senate races, suburban GOP leaders meeting here yesterday suggested the candidates winnow the fields themselves and spare the party a costly blood bath in next May's primary election.

Including Philadelphia, the suburban counties boast the strongest GOP voting block in Pennsylvania, with 43 percent of primary voters.

The meeting, held at the Days Inn near the Philadelphia International Airport, included a half-hour interview with each candidate. The discussions had almost nothing to do with candidates' positions on issues and everything to do with the mechanics of campaigning: How much money could a candidate raise? Would geography work for or against the candidate? How would gender affect the races?

The hopefuls included six probable candidates for governor and four for the U.S. Senate seat held by Democrat Harris Wofford.

The GOP leaders attending were: McNichol and Thomas Judge of Delaware County, Bill Lamb of Chester County, Herb Barness of Bucks County, Frank Bartle of Montgomery County and State Senate Minority Leader Robert C. Jubelirer. Those unable to attend included Billy Meehan and Don Jamieson of Philadelphia and Elsie Hillman and Henry Sneath of Pittsburgh.

1994

GOP SENATORS HOSTED BY SPECTER TO SPEND A WEEKEND IN THE BIG CITY

The Philadelphia Inquirer
April 13, 1994
By Steve Goldstein, *Inquirer* Washington Bureau

When a large contingent of Republican U.S. senators arrives Friday in Philadelphia for a weekend retreat, don't be surprised to catch them gawking.

Most of the GOP lawmakers represent states better known for exurbs than cities, for up-country rather than downtown.

"They are traveling to the nation's fifth most-populous city for an education," said host Sen. Arlen Specter, (R, Pa.).

On Saturday, discussions are scheduled from 9 a.m. to 3 p.m., followed by informal tours of the city. Dinner Saturday evening, sponsored by Bucks County developer Herb Barness, will be at Carpenters Hall.

United States Golf Association recognizes NANLYN GOLF CLUB as a Member Course

1994

I think that my dad just applied to the USGA for this recognition as a lark! He loved to play golf in his own backyard with his friends, and this gave official recognition to the course.

United States Golf Association®

Recognizes

Nanlyn Golf Club
as a MEMBER COURSE for 1994

The United States Golf Association,® founded "for the purpose of promoting and conserving throughout the United States the best interests and the true spirit of the game of golf, as embodied in its ancient and honorable traditions," extends its sincere appreciation for membership support of these same ideals.

F. Morgan Taylor, Jr.
Secretary

Reg Murphy
President

BARNESS & WELSH HONORED AT BCIDC ANNUAL MEETING
Bucks Prospectus
Spring 1994
Bucks County Industrial Development Corporation
In partnership with the Industrial Development Authority

On February 17, 1994, the BCIDC celebrated its 35th year of service to Bucks County.

Honored at the meeting, Herbert Barness and John T. Welsh, two of the CBCIDC's Founding Fathers, were applauded for their insight and ideas, which created the BCIDC 36 years ago. Both were presented with plaques that recognized and thanked them for their commitment, contributions and dedication in the creation of the corporation.

THE BARNESS ORGANIZATION: A VISION FOR THE FUTURE
Builder/Architect Philadelphia Edition
February 1994
By Dolores Little

Back in the 1920s, when the wheels of horse-drawn carriages defined the roadway we now call Route 611, Joseph Barness purchased some acreage for his home and chicken farm in Warrington, Bucks County.

It was a time when just about everyone was trying to improve their standard of living. Joseph Barness was no exception. Because he spoke several languages, he often assisted fellow immigrants with their housing purchases. Developing more than a casual interest in real estate, he envisioned a "total" community and toward that end, he worked for better housing, better roads and improved municipal services.

In 1923, the seeds for The Barness Organization were planted with the purchase and development of 80 acres in Bucks County. At that time,

Joseph Barness also made a guarantee few builders could make at that time—electricity in every home.

"This is a family business," said granddaughter Lynda Barness. "We have been in this community forever. This office is within a half-mile of the original Barness office in my grandparents' home."

Today, the company is headed by Joseph's son, Herbert Barness, who is chairman of the board …

Herbert Barness took the company into its expansion, an expansion that saw not only product diversification, but management and geographic expansion, as well. Going from a single-family home developer, the company began developing townhouses, multi-family residences, government-assisted housing for seniors, and office and commercial development. Geographically, the company expanded gradually over the years, with development not only in Pennsylvania, but in New Jersey, Delaware, and some international work in Mexico and the Caribbean.

1995

SPECTER UPBEAT DESPITE RIDGE SUPPORT OF DOLE
Source unknown
Undated

To U.S. Sen. Arlen Specter, it must be a bitter political irony that everyone wanted to know when Colin Powell, a non-candidate, would get into the presidential race while at the same time wondering when Specter, a candidate for eight months, would get out.

But yesterday, stepping off the train from Washington, D.C., Specter was upbeat and unbowed after a week that began with his wife Joan's loss of her City Council seat and ended yesterday with Gov. Ridge's endorsement of U.S. Sen. Robert Dole for the GOP presidential nomination.

Specter discounted the impact of Ridge's endorsement, noting that he had the backing of his Pennsylvania Republican colleague, U.S. Sen. Rick Santorum, and the state's two Republican national committee people, Elsie Hillman and Herbert Barness.

AT 71, BARNESS STILL GOING STRONG
The Intelligencer/Record
February 24, 1995
By Margaret Quann, Staff Writer

This article included a large photograph, two smaller ones, two boxes with information, and lots of copy!

Developer Herbert Barness looks at a family picture take in 1928 that hangs in his office in Warrington. He is the little boy on the left. Barness' father, Joseph Barness, an immigrant farmer, began selling houses to other immigrants in 1925. His son followed in his footsteps. Staff photo by E. Stace Leichliter.

WHETHER IT'S BUILDING OR POLITICS, HE SHAPES THE REGION'S LANDSCAPE

When Herbert Barness was a child in the 1920s, the region was bucolic. Rolling farmland. Cows grazing in open fields. One-room schoolhouses such as Castle Valley in Doylestown Township, the school he attended.

Electricity, that newfangled invention that lit the cities and small towns, still hadn't gone country. Kerosene lamps provided the lighting in farmhouses. And baths? Well, they were taken in a washtub of water that had been warmed on the wood-burning kitchen stove.

It was to this very rural area that his parents came in 1922 after arriving in Philadelphia from their native Poland and Russia. Joseph and Mary Barness were from farming families, and they wanted to farm.

They bought a tract of land about two miles off Route 611 in Doylestown Township.

Soon, Barness said, his father realized that "as an immigrant, there were a lot of other immigrants who wanted to live in the country, not the cities, so he decided to sell real estate while still farming."

In 1925, Joseph Barness built a house to sell. When it sold, he built another.

From those small beginnings grew The Barness Organization, one of the area's most dominant development firms. It celebrates its 70th anniversary this year.

Herbert Barness was just 1 year old when the company was founded. Now, he is chairman of the board and an influential businessman, civic leader and political aficionado. An engineer, he is a trustee of his alma mater, Bucknell University. Statewide, he is a political power. Nationally, he is one of only two Pennsylvania representatives to the National Republican Committee.

Last year, he was a co-chairman of Gov. Ridge's election campaign and contributed more than $60,000 to it.

"I've always had an interest in politics," said Barness, sitting in his fireplace-warmed office in Warrington. A cabinet filled with colorful candy to satisfy a sweet tooth and to offer visitors is situated nearby.

Ridge, he said, "will be very good for business" in the state.

Barness, himself, has been like a candy man to the Republican Party.

Harry W. Fawkes, chairman of the Bucks County Republican Committee, has been a friend for more than 30 years. "Every time a candidate ran, Herb always worked hard, always raised a lot of money for them," he said. "And he's been very good to the people ... with different volunteer groups."

For several years, Barness was a part owner of the Philadelphia Eagles, during Leonard Tose's reign.

More recently, watching from a distance as owner Jeffrey Lurie chose a new football coach, Barness declined to say much about Lurie's selection—Ray Rhodes, former defensive coordinator of the San Francisco 49ers.

"I don't even know who he is, never heard of him," Barness said the morning after Rhodes' selection.

But he had no yearning to be in Lurie's shoes.

"No, absolutely not," Barness said. "When you own a professional team, everyone feels it belongs to them in the community. And it's true, it does. It's a very interesting business, a very difficult business. I do not envy him at all."

Instead, Barness has put much of his energy into maintaining and expanding The Barness Organization. Headquartered along Route 611 in Warrington, it is a firm of international repute. It builds houses, apartments, offices, industrial parks and shopping centers along the East Coast and as far away as Mexico and Jamaica. The company has developed a number of housing sites in Bucks and Montgomery counties, as well as condominiums and parking garages in Atlantic City during the casino boom.

Still, when you visit Barness' office, you still get the feeling he is a hometown guy.

Looking over his shoulder in his office is an enlarged photo of his parents with him and his brother, Lewis, when they were young children. A model of the Castle Valley schoolhouse sits nearby.

Herbert Barness attended Castle Valley School, a one-room schoolhouse, when he was a boy. A model of it sits in his Warrington office. Staff photo by E. Stace Leichliter. [*Actually this was not a model of Castle Valley School itself. My sister and I bought this for our dad because it reminded us of the stories he had told us!*]

At 71, Barness is still going strong. Still a shrewd businessman. Still active in politics. Still looking to the future. Still building on the past. His father, he said, "had vision. He loved living out here and he knew other people would, too."

With the Great Depression, Joseph Barness' fledgling efforts to develop Central Bucks County received a big push. So many people were out of work and standing in food lines that the security of owning a piece of farmland where they could grow their own food became increasingly attractive.

During those years, the elder Barness "fought desperately to get electricity up here. He got together with the farmers and they finally succeeded," said his son.

Electricity did run along the road, now Route 611, to connect Doylestown to Willow Grove. But supplying it to outlying areas would mean more land could be developed for housing. Housing for those who wanted a country lifestyle close to the city—the new suburbanites.

Son Herbert is still at it, but now the commodity isn't electricity, it's water and sewer capacity. In Buckingham Township, where Barness' 734-unit Nanlyn Farms development is the symbolic centerpiece of a huge development corridor, he put up $1 million for a sewage treatment site.

New township supervisor Henry Rowan, long a foe of development in Buckingham, compliments Barness for his professionalism in developing the homes—despite slamming him on a project he says is no good for the township.

"He has shown a willingness to try and work with the issues," Rowan said, adding, "I don't think any of (Barness' development) is for the benefit of the township. It's being done for the benefit of The Barness Organization."

When Barness speaks of change, he talks about Lower Bucks.

"Buck County was ... all a bedroom community until 1950 when U.S. Steel came into Falls Township," he said. "That changed the complexion of Bucks County."

With the steel came the steelworkers who wanted affordable housing close to work. That led to the birth of Levittown and, eventually, expanded housing development countywide. The Barness Organization was ready and waiting.

Developers—especially ones as powerful and prolific as Barness—have become common targets of those who strive to preserve the remaining open space in the suburbs.

"A developer doesn't build unless there's a market," Barness said. "We fill a demand. If people don't want to move to an area, a developer won't build there. There's always the question: Do people follow industry or does industry follow people?"

Plus, he said, the nature of the region has changed.

"We were a great farming community. I farmed myself for many years," he said. "It is very difficult to compete today as a farmer. The younger generation doesn't want to work 24 hours as a farmer."

Major corporations from New York and elsewhere have moved to the Philadelphia suburbs, he noted, because they "found a good labor pool here. The work ethic is excellent."

Under Ridge's state leadership, Barness expects more tax advantages that will lure more industry to Pennsylvania. He expects less of what he calls "intrusion by government."

"We're overregulated, over-governed," he said. "Government is involved entirely too much in our daily lives. I certainly think municipalities are overregulated."

Barness has engaged in feisty battles with local officials over some of his development plans. Through court order, he and six other developers forced a change in Buckingham's zoning laws to allow for higher-density housing. The township appealed unsuccessfully all the way to the U.S. Supreme Court. Today, to the delight of some and the chagrin of others, Buckingham is one of the fastest-growing communities in Central Bucks. Barness, who resided on the 90-acre Nanlyn Farms estate in Buckingham, has moved to neighboring Solebury.

In 1980, when the company decided to sell the Warrington Country Club, a 144-acre private golf course, Barness offered it to Bucks County officials for $1.2 million. But county officials differed about the price and the wisdom of buying the property at that time. They asked Barness for a six-month extension to consider it, but he refused.

Six years later, the Cutler Group, a development firm in Montgomery Township, purchased it for the purpose of building more than 200 homes. By then, Barness had spent nine years trying to get township approval to develop the land. The township approved the property for development several months before Barness sold it.

When Barness needed a sewage system in order to build and sell homes in the Buckingham area, he opted not to wait for the Chalfont-New Britain sewage treatment plant to be expanded. Instead, he helped pay for a spray irrigation system to treat wastewater from the new developments, then allow the treated wastewater to be sprayed over fields and filtered back into the ground water. Like his father pressing for electricity, Barness sees spray irrigation as a wave of the future. More and more communities will use it, he thinks, "because it will regenerate the water supply ... It goes back into the soil."

As chairman of the board of The Barness Organization, he has no intentions of retiring.

His daughter, Lynda Barness, a vice president of the firm, sees her father's energy and commitment firsthand. He rises early to swim at 5:30 each morning. "He's in the office before anyone," she says. At home, he and Irma, his wife of 47 years, relish sharing in the lives of their offspring—two daughters and four granddaughters.

"Family is the most important thing for him ... the center of everything for him. He's a doting grandfather and wonderful dad," said Lynda. "I just consider myself so lucky to be able to work with him. He's very open, and willing to share ... a wonderful and patient teacher."

His daughter, Nancy, is married to Craig Stein, owner of the Phillies' farm team in Reading. His brother, Lewis, is a pediatrician and professor of pediatrics at the University of South Florida.

"If I had it to do all over again," Barness said, "I would choose what I've been doing, meeting wonderful people and doing great things.'"

Herbert Barness builds houses, apartments, offices, industrial parks and shopping centers along the East Coast and as far away as Mexico and Jamaica. Staff photo by E. Stace Leighliter.

QUOTES by Herbert Barness:

- On Gov. Tom Ridge: "He will be very good for business."
- On development: "A developer doesn't build unless there's a market. We fill a demand. If people don't want to move to an area, a developer won't build there."
- On farming: "It is very difficult to compete today as a farmer. The younger generation doesn't want to work 24 hours as a farmer."
- On government: "We're overregulated, over-governed. Government is involved entirely too much in our daily lives. I certainly think municipalities are overregulated."
- On the Philadelphia Eagles and owner Jeff Lurie: "When you own a professional team, everyone feels it belongs to them in the community. And it's true, it does. It's a very interesting business, a very difficult business. I do not envy him at all."

A (Small) SAMPLING OF PROPERTIES THAT HAVE BEEN OWNED AND/OR DEVELOPED BY THE BARNESS ORGANIZATION:

- Dalton Glen, semi-custom homes, Buckingham Twp., Bucks County
- Heritage Towers, senior citizen mid-rise, Doylestown, Bucks County
- Face Off Circle, ice-skating rink, Warminster Twp., Bucks County
- Glenbrook townhouses, New Britain Twp., Bucks County
- Keystone Race Track, Bensalem Twp., Bucks County
- Moreland Towers, senior citizen apartments, Hatboro, Montgomery County
- Montgomery Brook condominiums, Royersford, Montgomery County
- Ashford Glen townhouses, Sicklerville, N.J.

CHOOSE FROM THREE BARNESS SITES IN BUCKINGHAM TOWNSHIP: BEAUTIFUL DESIGNS, ATTRACTIVE PRICES
The Philadelphia Inquirer
March 10, 1995

Naturally the Barness Organization advertised its homes for sale. This was one description of the homes that were built on Nanlyn Farms.

The Barness Organization is celebrating its 70th year in homebuilding and is proud to present three different communities in historic Bucks County. These homes are beautifully designed and attractively priced.

- Fireside, a townhome community, has eight models from which to choose. Fireside offers first- or second-floor master bedroom suites, formal and casual living spaces, abundant storage, a one- or two-car garage and two or three bedrooms. Standard features in all Fireside homes include gas heat, decorator kitchens with full wall-height cabinets, elegant baths with ceramic tile floors and shower surrounds, and a sodded front lawn. Basements and fireplaces are available. The homes range in size from 1,220 to 2,074 s.f. and in price from $124,900 to $160,900.

- Hearthstone, a single-family home community, is a selection of exceptional homes. Inside each is a soaring foyer, a full basement, lots of storage space, a soaking tub, gas heat, and three or four bedrooms. And there are eight sparkling ponds in the community and intimate cul-de-sacs creating neighborhoods within neighborhoods. No two homes next to each other can have the identical elevation, so there is individuality both within the interiors and exteriors of the homes. There is a choice of siding, brick or stone facades and the homes blend into the natural landscape. There are five models from which to choose, ranging in size from 1,822 to 2,876 s.f. and in price from $179,900 to $210,400.

- Dalton Glen, a semi-custom home community, is the newest addition. This community offers many choices: four or five bedrooms, 2½ to 4½ baths, and master suites on the first or second floors. Standard features in these sophisticated homes include a grand two-story foyer entrance with hardwood flooring, a fireplace and basement, a dramatic staircase (or two), nine-foot ceilings, gas heat, General Electric appliances, including a microwave, a luxurious master bath with a soaking tub, Andersen windows, and more. The homes range in size from 2,666 to 3,540 s.f. and in price from $241,900 to $301,900.

Each of the three communities has a sales office that is open seven days a week from noon to 5 p.m. and at other times by appointment.

GOP MEETING SET FOR PHILADELPHIA
The Intelligencer/Record
July 12, 1995
By Edward Levenson, Staff Writer

Republican presidential candidates will converge on Philadelphia later this week for the semi-annual meeting of the Republican National Committee.

Herbert Barness, national committeeman from Solebury, Pennsylvania, said he expects the meeting, which runs Thursday through Saturday, will focus on routine organizational matters rather than a political platform.

That doesn't mean there won't be politics, however.

Most of the GOP presidential contenders—including U.S. Senators Arlen Specter, Bob Dole, Phil Gramm and Richard Lugar—are scheduled to address the committee at different times on Friday and Saturday.

Pennsylvania Republican Gov. Tom Ridge will be the speaker at Friday's luncheon. Speaker of the House Newt Gingrich will talk Friday morning, and national party chairman Haley Barbour will speak at Saturday's closing luncheon.

Barness is one of 165 members of the national committee, which sets the GOP's national policy and assists Republican candidates for political office. Each state, plus the District of Columbia and four U.S. territories, is represented by a committeeman, a committeewoman and the state chairman.

At least 145 members are expected to attend the meeting at the Wyndham Franklin Plaza Hotel in Center City, according to Barness. This is the first time the committee has met in Philadelphia.

"The party is not yet drafting a platform for next year's presidential convention in San Diego," said Barness, chairman of The Barness Organization, a residential and commercial development company.

"I think President Clinton is very, very vulnerable. I think we have an excellent chance (to regain the White House)," said Barness, who described himself as a "moderate conservative."

The GOP's unity, however, could become an issue.

"I don't know about a split between the ultra-conservatives and the moderates," Barness said. "There certainly is a difference of opinion. Hopefully, it will not be reflected in 1996."

The national committee will lay the groundwork for the elections this fall and in 1996, according to a press release.

Invitation from AN EVENING OF HONORS by the Pennsylvania Association of Broadcasters
October 16, 1995

THE PENNSYLVANIA ASSOCIATION
OF BROADCASTERS
CORDIALLY INVITES YOU TO
JOIN IN OUR SALUTE
TO

GOVERNOR TOM RIDGE

GOLD MEDAL AWARD

HERBERT BARNESS

AMBASSADOR'S AWARD

OCTOBER 16, 1995

LONGWOOD GARDENS, KENNETT SQUARE

R.S.V.P. CARD ENCLOSED

Please join in our celebration of two Pennsylvanians who have honored our state and country with their lifelong leadership, commitment and generosity.

We are honored to present our Ambassador's Award to Herbert Barness, a National Republican Committeeman, Developer, Engineer and devoted family man. Previous winners include Governor Richard Thornburgh and Senator Arlen Specter.

Our 30th Gold Medal will be presented to Governor Tom Ridge. We honor his services to our country in time of war, his 12 years of Congressional leadership, his devotion to family and the betterment of all Pennsylvanians. Previous Gold Medal winners include Walter Annenberg, Arnold Palmer, Dick Clark, Alexander Haig, James Michener, Roy Campanella, Shirley Jones and William Scranton.

POWELL WILL NOT RUN: Rules Out Race For President
The Intelligencer/Record
November 9, 1995

After months of "prayerful consideration" that captivated the nation, Colin Powell awkwardly embraced the Republican Party on Wednesday but said he would not run for president in 1996 because it was "a calling that I do not yet hear."

WHAT LOCAL LEADERS ARE SAYING ABOUT POWELL'S DECISION:
"I think, obviously, it helps Sen. Dole more than anyone else. He is the front-runner. I think a lot of people were holding back to see what Powell would do."—Herb Barness, president of the Barness Organization and a national Republican committeeman

GOV. RIDGE SET TO TOP $2 MILLION: The Governor's Ball should do it. More than $425,000 could be raised
The Philadelphia Inquirer
November 17, 1995
By Robert Zausner, *Inquirer* Staff Writer

By the time the clock strikes midnight at the Governor's Ball tonight, Gov. Ridge will have already turned into a multi-millionaire.

To be more precise, his campaign committee will have topped $2 million collected in contributions this year, thanks to the fancy affair to be held in Hershey.

That sum was the goal the campaign had set for itself for year's end. It won't have to wait that long.

Eight people signed up to be co-chairmen for the ball, which required a $25,000 commitment, while 17 signed up to be vice chairman, at $10,000 a pop, and 48 will be on the "dinner committee," an honor that comes with a $5,000 commitment. Those commitments alone add up to $610,000.

Among the chairmen of the ball are Bob Asher, the former Montgomery County Republican chairman, and Herbert Barness, a Bucks County developer and national GOP committeeman.

1996

FOCUS: BEHIND THE POLITICAL SCENES
Herb Barness '48 is a major player in the Republican Party at the State and National Level
Bucknell World
January 1996
By Kathie Dibell

Herb Barness dismisses GOP presidential hopeful Patrick Buchanan as "too far to the right," says of political gadfly Ross Perot, "I would like for him to disappear," and gives Newt Gingrich a seven on a scale of 10.

The average American voter may not have heard of Barness or care what he thinks, but his opinion is of upmost importance to politicians and potential candidates. Barness '48, a member of Bucknell's Board of Trustees since 1979, has never run for office, but the prominent Bucks County, Pa., developer is a major player on the political scene.

Sen. Arlen Specter, R-Pa., has known Barness since 1965. "He is an outstanding guy, very public spirited, very charitable, very active politically, a good friend of mine, well-respected around the country," Specter says.

Barness has been Pennsylvania's Republican National Committeeman since 1989, has been a delegate to seven GOP conventions, was on the site selection committee for the 1996 convention in San Diego and will serve on the convention's committee on arrangements.

He was co-chairman of the Pennsylvania finance committee in Ronald Reagan's presidential campaigns, state vice-chairman of the Bush-Quayle campaign, co-chairman of Pennsylvania Governor Tom Ridge's campaign and chairman of Specter's senatorial campaigns. He served on the President's Commission on Housing under Reagan.

Political mementos are surprisingly missing from Barness' office in Warrington, Pa. But after a visitor asked about pictures, Barness opened the door to his conference room, where the walls are filled with photos of political figures of the past 40 years. There are five presidents, including Democrat Jimmy Carter, and an assortment of governors, senators and congressmen. Even former Soviet President Mikhail Gorbachev smiles down from the gallery.

Most photos are signed. "With appreciation and warm regards," wrote former President Ronald Reagan. "To Herb with best wishes," said Senate majority leader Bob Dole, R-Kan. "To my dear friend with affection and appreciation," said Tom Ridge.

"Herb, you are a tremendous asset to the Republican Party and to our country. Thanks for all you do," wrote Senator Rick Santorum, R-Pa.

A rag doll of Bill Clinton serves as an office door draft dodger. The doll's not autographed.

The History of His Passion
Herb Barness has been interested in politics since 1940 when he was a mechanical engineering student at Bucknell and worked for the Republican presidential candidate Wendell Wilkie in the Hoosier's race against President Franklin D. Roosevelt.

"Roosevelt was running for a third term, and I didn't think anybody should have three terms," Barness says.

Barness' first venture into the political arena wasn't successful. FDR went on to win his third term, and Barness went off to war serving as an Air Force officer in the Pacific Theatre.

Back home following World War II, Barness graduated from Bucknell, married Irma Shorin'48 and entered the family development business,

The Barness Organization. The firm was started more than 70 years ago by his father and mother, immigrants from Poland and Russia. His parents bought a tract of land after settling outside Philadelphia and while still farming, began selling real estate to other immigrants. Today, with Barness as chairman of the board, the international firm builds shopping centers, industrial parks, homes, office complexes and is one of the nation's largest developers of senior citizens' housing.

Over the years, according to press accounts, the low-key and gracious businessman has personally contributed thousands of dollars to political campaigns—national, state and local—and is credited with raising millions more.

His Read on the '96 Campaign
In the early stages of the current presidential campaign, Barness backed the moderate Specter as a favorite son from Pennsylvania in the senator's short-lived bid for the GOP nomination. Before deciding to suspend his presidential campaign, Specter said, "I talked to Herb about it in detail, kept him fully apprised. I always talk to him regularly." With Specter out of the race, Barness threw his support to Dole.

Dole's current courtship of the conservative wing of the party pleases Barness. "Dole is a centrist. I think he is doing what former President Nixon told him to do. To get the nomination you go to the right, and then to win the election, go to the middle. I think Dole has always been in the middle."

"Dole will win the Republican nomination," Barness predicts, "unless there is some tremendous change."

Although the 72-year-old Barness is confident that the 72-year-old Dole can beat President Clinton in the general election, he acknowledges Dole's age is a factor. "I don't know how big a problem it is, but there is definitely a perception that he's too old. I hear my friends who are of that age saying the same thing."

He attributes the attitude to the fact that when his contemporaries were growing up, "society thought that 60 was real old, 65 was older and boy, when you get into the 70s, you should be put out to pasture someplace. I think that is changing because longevity has increased tremendously." Barness himself certainly has no intention of retiring.

Barness admits mixed feelings about former General Colin Powell's withdrawal from the presidential race. Although Barness backs Dole, "Powell would have made it interesting had he stayed in."

Even though Powell ruled out a vice presidential bid, Barness notes, "A lot of people say no in politics, but it doesn't always mean no." There is the possibility that Powell could be secretary of state under a Dole administration, or he could change his mind and run in four years, Barness says.

"A black man on the Republican ticket could change the dynamics of politics in the United States for generations."

The Republican Party has "been trying desperately" to woo blacks and other minorities into the party, Barness says, "but it's a perception that the Democrats care more for the minorities. We have to change that perception. We're building in this country a middle class minority. As it is being built, more and more are becoming Republicans, or not just automatically voting Democratic. Instead of pulling one lever, they are voting for a candidate. That in itself will change politics. Democrats have taken for granted the black population for years, because they had them."

Barness sees more and more members of minorities coming into his office, asking him how they can get involved. An Asian-American businesswoman stops by because she thinks it is important for Asian Americans to be active in politics. A black doctor is a regular visitor and a big GOP supporter. Initially he told Barness, "I always thought the Republicans didn't want minorities, didn't want African Americans." Barness asked him where he got that idea, and the doctor replied, "From the Democrats."

Although Powell may not seek the second spot on the GOP ticket, Barness sees many other good candidates. A candidate from the West or East is likely since Dole is from Kansas. Barness seems partial to New Jersey Governor Christine Todd Whitman. "She'd be a great candidate."

The Hidden Costs of Running

Politics have changed dramatically since Barness first worked for Wilkie.

"There's nothing sacred anymore," he says. "The media dissects anyone who is running for public office. You just have to lay yourself out there naked and say this is my life and this has been my life. There's nothing any more that is not unsaid, and that discourages people."

In addition, there's the tremendous cost of running for office. "Unfortunately money has become too important," Barness says. "It was always important, but there were limitations. But now with television ... Raising money has really become a burden, it's become almost obscene. The 60-second sound bite on news programs dictates that a candidate cannot rely on news coverage alone to get his message out," Barness says. He estimates that about 60 percent of a campaign budget goes for television advertising.

Every candidate running for president of the United States knows he has to raise at least $25 million, Barness notes.

Years ago, if someone gave $100 to a campaign, "it was a lot of money. Today, $1,000 is not a lot of money. I've said for years now the only growth industry in the United States is financing politicians."

Communication itself has changed politics and government. "We sat and watched the Gulf War, we saw missiles being shot, people being killed. Thirty years ago, it would have taken days to learn about it, to read it in the newspaper. We didn't watch news 24 hours a day."

Dedicated to the People

Even with the problems of 1990s politics, there is no dearth of candidates. "I think we have some outstanding individuals in government. Democrats and Republicans, dedicated and devoted people who are not in it for personal gain, but because they really believe in doing something for the people."

Barness cited Ridge as an example. "There's nothing personal he wants. He could go back to practicing law and probably make a multiple times of money. The same applies to Pennsylvania's two senators (Specter and Santorum)."

Barness also praised Edward Rendell, Democratic mayor of Philadelphia. "He was a very successful lawyer, could have made tons of money if money was his goal, but he loves the political scene, loves the activity, the excitement, the challenges. He's doing a great job.

"Private citizens have to support the good people," Barness says, "or we are not going to have qualified, honest individuals who are going to be interested in government."

That's what motivates Barness. He's never been interested in seeking public office himself. "I felt I could do more helping elect people, becoming involved in a broader scale than being a county commissioner or state representative."

His biggest reward in politics is "trying to get good people, qualified people, in office. That's always the aim."

Senator Specter notes, "Herb Barness is interested in politics for the public good, for no personal gain at all. It is very important to have people participate in drafting the platform, helping to establish policy and helping candidates."

The election of Ridge in 1994 is a great source of satisfaction for Barness, who was an early supporter. "I thought he had all the qualifications, and he does. The biggest thing he's done is to create a more business-friendly state. He has really turned the state around. He's doing what he said he was going to do. He is a fine governor now, and I think he is going to be a great governor."

Helping Reagan win the presidency was also gratifying. Although Barness considers Harry Truman the "best, most effective president we've had in the last 50 years," Reagan "was one of the tops."

Coming Changes

Barness welcomes the national debate on such issues as balancing the budget, Medicare, Medicaid, affirmative action and welfare reform.

"For the first time the major issues facing our country are really being discussed head-on. If we are going to have a balanced budget in seven years, we will have to face some of the divisive issues we are discussing ... Someone has to bite the bullet and say we have to make some changes. It's going to hurt. It's very difficult to take something away from someone that has already been given, but it has to be done."

He credits Gingrich for "leading the revolution. He's certainly changed the way government operates, moderately for the best I guess. He doesn't come across too well, needs a little better PR. He's done many good things; some not so good."

Even if the winner of the GOP presidential nomination has been decided by the time the convention convenes next summer, Barness anticipates some fireworks over the platform. The biggest fight will be over abortion, he laments.

"Abortion is the one issue that shouldn't be in politics at all," Barness says. "That's not a political issue. That's a moral issue, that's a religious issue, a personal issue, but it's not a political issue."

The Community Man

Lest someone think Barness' only interests are business and politics, consider that he is:

- A former part owner of the Philadelphia Eagles
- A former chairman of the Continental Thoroughbred Racing Association
- Chairman of the board of the Pop Warner Little Scholars
- Member of the Golf Course Superintendents Association of America
- Past president of the Bucks County Park Foundation
- Board member of the Bucks County Council of Boy Scouts of America

"I was always of the opinion that it was very important to be involved, not just in politics but in the community," Barness says.

He and Irma have two daughters: Lynda Barness who is a vice president of The Barness Organization, and Nancy Stein, whose husband Craig is an owner of the Philadelphia Phillies farm club in Reading. They also have four granddaughters.

[*Accompanying this article were photos of my dad with Pennsylvania Governor Tom Ridge, Sen. Robert Dole, R-Kan., and Sen. Rick Santorum, R-Pa.; President Ronald Reagan (with the inscription, "To Herb—with appreciation and warm regards, Ronald Reagan"); and Sen. Arlen Specter, R. Pa.*]

BUILDERS EXPECT GROWTH IN UPCOMING YEAR
The Intelligencer/Record
January 28, 1996

Builders planning for a productive year in the region included two who were not highlighted in the Jan 21. article on local development. [*The other was The David Cutler Group.*] They are:

The Barness Organization
The Barness Organization will open a new 30-home section of its popular Hearthstone development in Buckingham, called The Woods at Hearthstone, with some design changes. Homes will start in the low $200,000s.

Seventy new homes will be built in phase three of the Fireside townhome community with a starting price of $145,900, and a second phase has opened at Dalton Glen, a single-home community priced from the $240,000s. Both are in Buckingham.

"We are looking forward to '96; hopefully we will have new projects as well as new phases for the present ones," said Lynda Barness, vice president.

The company presently is in negotiations on other sites.

DEVELOPER: STRATEGIC LOCATION ATTRACTS HOME BUYERS TO AREA

Premiere Weekly
Week of February 14, 1996
By Julie D. Barth and Margaret Quann, Calkins Newspapers

With good access to roadways leading to the suburban Philadelphia and Princeton corporate areas, developers are cautiously bullish on the real estate market in both Bucks and Montgomery counties for this year.

Citing the lowest mortgage interest rates seen in several years, many builders will begin new developments and introduce new models in existing communities.

Following is a summary of existing and upcoming developments planned by major construction firms in the area.

[*The list included Heritage Building Group, Hovnanian, DeLuca Enterprises, Barness Organization, Calton Homes, C&M Home Builders Inc. Katz-Swerdloff Properties, Quaker Group, Toll Brothers, Cutler Group, Realen, Trafalgar House, A.P. Orleans Inc., and Westrum Development.*]

NEWSMAKERS
The Philadelphia Inquirer
February 16, 1996

This had a note on it in my dad's handwriting that said "Political file."

MOTHER LODE—The April Issue of Mother Jones, which inaugurates Mother Jones 400, a list of the country's top 400 political contributors, includes some names from the Philadelphia area, including Herbert Barness of Warrington [who] is president of the Barness Organization, a real-estate development firm. Contributed $119,150. He's a Republican.

DEVELOPER A PLAYER IN POLITICS; BARNESS AMONG TOP CONTRIBUTORS
The Intelligencer/Record
February 18, 1996
By Anne Freedman, Staff Writer

Area real estate developer Herbert Barness was one of the top 100 political contributors in the nation, according to a list compiled by San Francisco-based magazine *Mother Jones.*

Barness, president of The Barness Organization and a member of the Republican National Committee, donated $119,150 between January 1993 through June 1995. He came in 91st on the list of 400.

"I believe in the two-party system, and I believe in the candidates, and I think there are a lot more substantial contributors than I (who) they probably have missed," said Barness, of Warrington.

He was one of 13 Pennsylvanians and the only Bucks County or Montgomery County resident on the list.

"He's always been a contributor—for years," said Harry W. Fawkes, chairman of the Bucks County Republican Party. "It doesn't shock me that he gives because I know he does a lot for the party."

Barness said that he has never sought favors for his donations.

"I don't know what purpose people make contributions for, but I have never lobbied for anything in my life and I have been involved politically for 45 years," he said.

HOME NOTES: LOCAL FIRMS, AGENTS HONORED AT PINNACLE AWARDS DINNER

The Philadelphia Inquirer
March 10, 1996
By Alan J. Heavens, *Inquirer* Real Estate Writer

They're in. The winners of this year's Pinnacle Awards from the Home Builders Association of Bucks/Montgomery counties included The Barness Organization, Philomeno & Salamone, DeLuca Enterprises and Realen Homes.

The eighth annual Pinnacle Awards dinner honoring builders in the two counties was held Feb. 17, despite the snow that fell that night.

> Barness' Fireside was multifamily community of the year (average sale price below $150,000)...
>
> Single-family under 2,800 square feet went to Barness' Furlong...
>
> Most creative brochure (over $5 per) went to Barness Fireside.

U.S. WIELDS A BIG STICK: Sen. Specter Says We Should Define Vital Interests and Stick to Them
The Intelligencer/ Record
April 9, 1996
By Edward Levenson, Staff Writer

Developer Herbert Barness speaks with Sen. Arlen Specter on Monday at a luncheon meeting of 60 businesspeople in Warrington. The event was sponsored by his re-election committee. Staff photo by E. Stace Leighliter.

THE INSIDER
Philadelphia Business Journal
April 17, 1996

Bucks County real estate developer Herbert Barness is a finalist in the National Association of Homebuilders' Multifamily Council's Builder-of-the-Year award.

LOCAL BUILDERS WIN NATIONAL RECOGNITION: BARNESS NAMED 'BUILDER OF YEAR' FOR MULTIFAMILY HOUSING

The Intelligencer/Record
May 9, 1996

Herbert Barness, president of The Barness Organization, was named the 1996 Freddie Mac Builder of the Year at the National Association of Home Builders' 16th annual Pillars of the Industry Awards held at the Multi-Housing World Conference in Atlanta on May 4.

The award recognizes his achievements in the apartment-management industry.

In making their selection, the judges cited his half-century of dedication to the home building industry and his enormous civic contributions.

He was a charter member and first president of the Bucks County Home Builders Association and has maintained interest and involvement in promoting the goals of affordable and high-quality housing.

In addition, The Barness Organization has contributed to many philanthropic and community funds: land for the Warrington Fire Company and Rescue Squad, a Boy Scout building, a room at the Michener Museum in Doylestown, Barness Field and a dorm at Delaware Valley College.

Barness has continued as an active developer, builder and property manager. He has built residential communities, office complexes, shopping centers and industrial parks. His organization is also one of the largest developers of senior citizen housing, both on a subsidized and non-subsidized basis.

The Pillars of the Industry awards are sponsored by the NAHB's Multifamily Council in conjunction with *Multi-Housing News* magazine. This annual competition seeks to recognize firms and individuals who demonstrate commitment to the highest standards in multifamily design and promote a positive image of the multifamily industry.

Herbert Barness was named "Builder of the Year" for Multi-Family Housing.

LOCAL BUILDER RECEIVES NATIONAL ACCLAIM
The Bucks County Courier Times
June 9, 1996

Herbert Barness, Warrington, Pa., was recently recognized for his outstanding achievements, both professional and civic, at the National Association of Home Builders (NAHB) 16th Annual Pillars of the Industry Awards, held at the Multi-Housing World Conference in Atlanta, last month.

Mr. Barness received the 1996 Freddie Mac Builder of the Year award. In making their selection, the judges cited his half-century of dedication to the home building industry and his enormous civic contributions. Over the past 47 years, Mr. Barness has made people, community, promise and commitment the cornerstone of his career. Knowing it is important to build homes, he also knows that traditions, histories, roots, foundations and meaning for thousands of homeowners goes far beyond just sticks and bricks. Mr. Barness is a pioneer in providing beautifully designed and attractively priced housing.

He is a Charter Member and first President of the Bucks County Home Builders Association and has maintained interest and involvement in promoting the goals of affordable and high-quality housing. In addition, The Barness Organization has contributed to many philanthropic and community funds for example, land for the Warrington Fire Company and Rescue Squad, a Boy Scout building, a room in the Michener Museum, Barness Field, a dorm at Delaware Valley College, and others.

Mr. Barness continues as an active developer, builder, and property manager. He has built residential communities, office complexes, shopping centers and industrial parks. His organization is also one of the largest developers of senior citizen housing, both on a subsidized and non-subsidized basis. Multifamily housing in various forms has been a stronghold of the Barness Organization.

The Pillars of the Industry awards are sponsored by NAHB'S Multifamily Council in conjunction with *Multi-Housing News* magazine. This annual competition seeks to recognize firms and individuals who demonstrate commitment to the highest standards in multifamily design and management and promote the image of the multifamily industry.

KEEPING TRADITION: BUILDER OF THE YEAR
Multi-Housing News
June/July 1996
© 1996 Miller Freeman Inc.
By L.K.F.

This article was reprinted in The Intelligencer/Record *on May 20, 1998!*

PILLARS OF THE INDUSTRY

Keeping Tradition

BUILDER OF THE YEAR

In 1923, a young immigrant named Joseph Barness gave up chicken farming and bought 80 acres of land in Bucks County, Penn., to build homes. One at a time. Today, the 70-year-old Barness Organization, led by Joseph's son Herbert Barness, 71, is one of the most influential home builders in the state. Barness continues to adhere to his father's original ideals—commitment to quality, affordability and the community.

"A long tradition of continued success coupled with community involvement sets Barness apart," said one judge.

The Barness Organization has developed multifamily communities throughout the five-county Philadelphia area and southern New Jersey, as well as projects in Mexico and the Caribbean.

It has developed more than 3,500 government-subsidized units, and it is also a player in seniors housing.

The firm continues to pioneer attractively priced housing, stated Barness, but he feels that it should also give "something that goes far beyond just sticks and bricks." The contributions for which Barness was noted include his position as first president of the Bucks County Home Builders Association. He is also past president of the Bucks County Planning Commission, former partner of the Philadelphia Eagles Football Club, currently vice chairman of the board of trustees of Bucknell University, Lewisburg, Penn., and the list goes on.

He served on President Reagan's Commission on Housing and

Winner
Herbert Barness,
chairman, The Barness
Organization

Award Sponsor:
Freddie Mac

is a member of the Republican National Committee. Last year, he was honored by the Pennsylvania Association of Broadcasters. "When and if there is a 'cause,' everyone looks toward Herbert Barness to be the leader...it is the passion of [Barness] and the desire to fulfill his commitment that makes the event or candidate a winner," stated a supporter.

Barness still wakes at 5:30 each morning to swim and arrives earlier at the office than his colleagues. He and his wife of 47 years have two daughters, one of whom works for the family business, and four granddaughters. —*L.K.F.*

Reprinted with permission from MULTI-HOUSING NEWS, June/July 1996
© Copyright 1996 MILLER FREEMAN INC. All Rights Reserved.

DEEP POCKETS COULD BE KEY IN NOVEMBER; IN ATTORNEY GENERAL RACE, KOHN'S CASH AN ADVANTAGE

The Intelligencer/ Record
June 12, 1996

Both candidates for attorney general expect to spend millions of dollars before the campaign ends this November, but it appears only one will spend most of it out of his own pocket.

In fund-raising so far, Republican Mike Fisher is leading Democrat Joe Kohn by a wider margin, having collected about four times as much money. But Kohn may have the advantage in the end, being willing and able to spend several million dollars of his own and his family's money.

Fisher received $5,000 from Republican National Committeeman Herb Barness, an influential party insider, and $4,000 from political consultant John Brabender of Pittsburgh. Former Attorney General Leroy Zimmerman gave $500, as did fireworks king George Zambelli of New Castle. Pittsburgh attorney Art Rooney II, a Democrat, gave $350.

AROUND THE TOWN

The Jewish Exponent
July 11, 1996
By Leon Brown

Bucks County builder and developer Herbert Barness recently received the Pillars of the Industry Award and was named "Builder of the Year" by the National Association of Home Builders' Multi-Housing World Conference, held recently in Atlanta. Barness, who was a charter member and served as the first prez of the Bucks County Home Builders Association, has been a developer/builder for more than 47 years and is involved in the communities in which he builds.

THEY TOLD
Who-What-Where-When Magazine
July/August 1996
Central Bucks Chamber of Commerce

Herbert Barness, Warrington, has been recognized for outstanding achievements in the apartment management industry at the National Association of Home Builders' (NAHB) 16th Annual Pillars of the Industry awards, held at the Multi-Housing world conference in Atlanta in May. Barness is the recipient of the 1996 Freddie Mac Builder of the Year award. In making their selection, judges cited his half-century of dedication to the home building industry and his enormous civic contributions.

CAMPAIGN '96: POPULARITY
The Patriot-News
August 12, 1996

Bob Dole and Jack Kemp may be the most popular men at the Republican National Convention this week in San Diego.

But there is someone who is more popular among the delegates from Pennsylvania: National Committeeman Herb Barness of Bucks County.

Four years ago, the Pennsylvania delegation was housed in a nondescript Houston hotel near an airport about 45 minutes away from the convention center. No one was very happy about it.

"I heard a lot of complaints about Houston," said new state GOP chairman Alan Novak of Chester County.

The Republicans this year looked to Barness to fix the situation. And, according to delegates, Barness has passed the test with flying colors.

Through his wheeling-dealing, Barness was able to house the Pennsylvania delegates at the swanky San Diego Hilton Beach and Tennis Resort on Mission Bay. The hotel, with its swimming pool, tiki torches and sailboat rentals, is about 10 minutes from the downtown convention center.

PENNSYLVANIA DELEGATION ENJOYS SAN DIEGO'S CREATURE COMFORTS

The Intelligencer/Record
August 13, 1996

No more views of planes landing and taking off for Pennsylvanians attending the Republican National Convention.

What a difference four years make.

At the 1992 convention in Houston, the state's delegates were housed near the airport—a 45-minute bus ride if there was no traffic and a $45 cab ride for anyone who missed the bus. This year, they are within a 15-minute ride to the convention hall as well as to tourist attractions ranging from Sea World to the zoo.

Pennsylvania's Republican National Committeeman Herb Barness served on the convention committees that handled site selection and hotel accommodations for 1996. He visited several hotels in January and chose the Hilton.

PA DELEGATION LEARNS TO KICK BACK IN STYLE

The Philadelphia Inquirer
August 1996
By David Boldt: Commentary

Many Americans have the wrong idea about what political conventions are like.

I know I did.

Prior to arriving here, I had this picture of thousands of delegates working up a heavy sweat pounding out platform planks.

That was not the scene poolside at the Hilton Beach and Tennis Resort, where the Pennsylvania delegation is cooped up for the week.

There you had the likes of Gov. Ridge and state Senate Majority Leader Joe Loeper in bathing trunks, demonstrating diversity in physiognomy, but utterly united in their devotion to things Republican.

I suppose that it might have been possible, in the course of strolling over to the Banana Cabana for refreshments, to have stirred up a debate over abortion, or capital gains, or something. However, the question inevitably arose: Why bother?

Part of it, undoubtedly, is the setting. Herb Barness, the Republican National Committeeman from Bucks County, was continually accepting congratulations for snagging this hotel. Indeed, the story of how it happened took on a quasi-legendary quality as it passed from chaise longue to chaise longue.

Years ago, it was said, while the other members of the convention site selection committee frittered away their time at Sea World and so on, Herb tirelessly went from hotel to hotel, checking them out.

Something about the Hilton Beach and Tennis Resort—perhaps the harmonious meld of pink Spanish tile and tan terracotta, maybe the sun spangling off jet ski wakes in Mission Bay, or possibly the gentle "twock" of racket on ball in the distance—told him, "This is it."

Alan Novak, the new chairman of the Pennsylvania Republican State Committee, told the delegates: "If we can't have fun in this hotel—then we can't have fun."

MAJOR GIFTS INITIATIVE APPROACHES 60% OF GOAL; BARNESS FAMILY MAKES LEADERSHIP GIFT TO COMMUNITY PHASE

Foundation News, The Newsletter of the Bucks County Community College Foundation
Summer 1996

The College's Foundation has undertaken a three-year major gifts initiative to raise $1,000,000 to support scholarships, update instruction equipment, refurbish campus facilities, and build endowment. With the Community Phase of the effort in progress, the project is approaching 60% of goal.

Leadership gifts in the Community Phase have included $25,000 each from Pennoni Associates Inc., PECO Energy Company, and the Barness Family.

FREDDIE MAC WILL TAKE UP THE SLACK
Multi-Housing News
August/September 1996

... As partners in the effort to support the growth and endurance of the nation's multifamily housing stock, NAHB's [National Association of Home Builders] Multifamily Council and Freddie Mac co-sponsor the annual Freddie Mac Builder of the Year award, announced each year at the annual Pillars of the Industry ceremony during Multi-Housing World. This year's recipient was Herbert Barness, a developer, builder and property manager based in Warrington, Penn. According to the 1996 Pillar judges, Barness has committed the past 47 years to providing well-designed but reasonably priced rental and for-sale housing. His organization is also a large developer of senior citizen housing, both subsidized and non-subsidized.

"A long tradition of success coupled with community involvement sets Barness apart," said one of this year's Pillar judges.

Barness runs the company founded by his father, Joseph Barness, in 1923 and continues to adhere to his father's original ideals—commitment to quality, affordability and the community. He served on President Reagan's Commission on Housing and is a member of the Republican National Committee.

SCENIC SITES TO SEE AT THE WOODS AT HEARTHSTONE
The Intelligencer/Record
September 29, 1996
By Margaret Quann, Staff Writer

Have you ever walked into a sample home and said to yourself, "I wish I could decorate a room just like that."

If you choose to buy a home at The Woods at Hearthstone, the Barness organization's new single-family home community in Buckingham Township, it's easy.

Barness provides buyers with a home decorating book with exact details on the wallpaper, paint, fabrics and other materials used in their sample homes.

"It lets the buyer recreate what they've seen in the models," said Lynda Barness, vice president.

The book even includes specifications for moldings and other decorative trim. "You could go to a home improvements center and build your own," she added.

The Woods is the newest phase of Hearthstone, a community of single-family homes connected by jogging trails, acres of open space, with ponds and trees surrounding the neighborhood. There are 378 homes planned altogether. While the first section of Hearthstone is sold out, there are 212 homes planned for the Woods section. So far, 44 of those have been sold, said sales coordinator Joan Diaz.

The Woods will include six different models, all with four bedrooms, two-and-a-half baths, basements and two-car garages. Nine-foot first-floor ceilings come standard, as do turned staircases in the two-story-tall hardwood foyers.

Other standard features are volume ceilings in the main bedrooms, 42-inch tall cabinets in the kitchens and ceramic tiling in the baths.

Four of the models come with a first-floor study as well as a large family room. Starting prices range from $199,900 for the 1,981-square-foot Aquetong to $227,900 for the Durham III with 2,876 square feet of living space.

The homes have gas heat and central air-conditioning, 200 amp electric service and architectural roof shingles. They meet the requirements of the PECO Energy Company's SmartChoice program for energy efficiency.

The Durham III includes a first-floor study, divided staircase, and extra-large 17-foot,6-inch by 21-foot, 6-inch main bedroom with tray ceiling and sumptuous bath.

The Durham III has a bridge overlooking the family room, and "spectacular glass at the back of the house," Diaz said, explaining that there are slight revisions in the home from the popular Durham and Durham II, which were built in the first phases.

A new design, the Ferndale, offers a dramatic two-story family room and a split staircase going upstairs from both the foyer and the kitchen. A stucco exterior is available, adding to the home's appeal.

"It has a lot of dramatic flair," Diaz said.

Hearthstone is located in the Central Bucks School District. Real estate taxes are estimated between $3,000 and $3,500. There is an earned income tax.

The sales center is open daily, noon to 5 p.m.

HAPPENINGS
New Hope Gazette
November 7, 1996

Herbert Barness of Doylestown has been appointed to the board of trustees of the Pennsylvania Academy of the Fine Arts in Philadelphia. Barness is chairman of the board of The Barness Organization, a real estate brokerage, financing, development and property management firm in Warrington.

According to Gresham Rile, president of the Pennsylvania Academy of Fine Arts, Barness was appointed to the board as part of a five-year strategic plan currently under development at the institution, which expands the board both in size and geographic representation.

Barness is past president and director of the Bucks County Industrial Development Corporation, past president of the Bucks County Planning Commission, former partner of the Philadelphia Eagles, former trustee of Germantown Academy in Fort Washington and a former board member of the Philadelphia Regional Port Authority.

The Pennsylvania Academy of the Fine Arts, founded in 1805, is America's first art museum and school of fine arts.

HEADS ABOVE THE CROWD
The Philadelphia Inquirer
December 1996

Herbert Barness of Doylestown has been appointed to the board of trustees of the Pennsylvania Academy of the Fine Arts in Philadelphia. Barness is chairman of the board of the Barness Organization, a real estate brokerage, financing, development, and property management firm in Warrington.

He has served as president and director of the Bucks County Industrial Development Corp., president of the Bucks County Planning Commission, a board member of the Philadelphia Regional Port Authority, and a trustee of Germantown Academy in Fort Washington. He is a former partner in the Philadelphia Eagles.

1997

WANT ACCESS TO GOV. RIDGE? JOIN THE CLUB
The Philadelphia Inquirer
April 27, 1997
By Robert Zausner, *Inquirer* Harrisburg Bureau

Come June, you can go on a two-day golf outing with Gov. Ridge. In November, you can attend his private reception before the Governor's Ball. And on occasion you might dine with him at Le Bec Fin.

All it takes is $50,000.

A pledge to contribute that sum to Ridge's campaign fund over four years buys admissions to the Governor's Club board of directors—current membership is 97—and a half-dozen exclusive gatherings each year. Or, for $25,000, you can be a regular member of the club, as are 131 people, and still get some of the special invites.

Created after Ridge became governor in 1995, the club guarantees the Republican incumbent a minimum of $8.1 million toward his expected reelection bid next year. And he has yet to even declare his candidacy.

Some members don't get anything from the state and say their only interest is in good government.

Ridge says that there are no paybacks for donors and that "government isn't for sale."

A number of club members were major rain-makers for Ridge, giving not only on their own but helping bring out the unselfish side of others. In this realm, Herbert Barness, a Bucks County developer, is a regular thunderstorm producer, having brought in as many as 40 percent of the club's members, according to Simmons [Laurie Simmons, executive director of the Governor's Club].

"It was Herb's idea," she said of the club. "During the campaign your pitch is always the same—you've got to have money for media. We wanted to have a way to raise the funds during the off years ... I thought it was a great idea and so did the governor."

BARNESS NAMED WHARTON FINALIST
The Intelligencer/Record
June 29, 1997

The Barness Organization, homebuilder in the Delaware Valley for three generations, was selected as a finalist for the first "Family Business of the Year Award" by the University of Pennsylvania's Wharton School. Nine finalists from more than 600 nominated organizations were chosen.

The award process examined the history of each family business.

The Barness Organization is based in Warrington.

Program from THE 1997 FAMILY BUSINESS OF THE YEAR AWARDS
Thursday, May 29, 1997
The Warwick Hotel
Presented by The Wharton School Family-Controlled Corporation Program
The Wharton Small Business Development Center

The Barness Organization was one of three finalists in the medium-sized business (50-250 employees) category. The program read:

The Barness Organization
In 1925, Joseph Barness was a farmer in rural Bucks County when his community-mindedness compelled him to begin high-quality, affordable

homes for other immigrants in the area. Today, The Barness Organization retains its community spirit as a growing developer, builder and property manager that employs 65 people.

AROUND THE TOWN
The Jewish Exponent
June 12, 1997
By Leon Brown

The Wharton School of the University of Pennsylvania recently presented its 1997 Family Businesses of the Year Awards. Winner [*Finalist*] in the medium-sized businesses was the Barness Organization, started in 1925 when Joseph Barness, a chicken farmer in rural Bucks County, began building affordable homes. The Barness Organization also entered its third generation of leadership. Herb Barness came to the helm in the 1960s, and then was joined by his daughter, Lynda Barness, in the 1980s.

U.S. REP JAMES GREENWOOD'S CAMPAIGN COFFERS IN GOOD SHAPE
The Intelligencer/Record
August 8, 1997
By Edward Levenson, Staff Writer

Republican Congressman James Greenwood, who spent $608,000 to win a third term, already has raised $151,000 in his bid for a fourth term.

Greenwood, 46, has not formally announced for another term but he is expected to run again. He represents the 8th District, which comprises Bucks County, Horsham and part of Lower Moreland.

So far, no Republicans or Democrats have emerged to challenge him.

About 230 people, primarily from Bucks County, contributed to Greenwood's campaign during the first six months of the year. Contributors included developers Herbert Barness and Lynda Barness of Warrington [who gave] $1,000 each.

REPUBLICAN CLAMBAKE SATISFIES APPETITES AND REPLENISHES THE PARTY COFFERS

The Philadelphia Inquirer
August 28, 1997
By David Iams, Society

You don't have to be Republican to enjoy the annual Billy Meehan picnic at the end of August at the Bavarian Club in Northeast Philadelphia. But it helps.

This year, more than 1,000 guests attended the event named for the longtime political leader who ran it for years, said his son Michael Meehan, standing with Herb Barness. It's one of the Republican City Committee's main sources of revenue, raising about $50,000 according to committee chairman Vito Canuso, who was at the event last Sunday.

PA.'S POLITICAL, BUSINESS LUMINARIES CLUSTER: The Annual Pennsylvania Society Dinner in New York Sets Off a Frenzy of Socializing

The Philadelphia Inquirer
December 15, 1997
By Russell E. Eshleman Jr., *Inquirer* Harrisburg Bureau

... The stated purpose of the trip is the Saturday night Pennsylvania Society Dinner, but the real action, or at least the pretend action, occurs during the numerous receptions that come before and after.

Many receptions are purely political. For instance, GOP national committeeman and mega-bucks campaign financier Herb Barness of Bucks County hosted a gathering for [Tom] Ridge and members of his "Governors Club" of big givers on Saturday.

1998

NEW OFFICE BUILDING CONSIDERED ON PARK: WARRINGTON
The Doylestown Patriot
March 12, 1998
By Dana M. Eckman

As Warrington Township continues to grow by leaps and bounds, more office space is needed. That is why the Barness Organization Tuesday night presented township supervisors with a sketch plan to construct an office building on Park Road off Route 611.

The Barness Organization presented the plan, not for a motion for approval, but for input and guidance.

IN THE SUBURBS: TOWNHOUSES AT THE ENCLAVE
The Philadelphia Inquirer
March 29, 1998

Pre-construction prices begin at $179,900 at the Enclave at Fireside, a townhouse development in Warrington [*it was actually in Buckingham*], Bucks County, from the Barness Organization.

The 88 townhouses have stone facades and are grouped in buildings of four. Sizes range from 1,900 to 2,535 square feet, with nine-foot ceilings on the first floor. Standard features include master-bedroom suites on the first or second floor, a wood-burning fireplace and oversized closets. Most units also include a two-car garage.

The sales center is open daily from noon to 5 p.m. and by appointment.

DEVELOPER MARKS 50 YEARS OF BUILDING HOMES, DREAMS
The Jewish Exponent
May 28, 1998
By Leon Brown

In 1923, a Jewish immigrant named Joseph Barness and his wife, Mary, settled amidst the rolling meadows of Bucks County. Barness was optimistic that in America he could build his home, cultivate his farmland and savor the fulfillment of the American dream.

With the purchase of 80 acres of land and his vision for a better community, Barness planted the seeds of what is today The Barness Organization, based in Warrington.

Today, his son Herbert Barness, the organization's current board chairman, is marking his 50th year as a respected builder and real estate developer.

Barness, who served as commander of U.S. Army Air Force's 147th Airways Communications Squadron in World War II, from 1942-1946, graduated from Bucknell University in 1948. He then joined his father in the family business. Barness fondly remembers his parents building their first house. "It had a detached garage with a swinging door and a chicken coop in the rear yard," Barness said.

"Those options are no longer available with our homes. They have been replaced, of course, by homes that are very different in design," he said. "Yet, the pride that went into building that very first home is still something that goes with every Barness home."

Barness' recollections of the early years of building homes are part of his roots. He would visit the site of each home under construction, wearing work boots and work clothes. Although his wardrobe has changed, his love of the business has not.

Each morning, Barness arrives at his office earlier than his colleagues, to whom he dispenses candy and advice gleaned from years of experience.

His philosophy is that each and every home built is important because it is a major investment by every owner. Therefore, he never takes any part of the process for granted. He has demonstrated and taught that respect to his organizational family, repeating his father's credo that The Barness Organization "is developing better communities for better living."

The company's goal has not changed over the years, Barness said. "As in my father's day, the goal of The Barness Organization is not only to create neighborhoods, but to be a good neighbor."

Today, the company stretches far beyond the boundaries of Bucks County, building apartment complexes and private homes in the U.S. Virgin Islands, the Caribbean and Mexico.

Barness has been at the helm since the 1960s. He later brought in the third generation, his daughter Lynda, as vice president.

This year, The Barness Organization was selected as a finalist in the 1998 Greater Philadelphia Family Business of the Year Awards by the University of Pennsylvania's Wharton School.

In 1996, Barness received the Pillars of the Industry Award and was named "Builder of the Year" by the National Association of Home Builders' Multi-Housing World Conference. Barness, who was a charter member and served as the first president of the Bucks County Home Builders Association, is active in the communities he builds. Examples [of Barness' philanthropy] include the Joseph and Mary Barness dormitory at Delaware Valley College in Doylestown, the Warrington Fire Company and Barness Park in Warrington, along with other parks and open spaces.

He is a past president and director of the Bucks County Industrial Development Corporation and the Bucks County Planning Commission. Current vice chairman of the board of trustees of his alma mater Bucknell University, Barness has served on the Presidential Commission on Housing.

He has also served as board chairman of the Philadelphia Chapter of the American Technion Society and as a member of Technion's national board. He was honored by the Philadelphia Chapter in 1969.

Among his numerous honors, Barness received an Honor Role Service Award from Women's American ORT.

AGE-RESTRICTED HOUSING PROJECT GETS GO-AHEAD
The Intelligencer/Record
June 21, 1998
By Damon Levine, Staff Writer

The township planning commission unanimously recommended approval Thursday of a Barness Organization plan to build an age-restricted community of 241 single-family homes on 85 acres on Folly Road between Street and Bristol roads.

The proposed development, called Legacy Oaks, would be restricted to people 55 and older.

Plans for the development, which were shown at Thursday's planning commission meeting, are "very nice so far," said Phil Schwinn of Upper Southampton. Schwinn and his wife hope to purchase a house in the development when it's complete. "We've sold our house to our son," he said.

Commission approval was granted provided Barness met certain conditions.

Chief among those conditions was that Barness erect a traffic signal at Street and Folly roads. The commission also asked that Barness and the township engineer Richard Wieland meet with the development's neighbors to discuss both drainage and buffer issues.

"The requirement in the township is that the development of one property not increase the drainage on (to) another property," planning commission chairman Douglas Thomas said.

Thomas Hoff, whose land borders the proposed development, agreed to meet with township officials and the developer to discuss drainage issues. Hoff, however, is not enthusiastic about the project. "I think we've sort of resigned ourselves to our inevitable future," he said.

The commission granted Barness minor waivers, one of which was permission to put in a 580-foot-long street with a cul-de-sac. A township ordinance says cul-de-sac streets can be only 500 feet long.

The commission also allowed seven of the proposed development's 241 homes to have driveways situated 30 feet from an intersection. Township guidelines call for driveways to be no less than 50 feet from an intersection.

And Legacy Oaks will not have sidewalks. Standard sidewalks will be replaced with a winding pathway system which, said project architect David Minnow, senior citizens would appreciate. "You need to provide a really great pedestrian system but not necessarily standard subdivision sidewalks," Minnow said.

Legacy Oaks' streets will be maintained by a homeowners association. The development also will have restrictions on pets, fences, pools and home improvements.

The Barness Organization will go before the board of supervisors for final approval on July 14. Barness vice president Bob Brown said, "We'll be ready to start (construction) within a month of final approval."

HERBERT BARNESS: FOR 50 YEARS, PROVIDING THE AMERICAN DREAM
The Daily Intelligencer/The Record
July 12, 1998
By Kate Maclaren Johnson, Correspondent

For 50 years Herbert Barness has been in the business of building "dreams." You could say he grew into his job. His father, an immigrant farmer, planted the seeds of The Barness Organization when he began constructing houses in rural Bucks County 73 years ago. As a youngster, Herb worked for his father on Saturdays and during the summers—growing up not only with a firsthand knowledge of construction techniques, but also committed to his father's high standards and sense of community. For their home buyers, they were building the "American dream."

Although his long career with the organization bearing the family name began right after he graduated from Bucknell University, there was a little four-year detour—World War II. In 1942, before he finished college,

Barness heeded his country's call to arms, serving as Executive Officer 70th Army Airways Communications Group and Squadron Commander 147th Airway Communication Squadron (Pacific).

But fresh home from the war, Barness immediately took up the threads of his life, and in 1948, finished college with a degree in engineering, married his girlfriend, Irma, and started right to work with his father.

"I was in work boots the next day," he would recall. "We didn't have the luxury of 'finding yourself' in those days."

His lifelong interest in politics began about this time, according to his daughter, Lynda, who has closely worked with her father in The Barness Organization since 1989 [*actually 1985*]. "When Roosevelt was president, he began to be very concerned about term limits," she explained. "Politics are definitely something he is passionate about."

Barness' long active involvement with the Republican Party goes back 50 years. Currently he serves as a Republican National Committeeman for Pennsylvania. His daughter may only be half-joking when she laughingly refused to rule out her father's making a run for the White House. "You can never tell about him!"

In fact, for a man she describes as "really a behind the scenes person," he is becomingly modest. His resume reads like an entry in "Who's Who in America." In truth, he has been president or chairman of the board of a host of organizations of every stripe, including being a former partner of the Philadelphia Eagles. In his own field, Barness was not only a charter member, but also the first president of the Bucks County Home Builders Association. He is also a past president of the Bucks County Planning Commission.

In its 1996 Pillars of the Industry Awards, the National Association of Home Builders selected Herbert Barness as Multi-Family Builder of the Year. At that time it was revealed that in addition to the stylish custom homes which dot the five-county Philadelphia area and southern New Jersey, the Barness Organization has developed more than 3,500 government-subsidized units, and has also been involved in seniors housing.

Barness enjoys hard work. He has worked hard at everything he does, according to Lynda, now a vice president in The Barness Organization.

Knowledge gained from hands-on involvement at every level has proven invaluable in charting the achievements of the organization since he assumed a leadership role in the '60s. Instead of building houses, Barness wanted to build homes. Homeownership is a big part of the American Dream, and like his father before him, Barness enjoyed being a participant in fulfilling the dream for those who bought his houses.

But there have been a lot of nails in the walls since then. For example, such features as a chicken coop out back are no longer an option for a Barness home. And while the colonial remains the most poplar style, it has been transformed with much larger windows and open space inside.

Among the many communities Barness has developed over the years are Palomino Farms in Warrington, Silversmythe in Chalfont, Glennbrook in New Britain and most recently, Hearthstone, the Woods at Hearthstone, Dalton Glen and the Enclave at Fireside in Buckingham.

He also has built the Warrington Country Club, the Face-Off Circle skating rink in Warrington and the Chapman's Lane's shopping center in Doylestown.

"No, we don't build 'em like we used to," Barness says, "We build 'em better." He contends that not only are today's construction techniques better, but so are materials.

He predicts that the home of the future is here now—the "smart house"—distinguished by its incorporation of computers to handle everything from interior climate control to feeding the cat.

Herb Barness rises daily at 5:30 a.m., swims and then beats everyone to the office, including his personal assistant Terri Brodheim. He's chairman of the board but still makes the coffee. His sense of fun endears him to those who work for him. His habit of dispensing candy to visitors resulted in a surprise addition to his office. Lynda arranged that candy bins be included in the hardwood built-ins that line one side of her father's office.

"He's a chocoholic," she says fondly.

He freely admits that he loves that little touch and keeps the bins filled himself.

Despite the accolades that have been heaped upon him, and his tireless philanthropy, Barness says his proudest achievements have been his family. He and his wife have just celebrated 50 years of marriage. Irma Barness is an artist whose work can be seen throughout The Barness Organization's headquarters on Route 611 in Warrington just a half mile from its original home. Their daughters, Lynda and Nancy, have given them four granddaughters who often call their grandfather at work, "just to talk to him," says Terri Brodheim.

When asked how he would like to be remembered, Herb Barness replies with characteristic modesty as "part of the community" and "kind."

Herbert Barness, Chairman of the Board of The Barness Organization, relaxes in his Warrington office. Calkins photo by Kate Maclaren Johnson.

FULFILLING THE AMERICAN DREAM FOR 50 YEARS: The Barness Organization celebrates the anniversary of leadership by their second-generation president—Herbert Barness
Bucks County Courier Times
July 26, 1998
By Ruth Ann Roche

There's a celebration going on—one that is well deserved. For 50 years Herbert Barness has been building the homes that dreams are made of, and having a great deal of fun in the process.

He doesn't look like the shrewd business man that most people would conjure up when thinking about the leader of such a successful organization, and, although his education and business sense are quite extensive, he doesn't act like one either. Every day he opens up the Warrington office early in the morning and dispenses candy (Mr. Barness is a self-proclaimed sugar addict), maintains the growth of the business, and gives advice—good, sound advice learned from years of experience.

Seventy-three years ago, Mary and Joe Barness built their first home in Warrington. This stately abode had a few options that are rarely offered in new construction today, like a swinging garage door and a back yard chicken coop, but it did start a precedent for the Barness family. Herbert Barness grew up with a community being constructed around him, mainly due to the efforts of his own parents. It was no wonder that he put on his work boots and joined in at the construction sites.

"I look back upon those years with a fond appreciation of learning from involvement," explains Barness. "I learned to really listen to what people want. After all, a builder does not create the demand, but is there to fill the demand and make people's dreams become a reality."

Detours swayed the attention of Barness along the way up the ladder of the family business. In 1942 he was called to help his country fight World War II. No stranger to leadership, he became Executive Officer of the 70th Army Airways, and Communications and Squadron Commander of the 147th Airways Communication Squadron.

Another small setback from his building career came in a petite but quite pretty package. Barness married his sweetheart, Irma, in 1948. This same year he finished college, obtaining his degree from Bucknell University, and put his work boots back on his feet. It was then that he truly took his place in the building legacy that is so well known today.

Barness had two daughters, both of whom originally took off to follow their own dreams. But nearly 15 years ago, Lynda Barness sort of "fell back into" the building business, and today she is very happy as Vice President of the Barness organization.

"I never expected to be doing this, but I do love my job," Lynda says. Sitting in her office, her classic look is complemented by the surroundings that she designed. "We're always doing something different. Although our primary focus is in building residences, we have constructed parking garages, built skating rinks, and put together shopping centers. It's never boring."

Lynda has two daughters of her own, Jennifer and Melissa. Even though at this point they have no plans to join the family business, Lynda knows better than to try and guess the future.

"I'm afraid that if they do come to work with me, then they'll want my job!" says Lynda, with a joking smile. Speaking partly of her own experiences, "Never say never" has become one of Lynda's favorite quotes.

With successful communities in their background such as Glenbrook and Silversmythe, both located in Chalfont, and Dalton Glen, located in Buckingham, Barness is still going strong in making changes and supplying the demand of today's buyers. One of their best sellers, the Woods at Hearthstone, sold close to 70 homes last year. Joan Diaz, the sales manager for the community of 196 single-family homes, does an incredible job coordinating the sales force and overseeing all of the construction details.

"This is the type of community that people seem to want to be in," says Diaz, describing the neighborhood as having "seven ponds, bike paths, winding country roads, and a feeling of beauty and seclusion."

Also attributing to the success of the community is the list of standard amenities included in the price of the homes that are usually substantial upgrades.

"All of the homes in Hearthstone have nine foot ceilings on the first floor and fireplaces," continues Diaz. "We also take special care in preserving the look of the community by doing things like making sure that we don't put two of the same style homes directly next to each other."

At Hearthstone it is not hard to find a satisfied customer. People are eager to voice their opinions on everything from the quality of construction to the school district.

"One of the reasons that we decided to purchase a home in The Woods at Hearthstone is the look of the community," said Bob Tait, who just moved into the development early in June. "But the thing that helped us reach our decision the most is the fact that the homes here are built by Barness. I am familiar with most of the companies that build homes in the Delaware Valley, and I am very impressed by the quality and attention to detail that is found in a Barness home."

The homes available in The Woods at Hearthstone are base priced at $223,900, and generally go up to about $270,000. While there seems to be a style to suit everyone's taste, Barness will even customize a home, as far as the plans will allow, in order to meet the needs of the individual buyer.

"We respond to what people tell us that they want in a home," said Diaz. "The most common things are already there. Foyers are made of hardwood, baths are tiled, and so on."

One of the most recent customer requests that Barness is just beginning to meet is housing for people over age 55. Because people are living longer, and much of the population will be reaching the "over 55" age at the same time, there has been some concern about the fact that the most prominent type of housing built today will not meet the needs of the buyers in the future. All too often communities for seniors resemble an upscale version of a trailer park. Barness is now in the process of addressing these problems by building their first "over 55" community in Warrington called Legacy Oaks.

"We sent out questionnaires to find out what type of housing is needed in the Bucks County area," explained Lynda Barness. "After we deciphered that we are in desperate need of a retirement community, we obtained preliminary approval and ran two ads to let people know what we were doing. Immediately we received hundreds of calls from people who were all interested in purchasing a home in this type of community."

Legacy Oaks, located at Street and Folly roads, will be a community of single-family homes with first-floor master bedroom suites. Lofts and other items on the second story will be optional. Since approval has just been granted this past week, Barness is hoping to start construction by September.

For more information on Legacy Oaks, or any other Barness community, call the Warrington office at 343-0700 or visit their website at http://www.barness.com.

THE DAUGHTER ALSO RISES
The Player Magazine: Philadelphia's Journal of Power and Success
July/August 1998
By Miranda K. Salomon

Lynda Barness is a professional home maker.

In her 49 years, she has worn many hats—wife, mother, political fundraiser and chef, to name a few—but now, as vice president of the Warrington-based Barness Organization, she literally makes homes. She participates in nearly every aspect of the process that begins with a sheer inspiration and ends when a family moves into a brand-new, sparkling clean Barness-built house.

The 73-year-old real estate, development and property management company was founded by Lynda's grandfather, Joseph Barness; Herbert Barness, Lynda's father, is chairman of the board, and Murray Hirshorn is the president of the company. It's unusual for a woman to be in the building profession, but Lynda Barness has proven more than capable of running the property management, marketing and sales departments, not to mention being fully involved with everything except the actual construction.

"We're in the real estate development business," Barness explains. "We do everything from buying raw ground, to taking it through the development process—dealing with engineers, getting site plans—to working with architects and building, to marketing all of our communities, to dealing with the buyers at the end." Those communities are mostly in Pennsylvania, although The Barness Organization has done some building in Delaware and New Jersey. And though the company has built more than just homes, including country clubs, garages and shopping centers, today they're primarily homebuilders.

"We continue to take great pride in that, we really do," she says. "Today we're planning a community that will start in the $160,000 range, and we have another community that is closer to $300,000 a unit."

Growing up in Warrington, Barness did not dream of working for her father's company. "I did not ever expect to be in this business," asserts Barness, who studied political science at Tufts University and holds a Master's from Penn in international relations. Not planning but circumstance led her to the company that her father has run for most of the century—Herb Barness is currently celebrating his 50th year with the company—but working for the company suits her to a T.

Barness joined the business in 1985, when her position as eastern finance director of the Arlen Specter for U.S. Senate committee was taking up more time that she could spare. "My daughters (Jennifer, now 25, and Melissa, now 22) were young at the time," she remembers, "and I really didn't feel comfortable going out of town or being constantly on the go. So I went to my dad, and I said, 'What do you think?' And he said, 'Ok, we'll give it a try.'"

Today, Lynda's father is glad that she joined him in the family business. Working with his daughter, he says, has been delightful. "It's been a pleasure," he elaborates. "I enjoy it, and she's learned very quickly. Lynda is the third generation here, you know, and it has worked out very well."

Herb Barness is a man of many interests, and Lynda is clearly her father's daughter. He is a National Republican Committeeman of Pennsylvania, a member of the Pennsylvania Republican State Finance Committee, a charter member of the Bucks County Home Builders Association, and has served as president of the Pennsylvania Society and president and director of the Bucks County Development Corp. No homebody she, Lynda is on the boards of trustees of the University of Pennsylvania and Abington Hospital, and on the foundation board of Bucks County Community College. She is on the campaign executive committee for the Penn Medical Center and on the board of the Penn Veterinary School, and she is actively involved with the Homebuilders Association of Bucks and Montgomery Counties. And since 1995, Barness has served as a guest cooking-instructor at Kathy D'Addario's cooking school. "My mother, Irma, is a good cook, so I learned from her when growing up," says Barness. "I've taken lessons for years. Desserts are my specialty. The sweet tooth runs in my family. My dad has floor-to-ceiling candy bins in his office, so there's a pretty natural transition from candy to desserts."

In 1996, Barness decided to combine her love of cooking with her marketing responsibilities. She developed two "Home Sweet Home" cookbooks (a third is on the way) that have been given to the homeowners of Barness-built homes. "We are, in a sense, a small business, a family business, and we developed the cookbooks with a sense that this is a gift from our family to your family," she says. The first cookbook is comprised of favorite recipes donated by individuals who work for The Barness Organization; the second book is a collection of the specialties of the homeowners themselves. And the third, which should be completed this month, will contain dishes submitted by everyone and anyone associated with the organization.

"One of the themes in our business is family," says Barness. "I'm the beneficiary of what my grandfather did and what my father has done." Barness is very aware of her family's history, and the organization's promotional materials, which she wrote, tell the story of the Eastern

European farmer who built a solid business. "Really, my grandparents were pioneers," she says. "My grandfather was a chicken farmer when he first started out in Bucks County. They moved out into the country, and they built one house, and then another, and then another."

Herb Barness took over his father's business in the 1960s, and The Barness Organization grew as the Philadelphia suburbs developed. "In the 1960s, my father went to buy a piece of ground, and the price was $100 an acre," says Lynda Barness. "My grandfather had never paid more than $50 an acre. He couldn't comprehend that my father was willing to pay double that amount, to make this huge leap. And he went to my father and said, 'I think this business is passing me by. I can't fathom this. I think that you'd better take care of things from now on.' So my grandfather was still in the office, but my father took over and he really led it in a different direction.'"

When she first came to work for The Barness Organization, Lynda worked "school hours" so that she could be home in the afternoons and evenings. She shared an office with her father's secretary, which Lynda suspects was "an attempt to see if I was serious." One year later, she moved into her own office. She got her broker's license several years ago. Today, she shares a secretary with Hirshorn, who has been president of the company since 1979, and whom Barness describes as one of her mentors.

As for criticism from people who assume that she owes her job to her father, Barness says that it doesn't affect her at all. "I don't pay a lot of attention to it. I'm proud to be my father's daughter and I enjoy working with him. Having family in the business may get you in the door, but once you're there you have to make a place for yourself." And discrimination from others in the business who don't expect women to be in positions of authority has not prevented Barness' success. She finds that the most awkward moments are when a client, who wants to contact the builder, will ask to speak to "him." But since Lynda often has final approval of building plans, the client is politely told, "You can call her."

As for passing the business on to the next generation, Barness has chosen to wait and see. Her daughters are following paths of their own; Jennifer is currently getting a degree from the Tyler School of Art, and Melissa is working in public relations in Manhattan. "My father never influenced me to get into the business," Barness says. "I'd like my daughters to make their own career choices. Either way, I think it's important that they work elsewhere first. Our object isn't to make the business last forever, but really to make it thrive today."

At 74, Herb Barness won't be able to run the company indefinitely, but his daughter says that she can't imagine him retiring any time soon. "He loves what he does, and he does a lot of different things" she says. "He is still involved in politics on a day-to-day basis. So his entire day isn't about real estate, but he does keep a hand in the business. He doesn't do the nitty gritty, but he is deeply involved with the big picture."

Right now that bigger picture involves plans for The Barness Organization's next big project: Legacy Oaks at Warrington, a development for "active adults" over 55. The community will include a clubhouse, tennis courts and a pool, and will not allow children under 19 to live there permanently. Marketing the 240 units will occupy Barness for the time being. "This will be for people who are not necessarily retirees. But even if they are retired, these will be people who are very active, with many interests and hobbies; they'll travel."

For now, Lynda Barness has the best of both worlds: the opportunity to work full-time in a challenging field, while spending time with her father. She's learned to balance her interests, her career and her family, although she admits that keeping everything together has proven, at times, to be a juggling act. "It's always challenging, always thought-provoking; I'm always learning. I don't mean to sound like it's all rosy, but I love it."

For Lynda Barness, there's no place like home.

This photo accompanied the article. My dad has always had my back.

HERBERT BARNESS DIED OF CANCER ON SEPTEMBER 5, 1998

A memorial service was held on September 9, 1998, at Congregation Keneseth Israel. More than 1,000 people attended, and my father's brother, Lewis, along with his friends Don Meredith, Ben Alexander, Governor Tom Ridge, and Senator Arlen Specter all spoke beautiful, meaningful words about the person he was, and the impact he had on others.

There were many obituaries, resolutions, and other special mentions of my dad's death in the weeks that followed. I have an album full of them. I chose to include only a few in this book, because the main purpose of this project was to share and preserve the articles that I had collected about my father during his lifetime.

Since The Philadelphia Inquirer *and* The Daily Intelligencer *were responsible for most of the coverage of my dad throughout his life, I chose their articles about his passing to be included here.*

RIDGE: BARNESS 'GENEROUS' TO A FAULT
The Intelligencer/Record
September 7, 1998
By Harry Yanoshak, Staff Writer

Gov. Tom Ridge called him "generous to a fault."

Herbert Barness, 74, whose battle with cancer ended Saturday, often opened his home and showered hospitality "on so many friends—most of whom, he knew, never could return his generosity," Ridge said in a statement. "As I reflect on our friendship, what I remember the most are his kindnesses and countless acts of generosity."

Ridge called Barness, a millionaire real estate developer and Bucks County native, "a civic minded patriot" who loved the state, the nation and democracy.

"Pennsylvania is poorer without him."

Although Barness was generous with his contributions to the Republican Party and regional civic groups, he was more generous with his time, Ridge said, noting Barness was a "loving father and a proud grandfather."

Among the things Barness was—a political mover and shaker, shrewd businessman and a nationally prominent GOP leader—"family man" topped the list, said county Commissioner Charles Martin, board chairman.

Martin, who spoke with Barness three weeks ago about county government, will best remember Barness as an "honorable" man who despite his wealth lived an unassuming life.

"Together with his wife, Irma, Barness spread his generosity throughout the region," Martin said. "This is a real loss for Bucks County."

REPUBLICANS FLOCK TO BARNESS FUNERAL
The Philadelphia Inquirer
September 10, 1998
By Robert Zausner, *Inquirer* Harrisburg Bureau

Everyone who is anyone in Pennsylvania Republican politics crowded into a temple here yesterday to say goodbye—and undoubtedly, thank you—to a man remembered by a best friend as Herbert "Backseat" Barness.

Although that friend, retired Dallas Cowboys quarterback Don Meredith, was referring to Barness' place in a van during a trip to Europe, it aptly applied to the behind-the-scenes political role he played for decades.

It was the sage advice and fund-raising prowess of Barness, 74, a prominent Bucks County developer who died Saturday, that helped many of the more than 1,000 people at his funeral win their various titles—congressman, senator, governor.

Gov. Ridge, known for a somewhat still public demeanor, cried when he delivered the final words of his remarks, that Barness had lived "one perfect day at a time." Barness was one of Ridge's early backers and chaired the "Governor's Club," Ridge's current campaign apparatus for big donors.

Even Mayor Rendell, a Democrat, attended the hour-long service at Reform Congregation Keneseth Israel and brought with him the GOP national committee that has been studying Philadelphia as a possible site for the 2000 convention.

It was at the group's insistence, said Rendell, that the funeral was put on the day's agenda. Barness had served until his death as a Republican national committeeman. One member of the site-selection committee who knew Barness well, Jan Larimer of Wyoming, wept after the service.

Rendell said he joined the large club of Barness admirers when the developer invited him to his annual summer party following Rendell's loss in the Democratic primary for governor in 1986 to Robert P. Casey.

"My political career was, if not over, temporarily over. His kindness meant a lot to me," said the mayor.

The funeral service brought mostly Republicans, including the state chairmen from New York and Connecticut. Pennsylvania Republican Sens. Arlen Specter and Rick Santorum arrived together. Enough state legislators were there to convene a leadership meeting.

But it was Meredith, a former Monday Night Football announcer who presided over the service and recalled some of Barness' fondest observations, including one that took a shot at many in the audience: "You know, 99 percent of the lawyers give the rest of them a bad name."

He remarked on his unusual friendship with the soft-voiced, genteel Barness. "Talk about the odd couple," he said. "Where the hell did Herb and I get together? I don't know, but I'm sure glad we did."

Actually, Barness and Meredith owned a Bucks County radio station together, and Barness had more than a passing interest in football, at one time having owned 29 per cent of the Philadelphia Eagles.

Other nonpoliticians also met Barness on the indoor tennis court or nine-hole golf course he had until he moved to a smaller home several years ago. One tennis chum was Bill White, former St. Louis Cardinals player and past president of baseball's National League, who still lives in the area and attended yesterday's service. Meredith now lives in Santa Fe, N.M.

Most of his friends remembered Barness, a wealthy man, as simple and nice.

Specter said Barness was someone who "felt as comfortable at a clambake as he did in the governor's mansion or the White House."

Lt. Gov. Mark Schweiker, a fellow Bucks County resident, said that Barness came from a poor family and "never learned to ride a bike—not because he wasn't interested, but because they couldn't afford a bike."

He also remarked on Barness' courage in the face of a severe and protracted battle with cancer. "You'll see a thousand people come through here today," said Schweiker, "and not one who ever heard him complain."

U.S. Rep Jon Fox (R., Pa.) called Barness, who never ran for public office, a "humble hero" who "enjoyed being behind the scenes.

"A lot of people help in politics with the idea of 'How can it help me?' Herb just wanted to help others," said Fox. "He was a gem of a guy."

LIFE OF HERBERT BARNESS CELEBRATED: He was described as a unique and wonderful man with a zest for living
The Intelligencer/Record
September 10, 1998
By Edward Levenson, Staff Writer

Holding up a pair of overalls and a flannel shirt, sports broadcaster Don Meredith recalled the first time he met Herbert Barness.

Meredith, a former Dallas Cowboys quarterback, was invited to dinner at Barness' Buckingham estate, Nanlyn Farms, shortly after moving to Bucks County in 1973.

"Wouldn't you think that's a farmer?" Meredith said to an estimated 1,000 mourners who attended a memorial service for Barness on Wednesday at Reform Congregation Keneseth Israel.

Meredith said he wore overalls and a flannel shirt because "I was just trying to make him comfortable."

When Barness saw Meredith, he went upstairs and changed from a suit into blue jeans.

"I said, 'I think I'm going to like that guy'—and I did," Meredith related.

He became close friends with Barness, a prominent developer and Republican Party leader who died Saturday of cancer at age 74.

Meredith was among the public figures who attended the hour-long service for Barness.

The son of Eastern European Jewish immigrant parents grew up on a farm in Doylestown Township in the 1920s and went on to become chairman of The Barness Organization, a Warrington-based home, office and shopping center developer.

Pennsylvania politicians paying their respects included Gov. Tom Ridge, Lt. Gov. Mark Schweiker, U.S. Sen. Arlen Specter, House Speaker Matthew Ryan, Senate Majority Leader F. Joseph Loeper, Attorney General Mike Fisher and other members of the governor's cabinet.

Also in attendance were Philadelphia Mayor Edward Rendell, television anchorman Larry Kane, former National League President Bill White, former U.S. Transportation Secretary Drew Lewis, Bucks County state Sens. Joe Conti and Robert Tomlinson, Bucks Republican chairman Harry Fawkes, Bucks Commissioners Charles Martin and Michael Fitzpatrick and Bucks state legislators.

Meredith, who no longer lives in Bucks County, acted as master of ceremonies of the service, which combined humorous anecdotes and heart-felt emotion.

"I talked with Herb two weeks ago," he said. "Herb wanted a celebration. That's why we're here today, to celebrate the life of Herbert Barness."

Speakers spoke of Barness' zest for life, his love of family, his service to the community and his avid support of the Republican Party. Barness was a major party fund-raiser and Pennsylvania's national Republican committeeman.

Barness, who knew eight presidents, "treated the fellow parking cars in the parking lot the same as he did the President of the United States," said Charles Kopp, who was Barness' lawyer and friend for 30 years.

"With all his activities, his family always came first," Kopp said. Barness and his wife, Irma, had two daughters, Nancy and Lynda, and four granddaughters.

"Herb Barness was my friend, I'm proud to say," Kopp said. "He was a unique and wonderful man. It will be a long, long time—if ever—that we see another one like him.

Dr. Lewis Barness said his younger brother was a determined person.

"I think Herb had a great life," he said. "He picked his goals early in life and accomplished most of them. I think he would have liked to have lived a little longer."

Republican U.S. Sen. Arlen Specter said Barness could not refuse requests for public service.

"Herb did not have the word 'no' in his vocabulary," said Specter, a friend for 30 years.

Barness chaired a committee that recommended qualified nominees for federal judgeships in Pennsylvania and was working to bring the Republican National Convention to Philadelphia in 2000, the senator said.

Republican Gov. Tom Ridge said he attended hundreds of political functions with Barness, who would tug on Ridge's sleeve if the governor was getting too long-winded.

"At the end of the event, he'd say, 'I hope you didn't mind.' 'No, I did not mind,'" Ridge said.

"Herb Barness didn't waste time. He devoured life," Ridge said.

"We should live our lives as he did, one perfect day at a time," the governor concluded, choking up.

Rabbi Bradley Bleefeld ended the service by noting that "Barness" means "son of a miracle" in Aramaic, an ancient cousin of Hebrew.

"Herb was the son of a miracle by name, but Herb himself was a miracle by deed," the rabbi said.

He said this miracle touched Barness' wife, children and grandchildren and everyone who know him.

"Hallelujah for the life of Herbert Barness," Bleefeld said.

Epilogue

After my father's passing, I continued on with The Barness Organization until 2005, when I sold it to another local family builder. I wrote this article after the sale.

THE GIFT OF GOODBYE
Family Business Magazine
Spring 2007
By Lynda Barness

My father gave me many gifts throughout his lifetime, but one of the most important was the freedom to sell our 80-year-old family business.

My family's business had its beginnings in the days of Calvin Coolidge and the flapper dress. In 1925, Joseph Barness—a young immigrant with little money but much hope—and his wife, Mary, gave up chicken farming in rural Bucks County, Pa., and built a house for sale.

And then they built another. And another. Dedication, patience, and persistence were the building blocks of this effort. The goal was the American dream—home ownership.

Better roads were built, electricity was brought to the county and a community grew. Success was measured not in dollars, but by neighbors emerging in a farming landscape.

Joe and Mary Barness were my grandparents. They were pioneers, and they helped other families develop roots.

Those who worked on Barness homes became part of this kaleidoscope. Business was conducted with a handshake. Each house mattered, because the people who would live there mattered.

My father, Herb Barness, joined the family business full-time in 1948, after serving in World War II and completing his engineering degree at Bucknell University. His vision and courage changed the family business from a small local builder to one that encompassed shopping centers, a skating rink, apartment buildings, subsidized housing, a race track, golf courses, and the like.

I was privileged to work with my father for about 14 years before his untimely passing in 1998. I could go on and on about the life lessons I learned from him. My father never lost sight of what was really important, and he taught that to his children and grandchildren by example.

I continued the business until 2005. By that time, I could see that the real estate market had changed. Farmers would just call my father and ask if he wanted to purchase their farms. But shortly after his passing, I felt the need to establish a land acquisition team. National builders were entering our market, and local municipalities were making development more difficult. I saw the writing on the wall and knew it was time for a builder of my size to get out of this market.

My father and I didn't discuss succession while he was alive (we both assumed he would live to be a lot older than 74!), but I remembered an off-the-cuff conversation in which he said that if anything ever happened to him, I should sell the business and not risk everything that had been established in the decades before.

This is what I call the Gift of Goodbye. It was offered in the context of another conversation, but with it I was given freedom to use my best business judgment and not be clouded by expectations from the grave. I knew it was a gift then, but I had no idea what a huge gift it was until I was faced with his loss. There was no need to perpetuate the business out of emotion.

I looked for a buyer who was part of a family business, who would understand the values of The Barness Organization and honor those values by hiring most of the employees who had worked at Barness for years.

The sale was exceedingly emotional for me, because I was leaving people I had worked with for more than 20 years. But I was heartened by the fact that many of my employees were continuing on or had found other rewarding work.

The first house my grandparents built had a detached garage with a swinging door and a chicken coop in the rear yard. So much has changed—but maybe not everything. The Gift of Goodbye will last for my whole life.

Afterword

*S*hortly after I finished the draft of this book, I came across a letter I had written to my dad in the summer of 1998, shortly before his death. This book is full of the voices of others—friends, business associates, journalists, politicians—who shared their thoughts and recollections about his life and work. Now here is something just from me. I have added a few comments throughout so that future readers of this book can have a better understanding of our inside jokes, and of just how much fun, and how wonderful it was to be his daughter.

Dear Dad,
I bought this book [*Dear Dad, Thank you For Being Mine* by Scott Matthews and Tamara Nikuradse] for you and read it ... but thought I could do better, so I scribbled some things.
    Thanks—for everything.
        Love, Lyn

Thank you for ...

... bringing home goldfish in a big metal tub.

> *I was very young, and we lived in Warrington, and I remember that my dad brought home a big galvanized tub with goldfish in it. I think he found the fish in a pond on a job site, and somehow he obtained a tub, put the goldfish in it, and brought them home!*

... bending down gently to kiss us hello so that Sparky and Skipper didn't eat you.

> Sparky and Skipper were our dogs. They were Weimaraners—large, slim dogs that guarded my sister and me fiercely.

... wearing your big green winter coat for five years, and for not getting lost in the snow drift.

> We had a walk-out basement in Warrington, and one year we had a huge snowstorm that left huge drifts. I remembered being afraid that my father would be swallowed up in one of the drifts, but he had a long green coat with a hood that let us visually follow him. I can still picture him walking in that snow!

... making pizza on Sundays before it was fashionable.

> This became a family tradition. He went to a nearby store (Castignola's, I think) and purchased frozen pizza crusts, and then put tomato sauce and cheese on top. We loved it and looked forward to it every week.

... grilling out.

> My father was always a grillmaster. He had a built-in grill on the patio of our house in Warrington, which was definitely ahead of its time, and another one at Nanlyn Farms.

... making us think that three rows from the top of Franklin Field was heaven, or as close as we might get.

> We had family season tickets to the Philadelphia Eagles from 1959 on. It was a huge deal for my sister and me. We got picked up early from Sunday School, and then we all drove to the Hot Shoppes on Broad Street for lunch and went to the game. Our seats were on the 50-yard-line, three rows from the top of the stadium. My dad always said that this was as close to heaven as we might get. I can picture us sitting there like it was yesterday. There were no fancy seats;

> we sat on wooden benches. After we all stood up to cheer, we had to sit down again quickly, so that the person at the end of the row (usually my dad) would be sure to have a seat! We brought blankets to keep us warm, and my dad always bought us hot chocolate when the weather was cold.

... teaching your daughters to enjoy spectator sports.

> We were Eagles fans first and foremost, but we always appreciated watching sports.

... pushing us to play golf. Think of the hours we saved over the last 30-some years by <u>not</u> being on the golf course.

> My sister and I had every opportunity to play golf, from the country club that my dad built to the golf course in his backyard—but neither my sister nor I took up the sport. Now, of course, I wish I had.

... buying Mom a big green Oldsmobile.

> My parents' first house on in Warrington was on 30 acres (a farmer farmed most of it with wheat) so the houses in our neighborhood were pretty far apart. You couldn't just run across the street to borrow a cup of sugar—instead it was a long walk! My mother had grown up in Brooklyn, New York, so life in the country must have been quite a change, and isolating at times. When my dad bought her this car, it gave her the freedom to go anywhere—now she could drive to the general store and to Doylestown, rather than relying on him to take her. I still have a visual memory of this car!

... having a color TV before everyone else did.

> I remember the day it arrived. It was a major event for us!

... teaching us that FAMILY is the most important word.

> This needs no explanation!

... letting us know that food all ends up in the same place and that it's really OK to have dessert first.

> My father LOVED sweets. And from time to time he let us eat what we wanted, when we wanted it. I recall coming home from a trip to the Virgin Islands, and we had to stop in Puerto Rico first. We went to lunch at a restaurant at the airport, and we walked past a dessert trolley as we were taken to our seats. Of course we eyed the trolley with desire, and my father suggested that we start with dessert. What a memorable meal!

... teaching us that we have <u>only</u> two choices: earn more or spend less.

> My father was extremely generous with his children, but he made sure we understood his values.

... always keeping an umbrella over our head and keeping the floor firmly under our feet.

> We knew how much he loved us.

... always being there.

> He was.

... not sending us home to our grandparents when Nan and I spent a whole vacation arguing.

> That memorable summer, when we were traveling out West for a month, was not without its challenges. Every time my sister and I argued, we were threatened with a trip home to our grandparents.

... teaching us that speeders lose licenses, and then being pulled over during a trip out west *and* in Switzerland with us in the car.

> We saw our father get pulled over for speeding twice!

... living the maxim: Waste not, want not.

> That was part of my dad's value system. He meant it. It referred to food and to everything else.

... bringing doughnuts to Jen and Melissa every morning.

> Here was my dad's routine in the mornings: He would wake up, swim, go the supermarket and buy cheese and donuts, and then drive to Ambler (about a half-hour or more ride) to see his four granddaughters. He would bring my girls donuts and stay for a very short time, then move on to my sister's house and do the same with her girls, and still be at the office by about 7:30 a.m.!!!

... being mother and father.
... being grandfather and grandmother.
... stopping the world for your children or grandchildren, or at least making us feel that you would.
... listening to your mother when she called you at work to check to see if you had your raincoat.

> My grandmother was full of unconditional love for her family. When it rained, she checked on her grown son! It was one of the many ways she showed she cared.

... having Saturday lunch at Waterfields.

> When we lived in Warrington, my father, sister, grandfather and I would have lunch together every Saturday at a tiny restaurant not far from my grandparents' home. There weren't many restaurants in the area, to be sure, but this was our Saturday ritual.

... making birthdays into family occasions.

> Always! We made family celebrations out of anything we could. I learned that it was important to celebrate the good times, and we did!

... having us go over the river and through the woods for Thanksgiving.

> In the early years, our family went to New York City to my mother's parents' home for Thanksgiving. When my parents moved to the farm, Thanksgiving was held there. We always had extended family and friends join us, and that really became the definition of Thanksgiving for me.

... buying an extra snowmobile, even though it never snowed enough again.

> During the winter, the farm was, of course, a wonderland. One year early in our farm days, after a particularly big snowfall, my father decided to buy a snowmobile for my sister and me and our then-spouses. I think he bought one. And then it snowed some more, and he thought he would buy another one. He did ... but we were never there during a huge snowstorm again.

... giving us a Christmas tree and a Chaukkah menorah and letting us know the difference.

> My whole family is Jewish. Great-grandparents, grandparents, parents, and more. But when we lived in Warrington, we were one of the very few Jewish families there. When I was in 6th grade, Elaine Till was in fifth, my sister was in fourth, and Elaine's brother was in kindergarten. We were the only Jews in the school. So ... my parents provided us with a Christmas tree and all the trimmings, including a train that ran under it, so that we wouldn't feel left out. But we also celebrated Chanukkah, and my dad drove us from Warrington to Abington to go to Sunday School. After we moved to Rydal, the community was much more diverse, and my sister and I were older and understood more about our family's religious heritage—so we just celebrated Chanukkah.

... not getting upset when we turned off the alarm and you got up too late to drive us to Sunday School in Abington.

> OK, so we didn't always love going to Sunday School!

... asking why the "B" in math wasn't an "A." (I still don't know.)

> This was sort of a joke between us. I was an "A" student, so if I didn't get an A, my dad asked why. But it was without pressure. I was a self-motivated student.

… being proud of us.

… driving us to school.

… bringing us orange juice as a breakfast in bed, and using the intercom, and, if all else failed, sprinkling water on our heads to wake us up for school.

… teaching us that good government and being an informed and involved citizen matters.

> *My dad was so patriotic. He couldn't wait to defend his country in World War II, and he believed in voting "early and often." Good government really mattered to him.*

… having lunch with your parents every day.

> *For years, the Barness office was near my grandparents' home. And my dad would join them for lunch.*

… having lunch with your parents and me every day the summer I worked for you.

> *When I was 16, I worked as a receptionist in the real estate office, and I joined them for lunch too. Special.*

… knowing that the best way to spoil children is with love.

> *He did that in abundance.*

… taking *many* family vacations, and creating *many* extraordinary memories.

… showing us how to eat "cheese pie" and cheesecake from the Danish Bakery—with a fork, from the box.

> *My dad would go to this bakery when we lived in Rydal and buy a freshly made cheesecake, which was still warm when he returned home. He permitted us to grab a fork and dig in!*

… being "friends" with my friends as I was growing up—they have good memories of you and our house, too.

… setting an alarm clock on the stairs and having it go off so my date would leave.

… not letting Nan go to the shore. Boy, were you right! … Even though she won't agree …

> When she was a teenager, my sister wanted to go to Atlantic City with her friends. Permission denied.

… your unique sense of style!

> My father was definitely not a clothes-horse. He had a simple wardrobe, if you can call it that, and his clothes weren't always well-matched. We used to tease him about it.

… dropping bubble gum from the helicopter on Olympic Day at camp.

> My dad took a helicopter to visit my sister and me at camp. And one year, he dropped gum for the campers!

… the stunt with the "beer" at camp for Dede, Nan, and Leslee.

> My sister and her friends were teenagers, not old enough to drink alcohol, at least not legally. My dad asked a friend with a bottling company to put ginger ale—or was it 7 Up?—in beer cans, and he brought them to camp as a "gift." My sister and her friends secretly brought the cans to their bunk and, later that night, they shared and drank what was in the cans. They got tipsy! On soda!!! The power of suggestion …

… letting Leslee be an almost-sister at our house.

> This was my sister's best friend, and her parents and grandparents owned the camp we attended.

… telling us about the miles you walked to a one-room schoolhouse in the snow in hand-me-downs … and having it all be true.

… the tales about a boat built in the basement and other stories.

> One tale was that my father decided to build a boat when he was a young man. Unfortunately, he built it in the basement of their family home and had trouble getting it out.

... reminding me to put the newspaper back the way I got it.

> *I was taught to always return the newspaper to its original order so that the next person could enjoy it the same way that I had.*

... laughing—and crying—with me.

... knowing that licorice is an important food group, second only to chocolate.

... demonstrating again and again that inexpensive chocolate is infinitely better than the fancy stuff, and that there is nothing like a Snicker's bar.

... letting me call you "Herb" OR "Daddy," whichever suits my fancy at the time and place.

> *I started calling my dad by his first name the summer I worked as a receptionist in the real estate office next to my grandparent's home. I felt silly calling him Daddy in front of the business associates and buyers that came to see him. He was always fine with whatever I called him. As I got older, of course, I was more comfortable calling him Dad in the office!*

... letting me have an office next to yours.

... not overseeing everything I do.

... letting me make mistakes.

... trying to teach me everything I need to know about everything.

... dismissing me, unless I need to talk—and then letting me have your undivided attention whenever I need it.

... listening.

... always playing fair.

... showing us integrity as a way of life.

... making apple fritters a standard part of the work day.

... illustrating the salad-and-chocolate-diet by example.

... treating everyone equally.

... reminding us that you've been rich and you've been poor—and rich is better. But never forgetting how it was to be poor.

... letting a high school teacher force you to go to college.

... serving a grateful nation and winning WWII single-handedly.

… tantalizing us with the tales of the South Pacific. Anything else we should know??

… having parents who would keep a monkey for their soldier-son until his return.

… knowing how—and doing—all the jobs related to the real estate business.

… perpetuating the myth that dad was always home. It felt like it to us—but we know you worked hard and long. It always felt like you were there for us, though.

… buying a new car that was the same as the old car so no one would know.

… not buying too many new clothes—for decades!

… wearing 1960s shoes/boots in the 1990s.

… wearing short ties—and short pants.

… judging people by who they are, not their name or position.

… teaching your family that the true meaning of life is family.

… helping to pick me up when I've fallen.

… letting me be your employee and your daughter—together but, more importantly, separately.

… sending me cards.

… sending me and Nan Xeroxed (well, mimeographed) letters at camp and changing just the names.

… always <u>signing</u> your letters "be good, have fun, and stay well"—and meaning it.

… taking our phone calls regardless of who you are talking to.

… showing us that famous people are just people.

… giving us Republican blood in our veins.

… explaining that we should "vote early and vote often."

… knowing the difference between a German Shepherd and a Bishon Frise. No further comment!

> *My dad loved dogs, and he had a series of German Shepherds. My mother had her own yappy Bishon.*

... buying supermarket-brand soda 'cause it's cheaper.
... liking people, and teaching us to do the same.
... throwing great parties.

> My dad loved parties, and for a number of years he threw huge themed ones at the farm: Chocoholics Anonymous; Peanut Butter Factory; Strawberry Festival; Don't Stop the Carnival; Apple Dumplin' Gang; Decision '88 (political convention theme); and others.

... celebrating the good times.
... fighting lymphoma.
... having a limo but hardly using it. And letting *us* use it!

> He purchased a limousine after the sale of the race track. My sister and I used it from time to time, but we always asked the driver to park away from where we were going, so no one would see us get out of the big car.

... having a good attitude.
... keeping a roll-top desk in your office to remind you of your dad's.
... making "holiday" synonymous with "family."
... putting up with my "Jewish phase"—even though it lasted too long.
... helping others.
... having an impeccable reputation.
... building a petting-farm for your grandchildren, and changing the name on the sign as each child was born to include her.
... having an office over the hardware store.
... exercising every day—and not having it be a genetic trait passed down to me.
... explaining that it's better to buy low and sell high.
... having that entrepreneurial spirit.
... being a risk-taker—to a point.
... fighting lymphoma.
... stocking our refrigerators on family vacations.

... teaching us to start the day with pastry.
... washing down candy with diet soda.
... giving us a family vacation in St. Thomas and not telling us you had a recurrence of cancer until we got home.
... understanding how people are, but being willing to close your eyes when you have to.
... picking up the lunch check every day.
... sharing the profits all along the way.
... being "cultured" and going with mom to the orchestra and art museums—but preferring to be home with your family.
... stopping in to visit but never over-staying your welcome (a few more minutes would always be OK!)
... going to your children's school activities.
... going to your grandchildren's school activities.
... never making us feel that there should have been a boy in the family.
... giving Jen and Melissa their high-school diplomas. What wonderful memories!

> *My dad was on the Board of Trustees at Germantown Academy when my daughters were graduating.*

... taking trips with us to Makro—and buying out the store for us.

> *Makro was an early bulk-shopping store. My dad would take my sister and me for a buying spree ... we would take a huge cart and shop, and he would pay for everything. It was a fun outing for the three of us. And of course it was great to take home all the goods.*

... crying "happy" tears.

> *That's a family trait ... I remember my grandfather doing it regularly, and Nan and I do it too!*

... calling to just say hi and just making sure we're OK.
... getting us tickets for the Beatles concert but not letting us go because you thought it was too dangerous.

... exposing us to the world of politics, and showing us the positive side.
... giving me money and the freedom to manage it.
... hosting a family reunion and chronicling our family history.
... teaching us table manners by repeating the story about the date you liked—but you stopped seeing her because she pushed her peas with her fingers.
... getting angry at Mom because the curtains hadn't been delivered in the dining room—and then sending her roses the next day.
... having Wednesday as "date night" with Mom when we were growing up.
... letting me work for you. I like the work, but the best part is seeing my dad every day, even if it's only for a minute.
... getting Jen a Volvo, even though it's not American.
... believing in America.
... teaching us to dance in the basement in Warrington.
... having balloons made with my name on them when I ran for office in junior high school—and for telling me they really didn't cost anything.
... reminding us that "it skips a generation."
... high expectations.
... being first in, first out.
... walking 2 daughters down the aisle at the same time. I don't know how you did it!
... bringing apples to the office only once or twice—which meant that you listened—but going back to fattening goodies because you know that's what we really like.
... being "perfect" when I was a teenager—and staying that way as I grew up.
... preparing us for the world.
... fighting lymphoma.
... driving me to college and seeing my New England frame dorm and not pulling me out of school because I was living in a fire trap.
... letting me go to Russia—and all the other places.

... giving us money before vacations as we grew up.
... handing our children money on the sly.
... giving us savings bonds regularly but being surprised when we tally the total amount.
... letting us know the phone is for calling, even though sometimes it may be excessive.
... hardly using your car phone and not complaining (much) when I overuse mine.
... making pickled tomatoes in a crock in the barn.
... reminding us that there's no dress rehearsal.
... explaining the value of a handshake ... and that it was better without the lawyers.
... having a diet-delight platter with extra-crispy French fries.
... treating a chocolate soufflé with reverence.
... treating your daughters and granddaughters as the most special things in the world—even better than chocolate soufflé.
... loving us.
... taking care of us.
... sharing your values and your life with us.
... feeding us a steady diet of love and candy.
... giving.
... teaching.
... loving life.
... loving us.

Acknowledgments

I learned so much from compiling *The Man I Knew Was Once A Boy*. Yes, I learned so much about my father, and it touched my heart to read the letters he wrote as a young man. But I also learned about myself, and I knew that sooner or later I would have to tackle the box of press clippings and memorabilia that I had in my possession ... and that I could (eventually) do it.

Since the words in these clippings are not my own, I owe a huge debt of gratitude to the newspapers—principally *The Daily Intelligencer* and *The Philadelphia Inquirer*, along with others—and their publishers, editors, journalists, and photographers who covered my dad's activities with candor and caring. I am grateful to have this collection of articles that reflects the interests, causes, and story of my father's public adult life.

Ann Campbell has been "my" editor for *Once a Boy* and *In the Press*, and it is an absolute truth that I couldn't have done either without her. Her careful reading, deft hand, and gentle guidance were invaluable. The structure, editing, advice and more are so appreciated. I read these books now, and they make sense to me. Trust me when I tell you that Ann was responsible for this! And yet, I still hear my own voice (and of course my dad's) in both books. That is clearly the work of a stellar editor, and I thank Ann for all she did to help me along the way.

To say that I thank my father—truly for a gazillion things—is an understatement. I am eternally grateful that he was my dad.

And his legacy lives on. He is with me every day, and I see it in my children and grandchildren. I love when the little ones ask to hear stories about Popee's farm before they go to bed, even though they have never met him. Thanks to my daughters for keeping his memory alive. I hope my two books will help the next generations to know him also.

Lynda Barness
Philadelphia, PA

Appendix A: List of Articles by Year and Title

1920s
George Klein Bought First House sold by Barness

1932-36
What Is Home Without a Garden?

1940
Letter from Herbert Barness on Joseph Barness & Son, Inc. stationery

1941
Lion's Club 50th Anniversary Program

1955
Receive Prizes for Naming Development (Dawson Manor)

1957
Warrington—A Cross Roads from the Early 1700s to the Late 1930s, Today a Suburban Community

1958
Fortune magazine ad

1959
County Distinguished Service Award
Brochure from National Agricultural College

1960
Scouts Launch to Expand Camp; $360,000 Drive to Buy Poconos Site
Industrial Unit Picks Barness
Gifts for Generations
Valley College Dedicates Dorms
Barness Names 7 to Task Force
Please, Kris, Take Care of Our Friends

1961
Industrial Park Plans Bared for Warrington
Bucks Racing Assn. Awarded Liscense

1962
'Great Days' Are Under Way at Liberty Bell Park
Accepts Portrait

1963
$12 Million Community for Bucks Tract
Bucks Co. Board Names A. M. Moyer
Brochure from Welcome House
2 Phila. Groups in NBA Bids
Buck's Barness
Homes by 3 Builders Open at Palomino Farms
The Philadelphia Inquirer
Barness Says Group Still Seeks NBA Pact for City
The Jewish Exponent
Likely from *The Daily Intelligencer*
Herbert Barness Bids for Birds at 4.5 Million; Faces Fight from Paul Brown 7 Associates
Eagles' Stockholders Decide to Sell Team, Local Bid Presented
Realtor Barness Offers $4.5 Million for Eagles
Barness in Running to Buy Eagles
Barness Bid Shrugged Off, Brown Seen as Eagles' Buyer
Tellin' All About Sports
Planning Must Be Implemented
Tellin' All About Sports
Mum's Word on Eagle Sale
Tellin' All About Sports
Fire Blows Whistle on 'Cool' Eagle Talk
Tellin' All About Sports
Barness Withdraws Bid for Eagles After Failing to Get Cleveland Money
Tired of Delay, Barness Ends Bid for Eagles
Eagles' Sale Seems Unlikely Now
Hall Is Interested in Eagles
'Come Blow Your Horn' Premiere at County
Barness Pushing Novel Zoning Plan
Barness Named
Barness Wants Zoning Plans to Eliminate Slums
Bucks Developer Aims at Caribbean
The Jewish Exponent
Barness to Start Caribbean Project

'Brothers' to Seek Membership in UF
Barness Plans 116 Apartments
'Four Fields' Site Sold to Barness

1964

Barness Heads Race Group
Herb Barness Named Penn Racing Chief
Barness Elected Wm. Penn Racing Assn. President
The Bulletin
Work Started at Justa Farm
The Jewish Exponent
Construction Begun by Barness in Lancaster
Twin Double Trio Strikes It Rich Over Collar Itch
Bucks Co. Builder Builds in Islands
How 'Whiz Kids' Rang the Bell
Bucks' Bouncy Builder

1965

The Trenton-Evening Times
Growth of Warrington Shop Center Continues
Land Improvement Program Upturn Seen by Barness
Chalfont Post Office Geared for Growth
Gimbels Department Store Ad
Racing in Harness Enlivens Barness
Racing Group Here Moves to Sell Stock
Source Unknown
Liberty Bell Mutuel Handle Tops Individual U.S. Norm
Wm. Penn Prepares Racing with Outing
Liberty Bell Survives Hambletonian Needs, May Bring Classic to Track
Barness Says Real Estate Values Firm
Evening at Races
Joseph Barness Feted by 290 in Warrington
Tribute to a Man with Heart
Barness New Sponsor of Test: Philadelphia Golf Classic
Phila. Golf Classic Getting Fine Direction Which is Expected to Add Up to Success
Introducing ... New Members of the Golden Slipper Square Club
Barness is Quietly Efficient; Applies Business Technique to Golf
6 Pro-Am Teams Shut Out; Barness Trots to Sidelines
Barness Puts Golf Classic in 'Black'
New President of Classic is a Man of Action
Liberty Bell Sets Fast Early Pace
G. G. Amsterdam Heads NCCJ Dinner

1966
Barness & Son Honored
The Jewish Exponent
Bucks Construction Growth Continuing to Make Gains
Bucks Builder—Herb Barness: A Hand in Most Everything
Opening Night at Liberty Bell for June Fete
Barness Seeks Team in Soccer
Barness Backs Soccer Team Here; New Pro League Formed
Program from the 1966 Miss Pennsylvania Pageant
The Philadelphia Inquirer
Shafer in Tourney: GOP Represented
The Warminster Spirit
January Equal to Classic Pressure: Relieves Jack Nicklaus of Crown
Harness Folks Bet on Soccer Club
Barness Firm Plans 49 Million Development for Warrington
Justa Farm Wins Praise for Barness
Quiet Way to Awaken a County
Program from 25th Anniversary of Warrington Lions Club
New Team Harnessed
Warrington Presented Property by Barness

1967
Barness Named Pop Warner Youth Chairman
Opening Day
He's a Man of Many Faces—Sportsman, Realtor, Citizen
Pearl Buck Toasted at Belated Birthday
Barness Firm Gets 2D Renewal Job
Times Chronicle
International Blind Golfers' Tourney Scores an Ace
Bucks County Board of Realtors Presents Historic Bucks County
Herbert Barness Resigns as Head of Racing Group
Shafer Signs Flat Racing Bill, First for Penna.

1968
Racetrack Not the Road to Riches, Barness Says, But it Has Romance
Barness Seeks Buck ...
Barness Donates 15 Acres for Park
Technion Magazine
The Daily Intelligencer
Commonwealth of Pennsylvania Official Document—Votes for Delegate
Program from Pop Warner Little Scholars 1968 All-American Eleven: Service to Youth Dinner

Mid City Federal Elects Barness
Barness Park Dedicated to Kids of Warrington
Real Estate: Construction Caribbean-Style—A Local Builder Develops the Islands
GOP 'Group' Set Up for Convention Role
Suburban GOP Leaders, Delegates Play It Safe in Nixon-Rockefeller Fight for Nomination
'Scholars' Vacancy for Barness
Pop Warner
The Daily Intelligencer
GOP Delegates Uncommitted
Phila. Group Spearheads Campaign for $4 Million Technion Building
Pop Warner Program Thrives at Age 40
Two Flat Racing Licenses Ok'd for Bucks County

1969
Tose to Buy Eagles if Wolman Plan Fails
16 Men Will Direct Phila. Golf Classic
Jeff Keen Says
Tose Tops McCloskey's Bid, Gets Eagles for $16 Million
Pennsylvania Flat Sport Starts Today at Liberty Bell
Barness in Racing in a Big Way Now; Continental Head Owns PA. Farm
Continental Tries to Stem Losses
Barness is Eager to Open New Track: Because of Liberty Bell Losses
Persistency Fulfills a Dream for Tose; He Gets His Team
Barness to Receive 17th Technion Award
Technion Honors Herbert Barness
Round City Hall Square

1970
Program for The Mary Bailey Institute of Heart Research 1970 Golden Heart Achievement Awards
Wind Only Sign of Movement at Neshaminy Park
Tomlin Heads Youth Group for 42nd Year
Technion Magazine

1971
The Daily Intelligencer

1972
Talk Around Town: Barness Quits Racing for Politics
Tose Beefs Up His (Tax) Defense for Court Tilt as IRS Blows Whistle

1973
Apartments for the Aged Ok'd in Doylestown
Joseph Barness, 82, Dies
Editorial: Joseph Barness
Barnesses Donate $100,000 to Hospital
Penna. Probes Shamrock Racing License

1974
Warrington Ambulance Unit Dedicates New Headquarters
Modular Homes: An Idea Whose Time Is Passed

1975
Invitation to *Give 'Em Hell Harry*, a benefit performance for the Bucks County Playhouse in honor of the Barness Family
The Bucks County Playhouse *Give 'Em Hell Harry* Program
Letter from Herbert Barness to his mother
487 Warwick Townhouses Planned
Radio Station WBUX Photo

1976
Successful Apartment Developers Head for the Far Reaches

1977
Ad in *The Philadelphia Inquirer*
Certificate of Appreciation from Bayse Newcomb Lodge
Palomino Glen has Two Styles
Tose Rips His Former Banker
Strong Feelings for Leonard Tose

1978
Doylestown Housing
Warrington Country Club Going Semi-Public
Barness Sells his 29% of Eagles Team to Tose

1979
Vassar Square Apts. Sold to Pa. Partners
The Dynamos

1980
Most of $3 Million Damage Suit Against Tose is Dismissed

1981
Meredith, Fever Boss Want Phils
'Gong Show' Host in Interested in Phillies

Strike Threat has Barness Biding his Time
A Condo Rises from the Ashes of the Windsor
Corinthian Condo Provides Luxury Oceanfront
A Luxurious Bucks County Estate is on the Block

1982
Barness is Appointed to Judge Merit Body
Barness Named Fiscal Director for Scranton's Re-election Bid
Barnes Named to Presidential Housing Panel
Barness Named to White House Housing Panel
Bucks Builder Named to Presidential Panel
Barness Appointed to Housing Board
Carter Visits Area to Select China

1983
Program from "An Evening in Honor of Herbert Barness"
Group Paid No Cash for Cable Share

1984
Warrington's 250th Anniversary Pictorial History Calendar

1985
Snider Group Negotiating for Eagles

1986
Eulogy for Mary Barness
Barness is Leader of Pennsylvania Society
Hometown Boys Make Good: Jewish Athletes Have Played Major Positions in Philadelphia's Sports History

1987
Central Bucks Chamber of Commerce Honors 5
Minor League Baseball Can be Fun
Pennsylvanians Find Parties Aplenty in N.Y.

1988
Contribution to Michener Museum in Doylestown
People: VIP
Buckingham Approves Plans for Seven New Developments
New GOP Group Targets Center City Race for Funds
A New Federal Judge is Sworn in with the Prominent Looking On

1989
Program from The Bucks County Council and Boy Scouts of America's Friends of Scouting Annual Dinner
The Intelligencer/Record
GOP Is Off to a Slow Start in '90 Gubernatorial Race
Program from the Dedication Ceremony of the Irma and Herbert Barness Endowed Chair in the Fine and Performing Arts
George Anthonisen Sculpture Unveiled in Nation's Capital
Governor Taps Barness for Port Authority
Specter Already Filling War Chest for '92 Senate Race
Hafer May be Getting a Rival on the Right
Around the Town

1990
Transcript from KYW Newsradio 1060 Presents: The Delaware Valley: Backward into the Future
Capitalizing on Progress
GOP Abortion-Rights Group Names Bucks Man a Co-Chair
Pro-Choice Republican Group Selects Barness as Fund-Raiser
Washington Fax: Pro-Choice
Barness Given State GOP Post
Bucks County Developer to Represent GOP
Around the Town
Herb Barness—A Quiet Force in GOP Politics
Program from Lunch with the President
Experience Nets Barness GOP Committee Position
The Philadelphia Inquirer
GOP Fund-Raisers Look to Katz as Alternative to Castille or Rizzo
Presenting Torch of Life Award

1991
Program from The United Way of Bucks County's Leadership Giving Circle Recognition
At a Clearing in the Woods, 92 New Townhouses
Profile from the Republican National Committee Directory

1992
The Philadelphia Inquirer
Herbert Barness Selected VFC Citizen of the Year
Program from Citizen of the Year Award Ceremony
Boy Scouts Honor Barness
Herbert Barness Honored as Citizen of the Year
What Was Your Favorite Childhood Book?
Buckingham Eyes Zoning Exemption

Buckingham Approves 378 Homes
Membership in the Philadelphia Association of Golf Course Superintendents
Award of Honor from Top Farmers of America Association

1993
A Shakedown Run for GOP Hopefuls: Campaign '94

1994
GOP Senators Hosted by Specter to Spend a Weekend in the Big City
United States Gold Association recognizes Nanlyn Golf Club as a Member Course
Barness & Welsh Honored at BCIDC Annual Meeting
The Barness Organization: A Vision for the Future

1995
Specter Upbeat Despite Ridge Support of Dole
At 71, Barness is Still Going Strong
Choose from Three Barness Sites in Buckingham Township: Beautiful Designs, Attractive Prices
GOP Meeting Set for Philadelphia
Invitation from An Evening of Honors by the Pennsylvania Association of Broadcasters
Powell Will Not Run: Rules Out Race for President
Gov. Ridge Set to Top $2 Million

1996
Focus: Behind the Political Scenes—Herb Barness '48 is a Major Player in the Republican Party at the State and National Level
Builders Expect Growth in the Upcoming Year
Developer: Strategic Location Attracts Home Buyers to Area
Newsmakers
Developer a Player in Politcs; Barness Among Top Contributors
Home Notes: Local Firms, Agents Honored at Pinnacle Awards Dinner
U.S. Wields a Big Stick
The Insider
Local Builders Win National Recognition: Barness Named 'Builder of the Year' for Multifamily Housing
Local Builder Receives National Acclaim
Keeping Tradition: Builder of the Year
Deep Pockets Could be Key in November
Around the Town
They Told
Campaign '96: Popularity

Pennsylvania Delegations Enjoy San Diego's Creature Comforts
PA Delegation Learns to Kick Back in Style
Major Gifts Initiative Approaches 60% of Goal; Barness Family Makes Leadership Gift to Community Phase
Freddie Mac Will Take Up the Slack
Scenic Sites to See at The Woods at Hearthstone
Happenings
Heads Above the Crowd

1997
Want Access to Gov. Ridge? Join the Club
Barness Named Wharton Finalist
Program from the 1997 Family Business of the Year Awards
Around the Town
U.S. Rep. James Greenwood's Campaign Coffers in Good Shape
Republican Clambake Satisfies Appetites and Replenishes the Party Coffers
Pa.'s Political, Business Luminaries Cluster

1998
New Office Building Considered on Park: Warrington
In the Suburbs: Townhouses at the Enclave
Developer Marks 50 Years of Building Homes, Dreams
Age-Restricted Housing Project Gets Go-Ahead
Herbert Barness: For 50 Years, Providing the American Dream
Fulfilling the American Dream for 50 Years
The Daughter Also Rises
Ridge: Barness 'Generous' to a Fault
Republicans Flock to Barness Funeral
Life of Herbert Barness Celebrated

Epilogue
The Gift of Goodbye

Appendix B: Resume of Herbert Barness

Herbert Barness

1923 – 1998

His legacy lives on...

BIOGRAPHICAL RECORD OF

HERBERT BARNESS
975 EASTON ROAD, WARRINGTON, PENNSYLVANIA 18976

EDUCATION:
- Graduated Bucknell University 1948
- Military Service 1942-1946
- Graduate of Air Force Meteorology School
- Registered Professional Engineer
- Licensed Real Estate and Insurance Broker
- Attended Barnes Art Foundation
- Attended Fels Institute, Wharton Graduate School, University of Pennsylvania

MILITARY RECORD:
- Executive Officer 70th Army Airways Communications Group and Squadron Commander 147th Airways Communication Squadron (Pacific)

PRESENT BUSINESS AFFILIATIONS:
- Chairman of the Board — The Barness Organization
- Herbert Barness has been affiliated with The Barness Organization since 1948 and is active in all phases of real estate financing, brokerage, development, and property management.

PROFESSIONAL AFFILIATIONS:
- National Society of Professional Engineers
- The American Society of Mechanical Engineers
- The Society of American Military Engineers
- Pennsylvania Farmer's Association
- Bucks County Board of Realtors
- National Association of Real Estate Boards
- National Association of Home Builders
- Golf Course Superintendents Association of America
- Lambda Alpha International (an honorary land economics society)
- National Rifle Association
- American Legion

CIVIC AND PHILANTHROPIC ACTIVITIES . . . PAST AND PRESENT:

American Technion Society Philadelphia Chapter	Past President and Chairman
Annual Teenage Achievement Award Philadelphia	Director
Boy Scouts of America Bucks County Council	Advisory Board
Bucks County Home Builders Association	Charter Member
Bucks County Industrial Development Corp.	Past President and Director
Bucks County Park Foundation	Past President
Continental Bank & Trust Company of Philadelphia — Doylestown Region	Regional Board
Delaware Valley Philharmonic Orchestra	Past Chairman
Federal Judicial Nominating Commission	Member
The Pennsylvania Society	Director
Philadelphia Eagles Football Club	Former Partner
Pop Warner Little Scholars, Inc.	Director and Chairman of the Board

CIVIC AND PHILANTHROPIC ACTIVITIES ... PAST AND PRESENT: (Cont'd.)

President's Commission on Housing — Appointment made by President Ronald Reagan
U.S. Attorney Selection Commission — Member
Washington Crossing Foundation — Director
Welcome House, Doylestown — Past Chairman

RECIPIENT OF THE FOLLOWING AWARDS:

The American Legion (1972) Certificate of Meritorious Service
Big Brothers of America — Outstanding Service
Pop Warner Little Scholars — Outstanding Service to Youth
Schmidt's Sports Award — Outstanding contribution to the sports life of the Delaware Valley
U.S. Blind Golfers — Outstanding Service
Women's American ORT — Honor Roll Service Award 1967 Philadelphia Region
United States Harness Writers Delaware Valley Chapter Honorary Membership 1967
Scouting Service Award — Bucks County Council Boy Scouts of America — Outstanding Service
Bensalem Township Bucks County Annual Award for Outstanding Service toward Community — 1966
Bucks County Home Builders' Association — Charter Member and First President
Technion Humanitarian Award
Warrington Township Lions Club — Priviledged Member Award 1960

PARTIAL POLITICAL ACTIVITIES:

Pennsylvania Republican State Finance Committee
Bucks County Pennsylvania Republican Finance Committee
Delegate Republican National Convention 1968
Electoral College Pennsylvania 1972
Co-Chairman Pennsylvania Finance Committee Reagan for President
National Republican Committeeman of Pennsylvania

Appendix C:
Barness Brochures

This appendix contains my collection of brochures. The first, *The Expanding World Of ... Joseph Barness & Son*, is from 1966 or so. A *Daily Intelligencer* article from November 20, 1966, by Lester Trauch referenced this brochure.

During the more than 40 years in which our firm has been engaged in land development and building, tremendous gains in technology and facilities have been made. Whereas elecricity was not readily avaliable in our first venture into rural development, now, hundreds of projects later, we are on the threshold of having atomic energy available to us.

So too, having started in Bucks County, Pa., and then extending our operations into neighboring states, we have discovered new horizons for building and community development in the Caribbean area. Just as the need for advanced building methods and planning existed here, so now are they necessary and desirable throughout the world.

Joseph Barness & Son is prepared to meet this challenge. In fact, we have already embarked upon a course which will take us to any locality where we can be constructive. We look forward to smooth sailing.

Joseph Barness

HISTORY AND PROFILE

In 1923, Joseph Barness left Philadelphia, purchased 80 acres of land in Bucks County and entered upon his first subdivision effort. Before electricity lines could be extended to this property, Mr. Barness had to guarantee a minimum monthly usage of power. This was done and with it, the Barness firm was in business.

With this beginning, the firm advanced from the building of single dwelling units to residential developments of moderate size, and then to total community development. This transition, which became necessary to meet the needs of mass housing in undeveloped areas, entailed broad planning and required provision for full convenience facilities.

Joseph Barness & Son were prepared. Wholly owned companies were set up to take all steps from raw land to finished community: Engineering, architecture, water and sewer installations, roads, shopping centers, and recreational facilities. In end result, a full, self-sustaining community.

The requirements of tax ratables for financial support of such communities led to the entrance of the Barness firm into the building of Industrial Parks, which provide an orderly method for industrial development. From there, the firm has progressed into diversified fields, which include golf courses, country clubs and swim club construction.

All in all, Joseph Barness & Son is equipped and prepared to build anything, -- anywhere.

Herbert Barness, President of Barness & Son, is a mechanical engineer by profession. He has been a prime moving force in the broad expansion of the Barness firm. Ever active, he presides over the twelve subsidiary companies of the firm, yet finds time to be active in the community and business world.

Herbert Barness is past president of the Bucks County Planning Commission, past president of the Bucks County Home Builders Association, past president of the Bucks County Industrial Development Corporation, and past president of the Bucks County Park Foundation. He is a member of the Bucks County Society of Professional Engineers.

As an avocation, Barness is president of the Wm. Penn Racing Association, one of the four authorized harness racing tracks in the Commonwealth of Pennsylvania.

The St. Thomas House, largest privately sponsored apartment complex on St. Thomas, Virgin Islands, is nearing completion. Magnificence of location and quality of construction is illustrated above. Complete project calls for 400 units. The "Golden Roc" shown on left, is located on St. Croix, Virgin Islands, has been completed and is now fully occupied.

BARNESS *International*

Immediate future plans of Barness International call for additional apartment units in both St. Croix and St. Thomas. Continuing negotiations with the government of Jamaica should culminate shortly for the construction of single dwelling units and apartments. Negotiations continue for housing activity in Costa Rica and British Guinea.

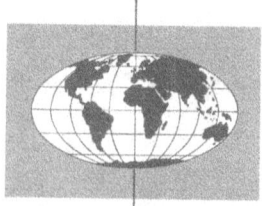

Appendix C | 433

ADMINISTRATIVE OFFICE
Joseph Barness & Son
U. S. Route 611
Warrington, Pennsylvania
Phone: Area Code 215-343-0700

SUBSIDIARIES
Warwick Water Co.
Palomino Farms
Palomino Water Co.
Palomino Sewer Co.
New Britain Water Co.
New Britain Sewer Co.
Chapel Hill Development Co.
Chapel Hill Sewer Co.
Barnsel, Inc.
Water & Sewer Utilities Services, Inc.
Earth Movers, Inc.
Recreational Pools, Inc.
Valley Sewer Company
Valley Water Company

OVERSEAS OPERATIONS
ST. CROIX V.I.
  Golden Roc Apartments
  Orange Grove Apartments
ST. THOMAS V. I.
  St. Thomas House
  Plantation Manor Apartments
JAMAICA B.W.I.
  Enson City Limited
  Seaton Hurst, Limited

RESIDENTIAL DEVELOPMENT SITES
FAIRFIELD
Warminster, Bucks
STORYBROOK HOMES
Warminster, Bucks
PALOMINO FARMS
Warrington, Bucks
LENAPE VILLAGE (Briarwood)
New Britain, Bucks
SANDY RIDGE ACRES
Doylestown, Bucks
RYDAL ESTATES
Abington, Montgomery County
HARTSVILLE PARK
Warminster, Bucks
JUSTA FARMS
Lower Moreland,
  Montgomery County
LAMPLIGHTER VILLAGE
Warminster, Bucks

APARTMENT PROJECTS
Lincoln Arms—Morrisville
Spruce Court—Doylestown
Penndel Apartments—Penndel
Spring Garden Apts.—Ambler
Jimmestown Village—Willow Grove
Pine Valley—Warrington
Lambertville, N.J.
Egg Harbor, N.J.
Warminster—Warminster
Valley Park East—Bethlehem
Valley Park Apts.—Bethlehem
Spring Manor Apts.—Lancaster
Elmwood Park Apts.—
  Bensalem Twp.
Middletown Apts.—
  Middletown Twp.
Plymouth Apts.—Plymouth Twp.

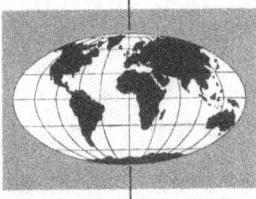

JOSEPH BARNESS & SON

This next brochure mentions the passing of Joseph Barness in 1973.

db

joseph barness and son, inc. 1352 easton road · warington, pa. 18976 · 215-343-0700

the
expanding
world of...

Joseph Barness,
Founder, 1893-1973

joseph barness an

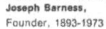

Joseph Barness, Warrington Township resident, developer and benefactor passed away in 1973 at the age of 80. His was the epitome of the American success story. He came to the United States as a young boy from Russia and moved from Philadelphia to Warrington in 1923, more than a half a century ago. Mr. Barness, quiet, firm, but never arrogant, dreamed, worked, planned, imagined and trusted until he achieved friends, success, and a great deal of satisfaction.

He worked within the system as it existed in lean, undeveloped, rural Warrington Township. He not only improved it from the inside, but also had the vision to extend its cultural growth far beyond previewed limitations.

His goals were good housing, good roads, good water and sewer facilities, good township government and, eventually, good, rich, full community living.

His generosity in many ways and in many things is known only to those whom he helped. Children will long enjoy the playgrounds, athletic fields and recreational areas he made possible.

Joseph Barness gave to his home in America endless gifts to display his joy in his adopted land. He also left an active, successful business and a philosophy of involvement that is its keystone today.

During the more than 50 years in which the firm of Joseph Barness & Son, Inc. has been engaged in land development and building, tremendous gains in technology and facilities have been made. Whereas electricity was not readily available during the company's first venture into rural development, now, hundreds of projects later, we are on the threshold of having atomic energy.

Also, having started in Bucks County, Pennsylvania, and then extending operations into neighboring states, the company has discovered new horizons for building and community development overseas. Just as the need for advanced building methods and planning existed here, so now are they necessary and desirable throughout the world. Joseph Barness & Son, Inc., is meeting this challenge effectively. In 1923, Joseph Barness purchased 80 acres of land in Bucks County and entered upon his first subdivision effort. Before electric lines could be extended to this property, Mr. Barness had to

history and profile

Herbert Barness, President

guarantee a minimum monthly usage of power. This was done, and the Barness firm was in business.

With this beginning, the firm advanced from the building of single dwelling units to residential developments of moderate size, and then to total community development. This transition, which became necessary to meet the needs of mass housing in undeveloped areas, entailed broad planning and required provision for full convenience facilities.

Joseph Barness & Son, Inc. was prepared. Wholly owned companies were set up to take all steps from raw land to finished community with: engineering, architecture, water and sewer installations, roads, shopping centers, and recreational facilities. The end results were fully self-sustaining communities.

The requirements of tax ratables for financial support of such communities led to the entrance of the Barness firm into the building of Industrial Parks, which provide an orderly method for industrial development. From there, the firm has progressed into diversified fields, which include golf courses, country clubs and swim club construction.

All in all, Joseph Barness & Son, Inc. is equipped and prepared to build anything—anywhere.

Herbert Barness, President of Joseph Barness & Son, Inc. is an engineer by profession. He has been a prime moving force in the broad expansion of the Barness firm, yet finds time to be active in the community and business world. He is past president of the Bucks County Planning Commission, Bucks County Home Builders Association, Bucks County Industrial Development Corporation and Bucks County Park Foundation. He is a member of the Bucks County Society of Professional Engineers. As an avocation, Barness was president of Wm. Penn Racing Association (Harness Racing) and a Director and former President of Continental Thoroughbred Racing Association. Mr. Barness has long been a supporter of the Artistic and Recreational activities of his community and is involved as a principal of the Philadelphia Eagles Football Club.

Here is the first brochure to use the new name, The Barness Organization. The name changed during the 1970s.

And the next brochure:

The Divisions

Developers, Realtors, Property Managers. These three interrelated roles encompass the diverse, specialized services provided by The Barness Organization to the commercial/residential development industry. Conceived as an autonomous branch functioning within the basic organizational structure, each division provides efficiency, expertise and experience, and increased flexibility to the investor, the consumer, and the business professional. Money and energy are more productively spent through conducting business with a long established firm with a participatory overview of the total industry.

Consider the definitive advantages of placing your confidence in a Development Company that has provided centralized, full-service capabilities at local, regional, national and international levels; a Real Estate Brokerage Division that handles tens of millions of dollars in transactions annually; and, a computer-assisted Property Management Division with years of experience accumulated in all phases of residential and commercial management. Then consider that these all-inclusive advantages emanate from one reputable source. The Barness Organization.

The Affiliates

Wholly-owned, yet distinct affiliates are an outgrowth of The Barness Organization. Correlated with the firm's objective to provide the ultimate in professional services while strengthening the cultural and economic base of the communities affected, each affiliate enhances the scope of the whole.

Among the more prominent of this growing number of affiliates are Stein-Urdang Securities, a broker-dealer registered with the Pennsylvania and U.S. Securities Commissions, participating in the selling of limited partnership interests in real estate syndications; Barness Insurance Company — a general agency writing commercial, home, auto and personal policies; Lincoln Abstract Company, specializing in title insurance; Barness International, sociologically and ecologically sensitive contractors for housing in emerging countries, and developers of prestigious communities in such places as Jamaica, Puerto Rico, Virgin Islands and Mexico; and, Warrington Country Club, a picturesque social and recreational facility in central Bucks County.

In addition, the organization controls substantial interests in the WBUX radio broadcasting company and Keystone Race Track, the only Thoroughbred racing facility operating in the Philadelphia area. For many years there existed significant involvement with the Philadelphia Eagles professional football team.

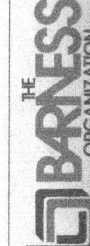

This next brochure was created after 1985 (when I started working at The Barness Organization). The address on the back shows we had moved to our new offices at 975 Easton Road in Warrington. And the last photo here is a view of Nanlyn Farm.

Seventy years ago,

a farmer named Joseph Barness
imagined the harmonious blending
of the land and its people,
a mosaic of flourishing towns,
prosperous farms, and comfortable homes.
Today, that vision thrives in the form of
The Barness Organization...

developing better communities for better living.

Today,

The Barness Organization

stretches far beyond
the boundaries of Bucks County.
During the 1960's,
Herbert Barness began his leadership role
in the corporation
and was later
joined by a third generation,
his daughter Lynda Barness.

*"The Barness Organization strives not only
to excel in the craft of building,
but also to create good neighborhoods
and to be a good neighbor."*
Herbert Barness

Under his leadership,
the corporation has thrived with wide-ranging
residential, commercial and industrial real estate projects
throughout the world.
And each one shares a common foundation...
a genuine concern for the
well-being of the community. &

THE BARNESS ORGANIZATION
Realtors • Developers • Property Management

Residential Development

* *Detached & Multi-Family Housing*
* *Rental Apartments*
* *Government Assisted Projects*

Joseph Barness and Son, Inc.

* *Real Estate Broker*
* *Property Management*
* *Land Acquisition*
* *Property Sales*

Investments

* *Shopping Centers*
* *Office Complexes*
* *Senior Living Facilities*

This final brochure was created after my father passed away. I continued to run the business for seven more years, then sold the ground we had in development and ended our family business in its 80th year. Note the items on the cover: building plans, a map, photos of my dad as a boy, glasses, a computer disk (!) and M&M peanut candies, which were a staple in the candy bins in my dad's office. All of this was styled on my dad's roll-top desk, with an American flag in full sight. This image really tells the story!

Appendix D: Barness Offices

This is a picture in front of my grandparents' home at 1334 Easton Road, Warrington. My grandmother is standing outside with an unidentified man and dog.

The very first real estate "office" (a single room) was in the addition on the right, and it opened into their living room by two separate doors. I can remember my grandfather watching television in his special chair in front of the office.

This photo was taken during the war years, with my grandfather, Joseph Barness, dressed in uniform.

After the office moved from its location in my grandparents' house, it was located in a small strip center to the left in this photo, not far from the sign.

The next office was over the hardware store in Warrington Shopping Center, behind my grandparents' home. My dad loved the low-key location!

And here is the very last "home" of The Barness Organization. We occupied the top floor to the left of the entrance door as you look at the photo. There was a fireplace in my dad's office, which he loved. Photo by Grant James.